Spencer Butte
Pioneers

The Indians called it Champ-a-te or Rattlesnake Mountain. Some people mistakenly call it Spencer's Butte. But the correct name of the prominent landmark which rises 2,065 feet above the Willamette Valley floor and so identifies the skyline and character of the city of Eugene, Oregon, is Spencer Butte.

According to Lewis McArthur's Oregon Geographic Names, "It was named in July 1845 by Dr. Elijah White who was making an exploration along the foothills of the Cascade Range for the purpose of locating an emigrant road to the eastern states. Dr. White and a companion, Batteus Du Guerre, climbed the mountain and the following passage, quoted from his book Ten Years in Oregon (compiled by Miss A. J. Allen and published in 1848), describes their experience on the summit:

> They now took a delightful survey of the general features of the landscape before them. On one hand was the vast chain of the Cascade Mountains, Mt. Hood looming in solitary grandeur far above its fellows; on the other hand was the Umpqua Mountains, and a little farther on, the coast ridge. Between these lay the whole magnificent panorama of the Willamette Valley, with its ribbon streams, and carpet-like verdure. The day was fine, and such was the clearness of the atmosphere that the scene was very distinct, grand and imposing. In enthusiastic admiration of the noble site, the doctor names the elevation Mt. Spencer, in compliment to John C. Spencer, the then secretary of war. . . .

"A. G. Walling's Illustrated History of Lane County has quite a different story about the naming of Spencer Butte. Based on tradition, Walling's version holds that the butte was named for a young Englishman named Spencer who wandered away from a Hudson Bay Company party and was killed on the mountain by Indians." (For more of this story see page 113 in this book.) One of the Spencer family descendants who lives in Eugene today claims the Spencers in these two stories were brothers, although she has not as yet been able to document that this is true.

Spencer Butte Pioneers

100 Years on the Sunny Side of the Butte
1850-1950

by LOIS BARTON

Spencer Butte Press
Eugene, Oregon
1982

The publication of this book has been aided by a contribution from the Lane County Historical Society Publication Fund and by local supporters of regional history through pre-publication subscription.

Library of Congress Catalog Card Number: 82-61837
International Standard Book Number: 0-9609420-0-9

Book Production by
Northwest Matrix
385 East Eleventh Street
Eugene, Oregon 97401

Book Design by
Vesta Creative Services

First Printing: November 1982
Second Printing: January 1987

Other books by Lois Barton:
Howard & Edith Holloway Family History, 1978
Lane County Historian Index, 1984
Daughter of the Soil, 1985
One Woman's West, 1986

Available from:
Spencer Butte Press
84889 Harry Taylor Road
Eugene, OR 97405

Dedication

For Elsie Swaggart Sutton (1906-1981) who was born here, went to school here, raised her family here and left her heart here. She knew the sunny side folks and where to find them.

Contents

Acknowledgments

This book could not have been written without the cooperation and support of a great many people. The late Martin Schmidt of the University of Oregon Library's Oregon Collection got me off to a good start. Ed Nolan and Marty West of the Lane County Museum Library and the staff of the Oregon Historical Library in Portland knew where to look and helped me find many names and pictures. Mary Rodman and Audrey Kuschke walked over the ground with me.

I am especially indebted to the families who lived here: to Elsie Swaggart Sutton and her brother Lester; Bertha Toll and Flora Toll Getchell; Walter and Bill Kindt and Maggie Kindt Toll; David and George Knox and Gertrude Knox Albro and her husband Merl; Merl's mother, Irene Carson Albro; Howard and Dorothy McBeth and Ruth McBeth Svarverud; Clarence Lombard and Helen Kerr Brown; Helen's mother, Ruth Lombard Kerr; Candace Haley Harris; Helen Osburn Meador; Mollie and Henry Christensen; Paul Ziniker and Ed Ziniker Jr. and Annabelle, his wife; Marie Ziniker Erdmann; Ralph Ruegger; John Napper; Emory and Mildred Pruett; Harry Taylor's family; Ethel Briggs who collected much of the Gay family history; Janet Bell Brown; John and Joyce Kommer; Florence Murdock; Quintin Barton and all the others who gave of their time so generously.

Special appreciation goes to Hal Barton who suggested the subtitle and to all my family who lived with an accumulating clutter of records, a single-minded chatter about "my homesteaders" and the clatter of my typewriter through five long years. It also goes to Barbara Hill for assistance with copy-editing. We have produced a unique record for those who come after us and I thank you all for helping it happen.

Lois Barton
Residing on the Jonathan Riggs
Donation Land Claim
May, 1982

Preface

Curiosity did it. Curiosity and Harry Taylor's stories.

My grandfather barely resisted the lure of the Oregon Trail. As for me—every wish I made on a star throughout my adolescence was that I might grow up to marry a Westerner and live in the West. Fate granted that wish. I've had a ringside seat to observe developments "at the end of the Trail" for a quarter of a century.

*Barton hayfield south
of Spencer Butte, 1953.
Lois Barton*

Covered wagon stories always ended with the promised land in sight. Then what happened? Specifically, what happened here on the sunny side of Spencer Butte? Whose axes rang out through the morning mist, falling timbers for a new home in the wilderness? Where did these particular settlers come from? How did they fare once they arrived? Was the land good to them?

As the oldest child on a family farm in Ohio, I knew first-hand about caring for livestock, about seedtime and harvest in the fields, about using and preserving the fruits of our labor to feed an active farm family the year around.

Much of that experience has fit into our Oregon subsistence lifestyle as my husband and I raised eight children on our place south of Spencer Butte. It also has been valuable background as I tried to understand how it was "in the early days."

Harry Taylor was here fifty years ahead of me. He knew some of the first and second generation settlers. He farmed and logged and helped sustain the schools and neighborhood. He was our nearest neighbor for several years and during that time shared his talents and memories with me.

Now, because fate took a hand, my curiosity prevailed and Harry told his stories, here is a sequel to covered wagons on the Oregon Trail.

Lois Barton

Introduction

For thirty years I've watched the seasons come and go on the Jonathan Riggs Donation Land Claim south of Spencer Butte. (Only through this study have I discovered it was the Riggs Donation Land Claim.) I've waded through the mud to do winter chores, rejoiced with returning bluebirds in the spring, shocked hay in the summer twilight, stored bushels of squash, apples and carrots for the winter—and wondered who cleared these fields before me and when.

This "doby" clay soil, a sharp contrast to the rich sandy loam of the Ohio farm where I grew up, is pernickety to work and not very productive. After the hardships of the wagon trail, it must have been quite a letdown for midwesterners to find the Oregon country was something less than paradise.

How did those plucky folks ever make it through their first winter? Many's the stormy morning I've sat gazing out the stable window with the smell of fresh warm milk billowing up from the pail between my knees, trying to imagine the details of feeding and caring for a family in some primitive shelter. Rain and fog and only wet wood to burn. Scarce food and little variety. Water to carry and heat and a scrubboard for doing laundry. Never quite warm, a dirt floor, and no established haven for temporary relief from the hardship and loneliness of the raw frontier.

In our first years here we had the good fortune to know Harry Taylor. He'd been on the sunny side of Spencer Butte since 1893 and he knew the land and the people. Our closest neighbor, he often ate with us. Daily experiences reminded him of past happenings which he recounted colorfully.

I was busy those years with small children, a garden, chickens, goats and cows to tend. But Harry's stories fascinated me. One time or another, I wrote down the ones I thought should be included in a history I would someday write. But where to begin? How does one learn about local events of one hundred years ago? Martin Schmidt at the University of Oregon said one must talk to the old folks, read old newspapers, look up records. At first I couldn't remember the name of the family Harry worked for as a boy, but the Christensens thought it was Osburn. A family member who was in real estate in Portland had visited them many years ago to see what the old home place looked like. Letters to all the Osburns listed in the Portland telephone directory brought a return-addressed postcard with the name of a granddaughter. What a thrill! A similar mailing to Riggs in the Moscow,

Edie Barton and goats circa 1955.
Lois Barton

Idaho, area was entirely unproductive, but I found enlistment papers in the Oregon Historical Library. When I got the Ruegger account book it was written in old German script. One clue led to another, and so the puzzle unraveled.

Now there is time. The original plan was to write about "our place" but one thing led to another. Osburn, for whom Harry worked, owned land clear to Dillard Road. Who had settled that? The Taylors traded their farm in Fairmount, east of Eugene, for a "brush ranch" on Spencer Creek. Someone else was there first. Who?

Boundaries for this study were set arbitrarily—Lorane Highway on the west, Camas Swale Road on the south, the eastern edge of the Christensen Valley on the east, and Spencer Butte on the north. I have studiously ignored tantalizing tidbits about territory all around the edge.

I started by learning what I could about the first settlers. I soon uncovered a trend toward large cattle ranches. Within a decade of settling, many of the homesteaders had moved on, selling their land, or abandoning it, for jobs in town or to try their hand in the gold fields. Family farms persisted, but usually provided only marginal subsistence in return for lots of hard work.

The following story touches only lightly on some of the area included because my sources were unfamiliar with those details. If your favorite acreage has been slighted, I hope you will add to this history.

The following quotes provide a description of that first winter after the long trek across the Oregon Trail and set the scene for what follows:

> Arriving in Oregon in late September or early October, the first concern of the pioneer was to find shelter. While some immediately set out to locate claims, many wintered wherever they could and waited until the next spring to look for available land.
>
> During the first winter the outfit that survived the trip across the plains became very important. Those precious tools, the broadaxe and auger, were used to construct crude shelters. Sound wagons and healthy teams were sold for cash or traded for necessities, or even land.

> All our outfit in the spring of 1853 was two yoke of oxen and one two-year-old heifer, having sold the wagon during the winter to get food and comfortable clothing. (From *A Piece of the Old Tent,* Lane County Pioneer Museum, 1976, p. 26.)

John Champion Richardson, who arrived in Oregon in October 1846, at the age of sixteen, wrote about living conditions that first winter.

> Came there too late [in the fall] to build, consequently we had to live that winter in a large tent brought across the plains. To this tent we made some additions, made of boards split out of timber that grew on the place. We had to go with ax and crosscut saw and hang a boy to each end of that saw and cut the timber into proper lengths and then with maul and wedge split it into what the western man called boards, but Yankey called shakes and with these boards make the necessary additional rooms, not by nailing them together for the reason that we had no nails. Perhaps there was not a nail in the whole tabernacle, neither sides nor roof. We made the boards stay in their places by means of green willows. Those on the roof we layed weight poles across the boards and fastened them there with willows too. . . . In this crude building we spent the winter in Oregon. . . . Occasionally mother would say, "Boys, how are you geting along with your work?" or perhaps [we would] see the tears falling from mother's face, or hear the remark, "This is an awful way to live."
>
> . . . Add to this hard way of living, my father, in laying in a supply of flour to last us till spring came, when we could haul from below, only laid in enough to last until the latter part of winter or early spring. However he had brought on some wheat for seed, but when the flour gave out we had to make a break on the wheat, so we had to live on boiled wheat and potatoes for six weeks. It was boiled wheat and potatoes and for a change it was potatoes and boiled wheat. (*Lane County Historian*, Vol. XIII, p. 25.)

> Winter was fast approaching, the farm operations for the season were closed. Few of the immigrants had money, the remnant of their stock was in no condition to sell, except at ruinous sacrifice, yet all needed supplies. It was a difficult matter to find employment and an absolute necessity to have such. Railmaking and hewing timber were almost the sole opportunity of the emigrant to procure food and raiment. As for houses, we stowed away as best we could in huts, sheds, shanties and cabins. . . . By dint of mutual good offices, much forbearance, a great deal of scrimping, patching and doing without, the winter wore away and search for homes began in earnest in the spring. (From *A Piece of the Old Tent,* p. 26.)

In the following pages you will find "unique" spellings, grammatical usage and punctuation in quotations from written records, telephone conversations, informal chats and tape-recorded interviews. I have tried to be faithful to the original copy where quotes were used and to give an authentic report from the people interviewed wherever possible because it allowed me to share more completely the adventure of my search.

Today's reader should understand the pioneers' attitude toward the Indians they dealt with, as reflected in this book, to be a product of the times. Hindsight allows us to perceive their very real conflict of interest more objectively, and to acknowledge that records available to us seldom shed light on the Native American point of view. □

CHAPTER 1

The First Settlers

By 1851 when the earliest settlements were made in the area south of Spencer Butte, most suitable acreage in the Willamette Valley from Portland south to Eugene already had been claimed. Newcomers were obliged to push ever farther into the wilderness away from any "civilization" which had developed to find available land that could be tilled or otherwise utilized for satisfactory homesteads.

This chapter includes tidbits about only part of the homesteaders who came to our area. For a complete list of the first settlers please see Appendix I. To understand where each claim was located you will need to consult the map on page 121. My purpose has been primarily to present the story of the relationship between the people and the land—to explore how the land either supported or hindered the settler. I have deliberately avoided detailed genealogies and sequential ownership data in favor of the broader picture. Index references will help you coordinate information about people whose names recur in later chapters.

Some of the homesteaders left a partial record of their lives in public places such as old newspapers, land ownership records and other public documents. I have no doubt that more fascinating details will emerge as time goes by, but for now we must shape the picture of the past from these incomplete fragments.

Because my search began with our "home place," I will tell first about the Jonathan Riggs Donation Land Claim. The other family stories are in alphabetical order.

JONATHAN AND MARY RIGGS

Jonathan Riggs, born in Kentucky in 1803, and his wife Mary, also a Kentuckian, were married May 12, 1825, in Monroe County, Missouri. With several children they arrived in Oregon November 16, 1852. By June of the following year the Riggs family had settled on 322.98 acres just south of Spencer Butte. The homestead certificate notes that the north half of their claim belonged to Jonathan, the south half to Polly (Mary). The 1860 census lists as household residents: Jonathan, Mary, twins Reuben and John, age thirteen, who were born in Missouri, Louise, eleven, also born in Missouri and Martha, ten, born in Iowa. An older son, Garnett, located a 320-acre claim adjoining his parents' homestead on the north and east. Son William settled a couple of miles east near what is now Dillard Road and Highway 99 South.

For twelve years the two Riggs families lived on their neighboring homesteads, building homes, clearing land and planting an orchard. Their buildings, of which nothing now remains, were apparently located at about the same place as those still in use on the properties 120 years later. Year-round springs of good water would have been one deciding factor in their placement.

Three reports indicate the location of the Riggs buildings. First, Garnett sold 240 acres of his homestead to Joseph Brumley in 1859, keeping only the 80 acres "on which his house and farm are situated." (Deed Book E, p. 178.) Second, when Lester Swaggart hunted and trapped across the Riggs Donation Land Claim in the early 1900s, the remains of a barn were still identifiable in the woods just north of the creek in the present barnyard. Third, John Taylor tells of finding old coins and broken dishes (indicating a homesite) on the knoll just south of that barn, an area where the Taylors grew their family garden.

The Riggs' orchard was just west of the farm buildings and downhill from a good spring which made watering of the young fruit trees feasible. Harry Taylor, then fourteen, came to work on the Osburn ranch in 1893 and often rode through the Riggs orchard to round up Osburn's milk cows. He said the fruit trees were fully mature at that time, and young pines just big enough to brush his stirrups were growing up among them. Many of those old apple trees are still producing usable fruit. Varieties include Baldwins, Newtons, Spitzenbergs, and a locally-identified Johnson Cider Apple which "apple historian" Lester McGraw says resembles a Rome Beauty seedling.

Garnett Riggs enlisted in 1855 to fight Indians in the Rogue Valley. Correspondence on file in the Oregon Historical Library in Portland indicates that he was a wagonmaster working under an officer named E. B. Matlock. Garnett's daughter wrote in 1903, "I was born February 6, 1856, in Oregon, Lane County, near Eugene City in a log hut and my mother has told me of the many times she had to run from the Indian before I was born. She was afraid of the Indian spys." Garnett's enlistment

The barn Harry Taylor built on Jonathan Riggs Donation Land Claim.
Lois Barton 1956

paper has this description of him: "Height, 5 feet 7½ inches, blew eyes, mouse hair, lite complexion."

In 1867 Jonathan Riggs' seventeen-year-old daughter Martha married Henry Padburg who was born in Prussia but was now homesteading just south of the Riggs place. The 1870 census showed Henry and Martha living on his homestead with their one-year-old daughter Mary.

In 1865 Jonathan and Garnett Riggs both sold their claims to George and James Emerick who had homesteaded a little farther south in 1853. Garnett's name appears in Amity, Oregon, in the 1870 census. Jonathan's family apparently was not in the state at that time. Five years later the Riggs property was resold to Thomas Judkins, and the Emericks migrated to

The hay mower must be oiled frequently.
Lois Barton 1953

Loading the hay. Harry Taylor and Barton children plus one neighbor.
Lois Barton 1953

Wasco County where they executed the affidavit of ownership.

Judkins ran sheep. In the summer of 1876 Nick Toll came to Oregon from California with his dad, Jonathan Toll, on an exploratory trip. "At eighteen he could handle a man's job. The Judkins had a large acreage in the Spencer Butte area. They wanted someone to care for their sheep. Nick took the job," according to his grandson Lester Swaggart.

On October 6, 1883, Lusina Judkins, widow, sold the Riggs property to Alex M. Osburn, who held it till 1894. After that almost the entire 2,000-acre Osburn place was resold eight times to local and out-of-state speculators between 1894 and 1910. The 1910 purchasers Samuel and Lydia Graham, established the Porter Acres subdivision which included the former Riggs Donation Land Claim.

A little more than a decade later Lawrence and Mollie Christensen rented a portion of the Osburn ranch, including the buildings, "from Chambers, the banker." The area was unfenced open range. During a 1976 interview Henry and Mollie Christensen said, "We used to farm that [Riggs] place all the time. Raised wheat and oats up there. We farmed them open fields for years. We'd pick apples up there every fall. That was a big orchard in them days. That was a beautiful orchard. It run clear down to your house, and then way up there."

During 1931 and 1932 Harry Taylor and John Gimpl bought the Riggs Donation Land Claims and additional contiguous acreage from P. L. Snodgrass, real estate dealer and financier, on a tax sale, paying on a stumpage basis for the timber. Later, Taylor bought out Gimpl's interest in the more than 900 acres and fenced the Riggs place at a cost of $3,000. He moved his family into a new cabin and built a barn, granary, shop, and chicken house. For ten years he farmed the Riggs fields, pastured mohair goats and cattle, cut many cords of firewood and hauled it to Eugene for sale. His wife, Belle, died on the place in 1941. Shortly after that he gave about 338 acres, including part of the Jonathan Riggs Donation Land Claim, and part of the Garnett Riggs Donation Land Claim to his son John with the understanding that John would look after him in his old age.

Into the haymow via a mechanical fork which dropped hay from an overhead track.
Lois Barton

John planted a two-acre commercial strawberry patch about 1940, but was drafted before the berries came into production and the deer got most of the crop. After discharge John logged another part of the acreage to pay for a college education, then sold the place to the present owners, Lois and Hal Barton, in 1951.

For most of the years between 1951 and his death in 1960, Harry Taylor lived in the old farmhouse on this place as our neighbor, usually eating his evening meal at our table. He helped us plant and harvest a few crops of hay in the cleared fields. He grubbed land for a small vineyard and a boysenberry patch. He put up clotheslines, built gates, repaired fences, erected another barn and an addition to the chicken house, and helped with the family butchering. He raised several acres of sweet corn two different years which I helped him market in the small local groceries. And he reminisced as he worked. He told stories at the table and rode with us to church, pointing out historical landmarks, recalling early events and people. Here the Osburns trapped a "wild" sow. There Orville Phelps had his nursery. This log house was built by neighbors to house a widow and her family. This is where they smoked salmon brought from tidewater on the Siuslaw river each fall—an overnight trip for team and wagon each way. So Harry planted the idea for this book.

This, then, is the story of the Jonathan Riggs Donation Land Claim. It is perhaps representative of land use on the sunny side of Spencer Butte, 1850-1950.

JAMES AND WILLIAM ANDERSON

According to Janet Bell Brown who taught school for thirty-four years in the Fox Hollow-LeBleu area, James and William Anderson were Canadians who came and took up claims together. One man's wife didn't like living in the "wilderness," so Janet bought his claim and paid him $135 for the work he'd done, namely building a shack and clearing a small piece of garden. The Andersons and a "Yankee" Irishman associated with them "built 'em a sawmill —a three-man sawmill, and they sawed out lumber. . . . My homestead shack was made out o' the lumber, and there wasn't any two boards the same width, the same thickness. They were put together with spikes and the

spikes kept—when the lumber dried out, the spikes *just* held them together. We'd look up and just wonder how long those spikes was a goin' to hold. They stayed just long enough to make a little something and split." (From an unpublished interview with JBB February 19, 1977.)

Janet earned full title under the homestead law to the claim she bought from one of the Andersons by 1925. Meanwhile she married. In due time she and her husband bought thirty-one adjoining acres of low-lying land with a good field on it in order to get a right-of-way out to the public road. They built a house and barn on that land and lived there until 1939.

HOLLEN BAILEY

Hollen Bailey was the fourth son of John Bailey, Sr., a Clay County, Kentucky, man. Tradition has it that John's father was James Bailey, a Virginian, who went from Virginia into the Kentucky Territory long before it became a state. All the members of this family were tall people. The shortest was Hollen's sister, Elizabeth, who was an even six feet tall. Most of the family came to Oregon during the years 1847 to 1853. Bailey Hill was named for the family. (*Lane County Historian*, Vol. VII, p. 8.)

Hollen was born in 1822. He married Elizabeth McCollum October 24, 1851, in Benton County, having arrived in Oregon prior to 1850. He settled on his claim in 1853 but was killed four years later by Indians in Cow Creek Canyon in Douglas County while helping drive hogs to California, leaving a widow with two children. She remarried James F. Amis and by 1870 was living in Eugene near Judkins. Hollen signed an affidavit for Samuel and Zilpha McCollum stating that he had known them as husband and wife since 1847, which would suggest that he may have traveled west with them and later married their daughter.

JOHN BLANTON

John Blanton was born in Jackson County, Missouri, April 29, 1833, and started to cross the plains with his parents in 1844. His father, a cooper by trade, died near Council Bluffs, Iowa, enroute to Oregon at age thirty-nine, leaving his widow and children dependent upon their own resources. The mother turned

Calloway Family. Front row: Charles and Elizabeth Ware Calloway. Second row, from left: Susy Calloway Wood, Mary Frances Calloway Roberts, John Calloway. Third row, from left: James, Tom and Henry Calloway.
Winter Photo circa 1895,
Lane County Museum

back to Andrew County, Missouri, and three years later remarried and continued to live in Missouri the rest of her life.

John lived with his mother until nineteen years of age. He worked as a farm hand for about three years. In 1853 he had an offer to go west as a driver of oxen, which he accepted. The train was on the road for three months and eleven days. He lived with an uncle, Isaac Blanton, near Salem for a short time. In 1861 he went to the mines of southern Oregon, where he met with fair success. In 1865 he married Catherine Shepard and they went to housekeeping on a farm near Eugene in Lane County. After five years they moved to Jackson County, where the Blantons raised livestock for a couple of years before moving to Polk County for four years and in the Waldo Hills of Marion County for a year.

Catherine Shephard was born in 1846 in Crawford County, Arkansas, and crossed the plains with her parents in 1852. The couple had twelve children. Blanton was a Democrat and a member of the United Evangelical Church. (Adapted from *Portrait and Biographical Record of the Willamette Valley, Oregon.*)

JAMES F. BOWDEN

James F. Bowden was born in 1832 in Devonshire, England. He came to America at the age of two years. An affidavit in Volume III of *Genealogical Material in Oregon Donation Land Claims* notes that James' father was a naturalized citizen before he became twenty-one years old. James married Mary Elston January 13, 1853, at Fort Boise, Oregon Territory. The Huddleston store ledger, page 70, lists purchases made by Bowden in 1854: boots, tobacco and merchandise worth $50, the bill for which was settled by a note and work. James sold the homestead to John W. Bowden October 5, 1883, for $600 in gold coin. Both buyer and seller were living in California when the deal was completed.

CHARLES CALLOWAY

According to family history, Charles traveled with Kit Carson and fought in the Mexican War. In 1840 his father, John, wrote a letter to a cousin in Kentucky and referred to Charles and his brother as "big wild boys." He said they had traveled to New Mexico and planned to go again in the spring. Charles was a big man, six-foot-two-inches tall and weighing around 200 pounds. Once during a flood a neighbor's wife called for help saying her cow was being swept down stream. Charles jumped into the swirling waters, grabbed the cow by the neck and pulled her ashore. In later years his wife Elizabeth suffered from an intestinal disorder and experienced great pain. Charles would pick her up in his arms and walk the floor to try and ease her pain.

In the spring of 1852 Charles, Elizabeth and the two boys, John, age seven, and Charles Henry, age two, left Missouri and traveled by wagon across the Oregon Trail. Robert Ware, Elizabeth's brother, was also with the wagon train. Family tradition states Elizabeth walked barefooted beside her brother's wagon to nurse

Andrew and Maria Carson and son Henry circa 1913. A portion of the third house on their homestead in background.
Irene Albro

his family through an illness on the trail. It is thought her mother was traveling with them and died along the way.

By May 16, 1852, the Callaways and Wares were along the Platte River, twenty miles west of Fort Kearney, Nebraska, and it was there Thomas Ware (probably Elizabeth's other brother) died. His widow, Sarah Mariah, may have been Charles' half sister. Their destination was finally reached when they arrived in Oregon September 25, 1852. Elizabeth gave birth to her second child, James H., eleven days later.

Charles and his family moved to their donation land claim on August 15, 1853. Charles was a farmer and raised hogs, driving them to California to sell. (From information provided by Joann Callaway of San Jose, California, in the summer of 1982.)

ANDREW JACKSON CARSON

David Carson, from Ireland, became a naturalized citizen on October 19, 1844, in Platte County, Missouri. He settled on a claim in Benton County in 1850. One of his heirs, Andrew Jackson Carson, was born in North Carolina March 20, 1832. He moved to Missouri as a child, then to Oregon in 1850. He lived in Benton County one year, possibly with his parents, and then settled on his Lane County claim in 1854. When interviewed later about these years, Andrew related:

There were only two houses in the Eugene townsite at that time, the Charnel Mulligan home in the southeast portion and the Eugene Skinner residence at the lower end of Skinner's Butte.

I was among the first citizens to vote for locating the county seat in this city.

[Our trip across the plains] required just five months, two and a half days for our caravan of ox teams to land in Oregon. The Indians were very troublesome and frequent massacres were reported to us as we came over the trail. On reaching the Snake river it was borne to our ears that an emigrant train ahead of us had been attacked. The Indians killed the mother and grown son in the affray and took captive the two daughters of the party. We heard afterwards that the younger girl died while a prisoner of the Indians, but that the other girl was ultimately rescued by the white settlers. (From an undated newspaper clipping, probably about 1911-1912.)

Andrew's daughter, Irene Carson Albro, recounted her father's experience driving hogs to southern Oregon.

The Baileys and my dad, they taken a drove of hogs to southern Oregon. But before they got there the Indians attacked them and they had quite a squirmish (sic) with the Indians and that was where Hollen Bailey was killed by the Indians. They lost all the hogs. The oxen were killed and the wagon destroyed that carried the supplies. They were driving two or three hundred head of hogs from here in this valley and out beyond Lorane. That was before my dad was married, and he was married in 1865. My dad mined after he went out there. He mined in southern Oregon. The Chinese was in there. . . . My dad stayed out there for several years and mined, then he came back here and taken up this place. He taken eighty acres here and eighty acres over there. The Simpson place was his. But they wouldn't allow—the government didn't want him to have only so much, so Mr. Moore, his friend, come and he taken the other eighty acres. They were very good friends. They run their stock together. I've heard Dad say that Mr. Moore came over and brought him a ham. And he said, "Well, Andy, I brought you a ham of meat. I don't know whether it was your hog or my hog." But that's the way they did. The stock run together and the hogs.

They had a boy named James, and one that was named Luther, but I don't remember Mr. Moore's name. See, that was way before my time. (From an interview with Irene Albro, November 10, 1977.)

Irene told another story about Indians on Spencer Creek. Her father used to tell the family that a group of Indians camped on Spencer Creek for several days—sometime before Irene was born in 1890. Their campsite was between the present Lutheran Church and the creek. They didn't bother anyone. Local residents found arrowheads in that strip of ground in later years.

About 1900 when Irene was ten or eleven years old and at school one day, a large Indian man came to the house and sat down in the rocking chair on the front porch without knocking or making any effort to come in. Her mother and sister inside the house were frightened. They took the gun and went out the back door to get Andrew who was cutting wood on the back of the place. He didn't want the gun, but left it in the woodshed when he came down to the house. Then he went around to the front to see what the Indian wanted. He could talk to them pretty well in jargon. The Indian was after deer hides to make buckskin. Andrew had one he never expected to use hanging in the woodshed, so gave it to the man. That ended *that* Indian scare.

Andrew married Mary Anne Ware and had nine children. Mary Anne's father, Thomas Ware, died of cholera while crossing the plains and Mary Anne came across with another train. The Calloways and Wares were relatives. Mary's mother was a Calloway. Her brother married a Ware. Irene still lives on her father's homestead.

PHILIP CONKLE

The only information about Philip Conkle I have discovered is in a newspaper clipping.

SAD ACCIDENT: On Thursday, December 8th a sad accident occurred about eight miles south of this city. A son of Philip Conkle, aged about 12 years, while hunting had the misfortune to slip while standing on a log, causing the discharge of his shotgun, the charge entering his body just below the heart, ranging upward causing his instant death. A younger brother

Irene Carson Albro's wedding picture.
Irene Albro

was with him at the time and brought the sad news to the famiy. Mr. Conkle and relatives have the sincere sympathy of all the neighbors in their sad affliction. (Eugene City *Guard,* December 17, 1881.)

JASPER AND ISAAC EEDY (EDIA)

Isaac was Jasper's son. Jasper took up a claim that had originally been filed by John H. Dinning. Charles Calloway and Thomas Bailey signed an affidavit before Joel Ware that John Dinning left and abandoned his claim after one year's residence, leaving the county in the "spring of 1856 and is not now in this section of the country." In 1871 Jasper sold his homestead to his son. On July 11, 1872, he married Mrs. Martha Winter. According to the 1870 census, Isaac was born in Indiana and Sarah, his wife, in Missouri. Irene Albro remembered that Jasper Edia (two spellings of this name appear on the records, a common phenomenon in early documents) went with her father and the Bailey men to drive hogs to southern Oregon.

Jasper Edia's homestead cabin.
George Knox

IRA HAWLEY

This account by Nirom Hawley from the *Lane County Historian* gives a picture of the early pioneers' experiences in getting settled on the land. His father, Ira Hawley, finally located at Divide, just south of Cottage Grove, but not until after high water discouraged the family from making the Creswell area their permanent home.

The Hawley family left Illinois in March 1852. They arrived in the Willamette Valley at harvest time. A brief summary of their search for open land precedes the account of actual settlement:

Soon after we struck camp two little girls came over and brought some muskmelons. We had a little visit and got somewhat acquainted. The young men came to camp too. Father asked them if there were any vacant cabins around. Father wanted to stay awhile here and let the stock pick up strength and flesh while he looked over the country. The man said there was a cabin about one-half mile away which had a good fireplace. There was a good spring nearby. It belonged to a fellow who had gone to the mines. He thought this man would not object if we moved in. We afterwards learned that it was this young fellow's own cabin. He was not twenty-one years old, so he held the land in this way. This family's name was Gear. Mrs. Gear was not at home when we first camped. The girls came over again and we learned that our families had come from near the same place. After we had been in that cabin for a while a new baby came to Mr. Gear's home. He secured Mother for a nurse. We moved over to their house. They had lived on that farm for a year or two. They had muskmelons and tomatoes. My, how we enjoyed them, and what appetites we had.

Father would take the light wagon and horse team and search for a place to settle. He went as far as French Prairie and Oregon City. He brought home some apples and groceries for the winter. While camped at Mr. Gear's, father sold one small mare for $200 and sold the one I had ridden for $200 in cash and he was to receive $100 worth of apple trees the next fall if we settled within reach. If not Mr. Gear was to send him the money. Mr. Gear was starting a nursery. After Father came back from Oregon City a light frost nipped the tomatoes. Mother preserved our big water can full of them. While camped here I lost my spotted pony. He broke his trail rope off. We could not corral him or drive him into a lane so we had to leave him. Mr. Gear afterwards sold him a-running [on the hoof].

I think we stayed in this locality for six weeks. Father bought a yoke of big steers. Our stock rested and picked up quite a little. We bought wheat for our winter's flour and started south.

We went to a little grist mill and store where we had our wheat ground. Mother bought some clouded blue dishes at the store. This was on the Santiam river. I think the town of Scio is located there now. We crossed the south fork. I think Lebanon is located near that place. After traveling four or five more days we came to Calapooya River where Brownsville is now located. Father went out away from the creek as the land along the creek was all taken up. We traveled along the foothills of Linn County prairie in the Willamette Valley. The land along the foothills where there were springs and along the creeks was pretty well taken. This place was a little south of Albany, about eighteen or twenty miles from the Willamette River. The old settlers told us that the country was so wet that it did not amount to anything. We camped in an oak grove which was a very pretty place. Two young men who were traveling with us began to dig a well. As they had poor tools they did not get along very fast. It took Father and I about one half day to take the stock to water and bring them back again. One night he decided he wanted a farm with a living spring on it.

The next day we drove on south and camped by a little creek that night. The young men were anxious to reach the mines. We had to travel so slowly with our winter's supply of provisions that Father decided to leave Mother and children in camp. He took the horse team and the men went on. Mother turned nurse again. I think it was a sick baby this time. Father went on about forty miles to a place near where Creswell is now situated. He picked out a claim and laid the foundation for a cabin and stuck up his claim notice. Then he came back for us. He was gone about a week. Again we drove south. I think we made the trip in about three days. We pitched camp on a slough which had a water hole in it. By digging in the side of the bank we got very good water to use. We afterward found a seep spring which furnished water for the house. The grass was big all around our camp. There had been a plague of mice and they had completely mowed the grass. It was good feed until the heavy rains came. Then the cut grass soon spoiled. I hunted in the bushes until I found a willow with three prongs. I cut two off short and left one for a handle. My small brother and I soon raked up enough grass to fill two bed ticks which were made from the wagon sheets.

I should have stated that we reached this place in November. A man had started a wet-weather saw mill not far away. We bought a few hundred feet of lumber, about one-half enough to box up our cabin. Then the mill broke down so we could not get any more lumber. Our claim cornered in a grove of small firs. Father cut small logs and built a lean-to on our cabin. We had to go five or six miles to get fir timber suitable to make shakes with which to shingle our house. That gave us two rooms. The boxed building was unfinished.

Two Robinson brothers and two Riggs brothers were our neighbors. The Riggs men had married sisters of the Robinson men. The Riggs family [no apparent relation to Jonathan] lived about four miles north of us. One of the Robinsons lived about five miles west and the other one lived about nine miles south. A number of emigrants came to that country during the fall of 1852.

During the fall and early winter Robinson and Riggs butchered Spanish cattle about once a week and sold it to the emigrants. They said people had better lay in their winter supply while the beef was fat. They advised salting the beef down. Feed would be poor when the grass began to rot. They would sell only dry old Spanish cows which had been brought from California. They sold them for fifty dollars apiece. An emigrant cow would bring about one hundred dollars. Father cut a big oak tree and hauled a cut of it up to the cabin. He dug a trough in it. He planned to salt meat in that as he could not get barrels.

About Christmas time we had a big snow storm. The snow became deep for that country. Father took his best yoke of oxen and went over to the Riggs place. Mr. Robinson got a couple of horses and then they hunted a fat cow. They corralled and butchered her. Then Father brought her home and salted the meat down in our oak trough. We had our winter's supply of meat.

The snow lasted for about ten days. There was no feed in the country. Quite a lot of the oak timber was covered with a long spiderweb moss. Father went out every morning and cut down several trees. The cattle ate greedily of the moss and small limbs. The cattle lived through the winter very well.

When the snow melted the river got very high. Father had never filed on this land. In January we moved fifteen miles farther south where we made our permanent home. (*Lane County Historian*, Vol. XIV, pp. 58-61.)

WASHINGTON JEWETT

Washington Jewett was born in Indiana in 1831. He arrived in Oregon November 20, 1847, and was living with his father, John Jewett, in Clatsop County when the 1850 census was taken. Washington settled on his claim near Spencer Butte November 19, 1855. He traveled with a group of men who went to Eastern Oregon in the summer of 1860 to look for the lost Blue Bucket Mine. The group was attacked by Indians in the south end of the Blue Mountains. The attack took place "June 7th, 1860 and 63 horses were run off in this surprise." A Mr. Leggett (or Liggett) wounded himself in the foot June 2, and was therefore not ambulatory. Two other men fell ill. It appears that the first Indian attack was to steal the horses and probably to stampede the men so the Paiutes could gather in their possessions as well.

"The Blue Bucket seekers decided there was nothing to do but start home with their remaining 37 horses. The Indians attacked them within two miles from the scene of the first affair. The valley men believed they killed some Indians but a Mr. 'Phips' was wounded. . . ." The men drafted an appeal to Governor Whiteaker asking for troops to "chastise" the Indians and explaining their troubles with the tribe. Washington Jewett was one of the signers of that appeal.

The story goes that the men eventually got back to the Willamette Valley on foot. As far as the records show no property lost by the Blue Bucket seekers was ever recovered even though regular army troops did go down into the Harney Basin where a reconnaissance party was attacked on June 23. It is probable that the attackers were the same Indians who had routed the prospectors from the Willamette Valley. (Adapted from *Lane County Historian*, Vol. XIII, p. 76-78.)

Washington Jewett's name does not appear in the Lane County census either in 1860 or 1870.

JOSEPH M. JONES

Joseph Jones was married in Pike County, Illinois, in 1839 and settled on his claim November 15, 1853, with his wife, Polly, and their two children. Two more children were born in Lane County before they moved to Sublimity in 1866. Joseph Jones won a premium for an Oregon-made plow at the first Oregon State Fair.

In an interview with Joseph's son, Reverend T. L. Jones, he told Fred Lockley:

My people were Southerners. I was born in Pike County, Illinois, February 4, 1841. . . . My father, J. M. Jones, who was born in South Carolina, was a farmer. My mother, whose maiden name was Polly L. Davis, was born in Missouri. Her parents were natives of Kentucky. They were married in 1839. I am the second of their eleven children. . . .

I was 12 years old when we started for Oregon, in the spring of 1853. We came across the plains by ox team and prairie schooner. I walked barefoot from the Missouri River to the Willamete Valley, a 2000-mile walk. My job was to drive the loose cows. Father drove the oxen. Father took up a donation land claim eight miles south of Eugene, not far from the present city of Creswell. At that time there were only four houses in Eugene. Father taught school in a log schoolhouse near our claim. The school usually lasted three months in each year. (From Mike Helm's *Conversations with Bullwackers, et. al.* citing the Oregon *Journal,* September 24, 1922.)

ERNEST AND CHARLES KNOOP
An early history provides this biography:

Immigrants from Germany. Charles Knoop is the owner of an attractive fruit ranch of eleven acres located a mile and a half northwest of Eugene on Pacific Highway, that he has been cultivating for six years. Born in Germany in 1859, second child of H. J. and Christina Knoop, Charles was reared and educated in his native land. At age 22 he emigrated to the U.S., first locating in Chicago. He worked at landscape gardening there for a year, then started west to San Francisco. He spent a short time in British Columbia, then went to Portland. After following various pursuits in Portland he went to eastern Oregon and engaged in sheep raising. Four years later he came to Eugene (in 1893) and invested his capital in four hundred eighty acres of land in the mountains and homesteaded a quarter section and engaged in raising Angora goats. The undertaking proved to be lucrative although he had to ship all of the wool to New York, that being the nearest market. He continued to be identified with the sheep business until 1905, when he sold his ranch and bought forty acres northwest of Eugene.

He is a man of great versatility and while living in the old country studied art. Although he has never followed this as a profession, he finds his chief recreation and keenest enjoyment in his paints and brushes. He is now working on a number of pictures which give evidence of ability and much inherent skill. (Joseph Gaston,

Atmer and Elizabeth Lombard wedding picture. Helene Brown

Centennial History of Oregon, Chicago: Clark Publishing Co., 1912, Vol. II, p. 503.)

His brother, Ernest, homesteaded adjoining property which he eventually sold to Charles after he moved to San Francisco. Charles traded the Fox Hollow acreage to Fred Knox for land on Knoop Lane in 1903.

J. LYMAN AND ATMER LOMBARD
These Lombards were sons of a sea captain who apparently drowned at sea. He left a note giving the name he chose for his yet unborn son, and Atmer was all they could make of his writing.

Atmer was fourteen when his mother remarried and the boys left for Wisconsin and later Iowa where they learned their trade— plastering, brick-laying and stone masonry. They were master masons and came West to work on Deady Hall at the University of Oregon in 1888. Much later, in 1925, Atmer was given the contract to build the Masonic Lodge in Eugene (*Lane County Historian,* Vol. I, No. 3, p. 16).

The two brothers took up adjoining homesteads southwest of Eugene. Lyman was one of the most successful contractors in Eugene (in 1903). At one time he owned 240 acres seven miles south of Eugene on fifteen acres of which he raised large quantities of fruit.

His maternal great-grandfather Hobbs fought in the Revolutionary War. His paternal grandfather, Cornelius Lombard, was born at Cape Cod and settled in Bangor, Maine, October 15, 1858. He learned the stone mason's trade in Sioux City, Iowa. He married Sarah E. Bowser of Argyle, Wisconsin, in Battlecreek, Iowa, and

Sawmill on McBeth place.
Ruth Svarverud

arrived in Eugene in 1887. Nine children were born to this union. (*Portrait and Biographical Record of the Willamette Valley, Oregon*, pp. 1086-87.)

One of their children, Ruth Lombard Kerr, wrote in 1978 some of her recollections of family life on the homestead:

My father planted the orchard and did a lot of the work on the farm. He worked all week in Eugene and had to walk back and forth to his job. . . . I recall the night our barn burned and how my oldest sister kept all of us in the house. It was a real sight and neighbors came to fight the fire. My father was in town.

One time my oldest sister and brother, probably only 10 and 12 years old, had to drive to town and get some barrels of cement for my father. It was dark when they reached the timbered road a couple of miles from home, when a huge cougar jumped at the wagon. The horses were terrified, as were the children. They made the horses gallop all the way home. The barrels of cement fell out of the wagon, but dad was so glad they arrived home safely. Those events and my mother's death convinced him he must give up his farm and move to town. My mother died in childbirth because it was winter and the doctor could not get through the terrible roads in time to help her. Mother had been a teacher before her marriage and her sister taught at the Fox Hollow school one year.

J. L. Lombard sold his property to L. D. Herrington in 1891. The place changed hands again, perhaps more than once before 1913. That year David Ross McBeth and his son Walter Herbert bought it from Charles Walker. The McBeths were from Kansas. They started with Lombard's 160 acres and bought

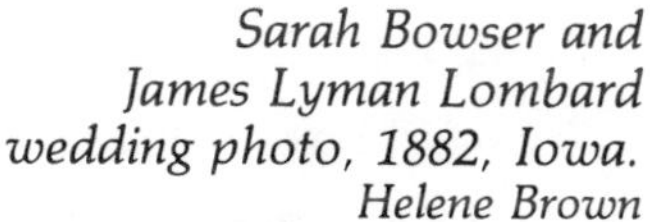

Sarah Bowser and
James Lyman Lombard
wedding photo, 1882, Iowa.
Helene Brown

Nina McBeth and her sheep.
Ruth Svarverud

McBeth Family. From left: David, Ralph, Nina (mother), Herbert (father), Howard. Children in front: Ruth and Edith.
Ruth Svarverud 1926

surrounding land until they had 1000 acres. In a taped interview on November 17, 1977, Howard McBeth said:

> They bought east of us clear up to and including the Goodpasture place [part of Martin Gay homestead]. My Uncle Harvey was on the Goodpasture place after grandad passed away. I was three when we came from Beloit, Kansas.
>
> We planted some grain. We'd thrash some. We put up hay too for our animals. We had a few cows and later after we got the Goodpasture place we had a bunch of sheep. We used to farm those fields along the road. We sold a little cream in those days. Had a few chickens and milk cows. We had some beef cattle, a little bit of everything. I went to school at Fox Hollow.
>
> Years later sister Ruth's husband, his cousin and I put a sawmill in on the folks' place and cut cants [a log slabbed on one or more sides]. Worked at that until about 1950.

ROBERT MATHANY

Robert Mathany was born in Kentucky in 1829. He arrived in Oregon September 20, 1850, and settled on the claim November 20, 1853. From the information on a claim he filed for services rendered in the Oregon Territory Indian Wars of 1855-1856, we have this description of the man: six feet tall, light complexion, grey eyes, black hair. He described himself as a farmer and said he served 128 days as a private under Captain John M. Waldons, and lived six years at Eugene and forty years in Benton County after his discharge. He named three men who served with him during the Indian Wars: Samuel Mathany, of Gaston, Oregon, Charles Tedrow of Marshfield, and Charles McClure of LaGrande. The period of service was from February 13 to June 19, 1856. Mathany sold his claim to James Emerick in 1865.

BOYD MAUPIN

Boyd Maupin was born in 1820 in Cole County, Missouri, and married Amanda R. Richardson on December 22, 1843, in Franklin County, Missouri. They arrived in Oregon September 13, 1853. Some homestead property belonged to wives and when Boyd's wife Amanda died, apparently a second guardian was appointed to help care for their five minor children. This entry appears in Deed Book B, page 184 in Lane County land records:

> *12-27-1857.* Boyd Maupin and Margaret Ann Maupin, Thos. Gillion Maupin, Sarah Lorinda Maupin, Nancy Adeline Maupin and George Washington Maupin, infant children for whom Boyd is guardian of the first part; and Henry G. Hadley of second part, by order of court 10-6-1857, that Boyd Maupin, guardian over the persons and property of Margaret Ann and other minor heirs of Amanda F. Maupin deceased, proceed to sell real estate of Amanda, the land claim now held by Boyd Maupin, their father. The sale properly made, this court ordered conveyance to H. G. Hadley. $700 pd. (Description of the property follows this entry.)

Boyd Maupin's second wife was Mrs. Minerva Crabtree Alexander. Old-timers in the Fox Hollow area report that the first school there was the "Maupin" school. His land was later part of the Knoop-Knox holdings.

AZARIAH PARK

Azariah Park was born in Virginia in 1818, according to census documents. His wife, Elizabeth, was born in Illinois. He arrived in Oregon on September 17, 1852, a man thirty-four years old. He settled on his claim February 15, 1854, and married Elizabeth A. Moore August 24, 1854, in Lane County, Oregon Territory. I quote from a handwritten paper from the National Archieves in Washington, D.C. where the original homestead papers are kept:

Azariah Park of Lane County in the Territory of Oregon, being first duly sworn, says that he is a white settler on the public lands in Oregon and was a resident thereof on and before the eighteenth day of September, 1852, and above the age of eighteen years on the first day of December, 1850, and is a native born citizen of the United States.

And that he was born in Hampshire County, Virginia in the year 1821 (sic), that he has personally resided upon and cultivated that part of the public lands in Oregon particularly described in Notification No. [illegible] hereunto annexed continuously from the 15th day of April, 1853 to the 24th day of November, 1853 and he further says that he is not a married man, has three brothers, Abraham, Silas and Jacob Park, five sisters, Mary Brickell, Rebecca Park, Anna Hyatt, Elizabeth Rudolph and (Margaret Shelly, —½ sister).

Signed: *Azariah Park*

Subscribed and sworn before me)
this 24 day of November, 1853)
Witness my hand and private seal)
no official Seal being as yet)
provided at Eugene City the)
day and year above written)

E. F. Skinner (seal)
Clerk District Court
Lane County, O.T.

An undated newspaper clipping from an unidentified paper reads as follows:

FELL INTO THE FIRE
Lane County pioneer drops dead in Eugene.

Eugene 3-26-1898—Ezeriah Park, about 80 years of age, dropped dead last evening at his home about 6 miles south of Eugene. About 8 o'clock he was sitting in front of his fireplace, when he complained to his family of a pain in his side, and suddenly fell forward into the fire. He was rescued before being badly burned and found to be dead. Heart failure is assigned as cause of death. Mr. Park has been a resident of Lane County since about 1850. He has always led a quiet life. (From Oregon Historical Library *Scrap Book 56.*)

ORVILLE PHELPS

Orville Phelps, who came to Oregon in 1850 from Illinois, apparently never married. Twenty-seven years later, in the spring of 1877, he built a sixteen by thirty-two foot log house just below the road on the west slope of Spencer Butte as the first step in establishing a homestead of 158.77 acres. Mr. Phelps described the place on his Homestead Proof form. "It is rolling land, some timber, good

Pruetts with a load of hay on Phelps homestead west of Spencer Butte.
Emory & Mildred Pruett

grazing or fruit land, some good farm land." The form tells us his "first house was built in 1877 and I established residence on the 17th of May, 1877. Present occupied house was built last year (1899). I have two log houses 16 x 32 and 14 x 32, and a box barn, fencing and orchard, value $500 to $600. I am unmarried. I have resided there continuously, have been away from my house but one night since 1877." He had cultivated about fifteen acres and raised crops every seasons since 1878. Witnesses to his paper mentioned a good young orchard and a nursery. An ad in the Brevities section of the Eugene City *Guard* dated November 1, 1890, reads as follows: "Go to Orville Phelps Spencer Butte Nursery for 3-yr-old apple, pear, cherry trees, etc."

The unsold nursery stock is still plainly identifiable below the road just west of Spencer Butte Park. Seedling fruit trees flourish all up and down the butte, scattered there by birds and deer.

Old-timers in the area remember a time when the local school teacher took pity on this old bachelor Orville and baked him a birthday cake. He was so impressed by her act of kindness that he became quite infatuated with her. As Lester Swaggert remembered, she "couldn't hardly get away from him. He was trying to court her and she didn't want to have anything to do with him in that respect."

On October 28, 1899, Orville Phelps, then seventy-six years old, sold his homestead to Rebecca A. Porter for $1,000. Albert Ruegger, a cattle dealer who lived on the Martin Gay homestead to the south, paid Orville Phelps

$80 on September 11, 1899, for three cows, and $290 on October 16 of that year for eighteen head, according to entries in the Ruegger account book.

After Orville Phelps sold the place to Mrs. Porter a number of people lived there. The Pruetts moved onto the place in 1932 and eventually bought all but forty acres of the land. That forty had been sold to the city for an entrance to Spencer Butte Park. Emory Pruett said in a recent interview:

> We didn't do a lot of farming, but we did farm this hillside above the road and below. We grew grain, wheat and oats for the stock. We sowed hay. Mostly we grew oats. That field raised a whale of a crop of vetch and oats. It was so thick that after Dad went through and cut it with a team and mower we kids would have to go by and tear it apart with a fork so he could make another cut.
>
> Dad raised cattle and sold cream. There was a barn with sixteen cow stanchions in the back part of it.
>
> I guess we've got the only mulberry tree in Lane County. This big tree that stood just in front of the barn. We used to hang our butchered animals from a block in that tree. It was something Phelps musta planted when he had the nursery here.

WILLIAM D. RENSHAW

Another pioneer who settled south of Spencer Butte was William Renshaw.

> William Renshaw was of Scotch-Irish ancestry and settled in Springfield, Missouri, in 1837. He had been born near Nashville, Tennessee, in 1823. He sold his large farm, outfitted himself with ox-teams and provisions and crossed the plains with his wife and two children in 1851, encompassing the distance in six months to the day. He had comparatively little trouble with the Indians, although some more courageous than others helped themselves to some of his stock. In the spring of 1852 he settled on a donation claim six miles south of Eugene, composed of three hundred and twenty acres of uncultivated land, and there built a small log house and began to prepare for such crops as could be planted on short order. He was quite successful from a financial standpoint, and was popular in his neighborhood. His death at the age of sixty-five, which took place in 1888, was regretted by a large circle of friends and well-wishers. He was a Republican and a Presbyterian. In his youth he married Mary J. Walker, born in Tennessee, and who removed with her parents to Green County,

Missouri, before coming to Oregon. Mrs. Renshaw was born in 1828 and died in 1887. His son, William M., was owner and operator of the Smeed Hotel in Eugene for a number of years. (*Portrait and Biographical Record of the Willamette Valley,* p. 1428.)

There is good evidence that the Renshaws crossed the plains with the Martin Gay family; they both left from Springfield, Missouri, and both families were on the road for six months. Martha Gay mentions that some of their traveling companions settled near them in the Camas Swale neighborhood, and there is a May 30, 1851, entry in the James Gay diary of their trip (an entry which was crossed out but is still legible) saying "buffalo seen, antelope killed by Mr. Renshaw."

The *Lane County Historian* notes, "The Renshaw lands at the extreme end of the old Dillard Road, then called Alder Street, was hilly, rocky and covered with fir and oak trees. A small school house was on the land, also used for church services on Sundays." (Vol. XVI, p. 18.)

THE LEWIS RINEHART FAMILY

The Rineharts settled ten miles south of Eugene on Camas Swale in 1853, according to their youngest daughter's account. Lewis raised cattle and a few sheep, also hay and enough grain to take to the mill for the family flour. Lewis also sold enough cheese, butter, lard, eggs, bacon, and other things to supply his family with food and clothing. He owned quite a herd of cattle, some sixty milk cows at one time. He lost forty of them over the hard winter of 1861-62, which was the winter of the flood all over the valley.

There were no schoolhouses near their home, so what schooling the boys got before Sarah, the youngest, was old enough to go to school, was taught by a man in an old cabin near home. The pupils were all large boys—no girls. Later on Jim, Frank, Lew, and Henry went to college in Eugene. The college burned down the winter they were there.

In about 1859 Lewis moved to Eugene so the three younger boys could attend the winter school. Sarah attended a short time as she was only six years old. The children's next school was on the Coast Fork near their brother, George Rinehart, where the younger children

Lewis Rinehart, Sr. and Elizabeth Ellis Rinehart before 1881.
Charles Wilkins

stayed for three months and walked one and a half miles to school. When Sarah was eleven and twelve years old, her father again moved to Eugene for the winter schools. Only two brothers were at home then, as the older ones were off teaching or taking care of the home place. When Sarah was fourteen she again stayed with brother George for the school term. The next year there was a three-month school in an old log cabin taught by a woman; the following year it was taught by a man. The next year a new log school was built and one three-month term offered.

In the spring of 1870 Lewis rented out the old home and moved to the Grand Ronde Valley because the boys had gone there with cattle several springs before and were doing well. Jasper Rinehart was the only boy at home and he was anxious to go, so they bought some more sheep. Lewis and his son, Lewis Jr., by this time had 1,800 head they wanted to drive east of the mountains. Jasper and some boys drove the sheep while Lewis and his wife drove a team across the mountains. They went to John Rinehart's place by the Willamette route to Prineville, down the Deschutes River and over the John Day River and up Rock Creek five miles above where Olex now stands. They lost many sheep on the road, arriving at their final destination with only 300 head. From that point on the Rinehart family centered their operations in eastern Oregon.

GEORGE W. RINEHART

Lewis' oldest son, George, preceded his family to Oregon by one year. He homesteaded what is now known as the Christensen Valley, but sold the place to Joseph Brumley in 1860 and bought land just south of Creswell.

A news story under Creswell items in the Eugene City *Guard*, dated January 8, 1881, notes: "Mr. G. W. Rinehart of Creswell received a silver headed cane as a Christmas present from his son, W. N. Rinehart of Tuscarora, Nev." The *Oregon Historical Quarterly*, Number 47, reports that George W. Rinehart was postmaster in the Coast Fork Post Office

The Rinehart Family. Seated from left: Unknown, Elizabeth (mother), Sarah. Standing from left: John, Henry, George, Lewis Jr., James, William, Frank, Jasper.
Charles Wilkins

George and Maggie Toll's tent-house overview.
Elsie Sutton

established December 28, 1867, and closed October 1, 1872.

JONATHAN AND NICHOLAS TOLL

This family is almost the only one of the homesteaders in the area whose descendants are still living on the land they homesteaded.

Jonathan's father came from Wales at the age of eighteen. He was a shoemaker. Jonathan's first wife died in childbirth after they reached California. Jonathan came to Oregon after her death in the 1870s. He lived for a year in the old Burdick's tannery on South Willamette Street at about 50th Avenue. He walked from there every day over to near where Stella Magladry School is now, working as a farm hand. His son Nick found work as a sheepherder for Judkins south of Spencer Butte. It was a lonely year for Jonathan and he returned to California where he married Sarah Almira Applegate Moomaw, a cousin of Jesse Applegate's. Other family members had gone back with him and they spent the next few years in California where Nick married Melissa Jane Moomaw, Sarah's fifteen-year-old daughter. Sarah had come west in the same wagon train as the Tolls.

The Tolls came back to Oregon in 1882. Nick's sister Lydia married a Westrope and several of the family settled along Fox Hollow in those years. Another sister Kate married William Winter. Jonathan had two other sons, Layton and George. George married Maggie Kindt and they lived for many years in a log house which still stands near Fox Hollow Road.

Lester Swaggart, Nick's grandson, told about the family settling on the land in Fox Hollow:

In about 1885 they built a nice log cabin and they cleared land. The log house they built was over forty feet long. It consisted of three rooms —two bedrooms and a living area. A door was made to each room from the outside on the south wall. A large fireplace was constructed on the east end out of sticks and clay after the early Lincoln-type back in Illinois. The bedrooms had only dirt floors. Clay and long strips of wood battened the cracks between the logs. Wide shakes were used for the roof which projected along the south side to make a sheltered walkway that ran along by the doors. A shed adjoining the house was built at the west end. This annex was where their bacon and ham was hung and smoked.

Nick's first child, Luella Matilda, was born in the log house shortly after it was completed. Nick's and Jonathan's families both lived in the log house for four or five years. Nicholas then made another home out of hewed logs which was still standing in 1978. Sometime later he built a good house of lumber from Charlie Knoop's sawmill down the road. This house burned in 1952.

Nick's brother George married Maggie Kindt and they started housekeeping in a different kind of abode—a tent house. Apparently this kind of shelter was not too uncommon as a temporary arrangement. The tent covered a floored area with lumber sidewalls up to a height of about three feet; this was used as the

Inside the tent-house bedroom.
Elsie Sutton

bedroom. In this case, at least, the kitchen-dining room was set up under a separate roof adjoining the tent-covered bedroom. George and Maggie later bought a portion of the James Breeding Donation Land Claim.

Nick's daughter, Bertha Toll, said, "When dad and grandpa came here in 1882 and home-steaded it was all open range and the stock could run everywhere. We didn't do too much feeding. That first year we didn't get any hay. By the time we needed hay it had already been bought by others. We lost quite a few head of cattle that winter.

"You depended on goats to clear the land—mohair goats."

Bertha recalled that her family met Cal Young and his brothers headed for eastern Oregon with some stock as they came west over the pass on their way to the Willamette Valley. She said her mother never really learned to make "light" bread. They usually ate sourdough when she was a child. Her mother was born in California in 1864 and came to Oregon as a new bride. Much of the cooking in California on the big ranches where Nick worked was done by Chinese cooks. These cooks were known for carrying their yeast made from hops with them.

The Tolls took their grain over Bond Hill to Trunnel's mill near Creswell to be ground into flour.

Lester recalled that the family had a difficult time making any money in the early years. "One of the things they did," he said, "in the spring especially was getting tan bark for a tannery down here—Burdick's tannery—located just off South Willamette near 50th. Tan bark is the part between the big bark and the trunk of the tree on big fir trees.

"And I know they worked for Mr. Good-pasture, clearing up land. They'd fell the second growth timber and bunch it together. Made log piles and burned it."

According to some of the old-timers, Nick worked for Alex Osburn who hired several

Four generations in front of Nick Toll's home-stead cabin. From left: Elsie Swaggart Sutton, Melissa Toll, Luella Toll Swaggart, Luella Sutton.
Elsie Sutton

men to go over his pastures with grubbing hoes and cut out the young oak and cedar trees that were getting started. Like most of their neighbors, the Tolls made shakes and shingles to sell for cash income.

"Granddad was an excellent hand with the axe and crosscut," Lester said. "I remember the place near the house where he unloaded his shake bolts. He had a profession of riving out beautiful boards with his mallet and fro. He took orders from those who lived far and near. At times one would see stacks and stacks of the riven shakes ready for market."

Jonathan worked on the Spencer Butte Road with a pick and shovel. The road was hub-deep with mud in the winter and thick with dust in the summer. Bertha recalled, "There wasn't many families lived out here in those days—early 1900s. If your neighbor went to town he'd stop and ask you, 'Is there anything you want from town? You want to go to town with me?' It took all day. The women folks didn't go very much. It was the men folks that went. That way one neighbor would go in this week and another next, and helped each other. Grandpa Knox would come by in his big wagon, stop down here and take Dad with him."

Lester shared further recollections of Nicholas:

> In his later years Nick practically lost his eyesight. He had cataracts on both eyes. My grandmother spent a lot of time in the garden

Nick Toll and his fiddle circa 1912.
George Knox Album

during the summer. The boys had hewed out troughs from young trees to bring water to the garden from a spring up the hill.

> Grandfather Nick was a fiddler. In the evenings by the fire he would get out his old violin and we'd take turns playing tunes and Sam would bring a pan of apples from the fruit house which we peeled and ate there by the fire.

> As Granddad got older he didn't like to be confined. In the better weather he would take his cane, put on his broad-brimmed hat and get out for a walk in his shirt sleeves. As far as I can remember he seldom wore a coat. His steps were short and hitchy. In his strolls he would give everything he came to a good looking-over. Granddad was still quite a hand to talk and entertain. He said, "I used to work out my

Toll homestead
circa 1920.
Lester Swaggart

William and Mary Shields Walker.
Marty West

poll tax on the county road when I was young." The neighbor asked, "How old were you?" "Oh, about seventy." At this time Granddad was some past ninety. He passed away at his Fox Hollow home at the age of ninety-eight and a half.

Jonathan's wife, Sarah, and four of Nick's unnamed infant daughters are buried in a family plot above Fox Hollow Road not far from where John Toll lives today.

Nick's son Carl later homesteaded a "timber" claim in the hills southwest of the earlier Toll homestead.

WILLIAM AND THOMAS WALKER

William Walker was born in Knox County, Tennessee, in 1800. He arrived in Oregon in 1853 and settled on his claim that year in November.

His great-grandson, Cecil Robe, said in an interview with Dan Sellard of the Eugene *Register-Guard* in 1979, "I remember my grandmother (Eliza Ann Walker Robe) telling me that on the way out here her father got to joking with some Indians and kinda playfully suggested trading her for some ponies. Anyway, when Grandma and her mother found out what he had done they gave him whatfor. And they gathered up everything they could and got out of the place as fast as they could so the Indians wouldn't find anyone there."

Walker apparently stayed on his homestead only long enough to "prove up" because by 1858 the *People's Press* in Eugene City was carrying ads for his store. An ad dated February 25, 1858, reads, "Just received a large supply of Dr. Jaynes' family medicine direct from Philadelphia. Also 300 almanacs gratis." Then on March 8, 1859, "The undersigned having fitted up a new store house on 9th St. one door west of Goldsmith and Co's store is now receiving and opening a general stock of medicines and groceries. [An extensive list of items follows.] Signed: Wm. Walker." And again, November 19, 1859, "Wm. Walker moved his store from 9th to Willamette St."

Williams' daughter Nancy married James Galloway in 1860. Martha Gay told a story about a Mr. Galloway who visited their camp near Albany in 1851. Probably it was another Galloway, but the story is timely and interesting:

Shortly after we had camped on a Sunday afternoon, we saw a man riding rapidly towards our tent. We could not imagine who he was or why he was riding so fast. As he came nearer we saw that he was riding a fine horse and had a long rope dragging after him like a Spaniard or Indian.

He was well-dressed and a nice-looking man. He rode near us and dismounted, taking the rope in his hand and allowing the horse to walk away the length of the rope to feed. Father went forward to meet the visitor, thinking he was some old friend who had heard of our arrival and come to see us, but was rather surprised when the man asked if his daughter was there, saying that he wished to see her.

He said he was a single man and was in search of a wife and handed Father a letter of introduction. It was written by an old friend stating that Galloway was a very fine gentleman and financially well-off and was in haste to marry and save a half-section of land. The law stated that all married men were entitled to a certain amount of land if married before a set date. If not they lost the land. Hence he was in a great hurry as he had only a few more days to find a land partner!

The man insisted on seeing sister Mamie. Father said, "No sir, I have no daughter to barter for land. You had better go as you came, in haste!" It was storming so Father loaned him a cloak and told him of other emigrants near by. We heard later that Mr. Galloway found a woman willing to marry him and help save the half-section!

It is possible that the marriage mentioned above didn't last and that James Galloway remarried. I have not been able to solve the mystery to date.

W. T. WALKER

W. T. Walker, known as Thomas, was the fifth child of William and came to Oregon at the same time as his father. His next older sister was the wife of William Renshaw, who took up the neighboring homestead. He settled on his claim in August, 1854, and married Ardelia Zumwalt on Valentine's Day 1855. One might assume he helped his father get settled before moving out on his own a few months later as a man of twenty-four years. His claim was sold to his half-sister Nancy Galloway and her husband James in 1866.

JOEL WARE

Joel Ware was born in Mahoning County, Ohio, February 19, 1832, of Quaker parents. He crossed the plains driving an ox team to California, arriving in August 1852. He settled in Sacramento where he was in the printing business until 1857 when he came to Oregon by boat and located in Portland. He came on to Eugene in 1858. He married Elizabeth F. Cochran of Klickitat County at the residence of the bride's father. The ceremony was performed by Nelson Whitney on June 5, 1861. In 1858 Joel Ware was employed on the *People's Press,* a Free Soil paper, established during the previous summer, as typesetter, proofreader and pressman. He also wrote a local column. In 1861 he was appointed to the Surveyor General's office as chief draftsman and chief clerk. In 1870 he became Lane County Clerk, a post which he held for twenty years. After retiring as county clerk, he engaged in abstract and real estate business.

During his twenty years as county clerk, Joel Ware obtained homestead certificates for many properties in Lane County. As such, he is included in this history, although it remains unclear whether he actually lived on any property in the Spencer Butte area.□

CHAPTER 2

The Trip West

The first sizeable trek overland to Oregon in 1843 brought approximately 900 persons to the territory and demonstrated that wagons *could* be driven as far as The Dalles. From that year on, emigrants arrived in increasing numbers, an estimated 2700 in 1846. The gold rush brought "hordes" of fortune seekers in 1849 and 1850. Many of these people came with no intention of staying to settle, but their passage over the trails resulted in continuing improvements and a clearer track. Two hundred thousand people traveled west during the decade of the 1850s including most of those who settled near Spencer Butte.

The Mormons had arrived in the Salt Lake Valley in 1847 and by 1850 had established a community which was able to reprovision the overland travelers who reached that point, a sort of half-way station which reduced the necessity for starting with such heavy loads if travelers planned accordingly. Private protection was established at several points along the route by the time our travelers passed that way.

According to John Unruh in *The Plains Across*, "The number of whites killed by Indians has been vastly exaggerated." This is an important perspective for readers and authors of regional histories to keep in mind as more factual and enlightened information is uncovered about what actually happened between the settlers and the Indians. A widespread disdain by the overlanders for the Indian "right" to toll for passage across their lands was one of the issues which provoked the Indians to rude and hostile acts of resistance. Relationships worsened as the years went by. The Indians were more of a threat to travelers by 1860 than they had been in the 1840s.

The following account reflects the experiences of 67 families who traveled the Oregon Trail to settle in the Spencer Butte area between 1851 and 1863.

Four of the families who settled in the Spencer Butte area left written records about their trips. They are the Martin Gay family, the Lewis Rinehart family, the Jonathan and Nicholas Toll families, and the Jonathan Butler family. The following passages are excerpts from those family journals.

THE MARTIN BAKER GAY FAMILY

(From an unpublished manuscript titled *The Sunset Trail* by Martha Ann Gay Masterson, handwritten and later prepared for permanent family records by her niece, Celeste Campbell.)

We had lived in Springfield [Missouri] three years. . . . Father got the Western fever and longed to go to the new country, away off towards the setting sun.

He had talked of Oregon and the Columbia River for years and wanted to take his sons where they could have land, as the Government promised to give homes to all who would make the journey to Oregon. Mother did not want to go, to undertake the long and dangerous trek with a large family of small children. She begged father to give up the idea but it seemed he could not do so.

Father received a letter from an old neighbor who had been in Oregon for two years and he insisted on Father's going West. The neighbor spoke of what a lovely land it was and of the genial climate and the rich gold mines in California. Mother finally reluctantly consented to go and Father at once set about making arrangements for the long journey across the plains. He told of his plans and said he wanted us all to go with him to the new land of the sunset. . . . Then he asked if we wanted to go. We

Wagon train, probably in Wyoming, 1902.
Ray Baugh Collection, Lane County Museum

rather thought we would like to stay where we were. We had our beautiful home and friends and it was hard to give them up. But children in those days did as their parents asked them to, so all our contacts were broken and we came to Oregon.

My oldest brother, James . . . was about to be married. He told his intended wife, Frances J., that he expected to go West the next spring, and she promised to go with him and that was the understanding when they were married.

Father had been busy for several months selling off his property and settling up his extensive business affairs. He soon realized that it would be a great undertaking to prepare for a journey across the plains with such a large family. Everything must be serviceable and of the best. Just the clothing for so many for such a trip was no small matter. The provisions necessary to last five months were enough to stock a small grocery store.

The wagons were strong and water-tight, to be used as boats if necessary in crossing swollen streams. . . . The oxen were selected, the strongest and quietest. None of inferior grade could be depended on to take us through the many dangers of the trail.

Only a few horses were needed for the riders —none for the wagons. Plenty of firearms and ammunition were stored in waterproof boxes and side arms provided for all old enough to carry and use them.

Bolts of heavy canvas were being measured off for the four enormous wagon covers. Also the great tent was cut out and a dozen or more people were working on it.

Great stacks of garments all sizes and colors were in the process of being made for weeks and months, yes, and for more than a year the sewing went forward. There were no sewing machines in those days; everything was sewed by hand. The neighbors would come in crowds and have "sewing bees" as there was so much to do.

For days the great white tent stood in the yard and the four covered wagons, loaded with supplies, were ready to roll out on the journey.

The tenth day of April, 1851, was set for starting and I think all of the town and part of our county must have known it from the crowds of people who filled the yard and street.

The great tent was folded and put in its place. It was to be our home for five months. We had a light table and sheet iron stove and expected to be quite comfortable. The sleeping berths were in the wagons as Father thought it more healthful than sleeping on the ground and less danger from reptiles and Indians.

The first day of our journey we arrived at our old farm neighborhood. Next morning we went to our aunts for a short stay, then to Grandmothers who lived in the next county. We waited here for our sister-in-law who had not started with us from Springfield. Her parents coaxed her to stay, saying that if she would not go, her husband would remain with her in Missouri. But when they saw him start out with his wagon and team they gave up that plan and consented for their daughter to go with her husband, as she had promised before they were married.

We had a nice visit with Grandmother and late in the evening of the third day we saw the coach coming with sister-in-law, who was accompanied by her father and brother. The next morning we parted with dear Grandmother, knowing full well that we would never see her again.

After a few days travel, the Gays reached the place agreed upon for organizing the company:

After the evening meal the men and some of the women of the company assembled around a great campfire where a captain was elected, sentries were appointed and the rules of action and movement were made known to all concerned.

All were to be ready when the leader started out and a different leader was appointed for each day so that no one had preference. In a long train, the leading teams have the best position on account of the dust which is dreadful at times and almost suffocating.

One morning soon after the long train of wagons had got straightened out and started, I was aroused from my musings by a roaring noise approaching from behind us and the next moment the herd of loose cattle and horses came rushing past, causing the teams on the wagon to run, giving us a fast ride. It was our first stampede but not the last! We never knew what caused the cattle to run that first time. Perhaps Indians or buffalo were near.

We often saw great trains of emigrants and occasionally talked with some of them and heard tales of strayed cattle; of their hired help deserting them and of others who were going back to their eastern homes.

We were now well into Indian country and getting along nicely. We scarcely ever saw an Indian and those we did see were friendly so we hoped we were mistaken about them, as we thought they would all want to fight with us! One morning in May we entered an Indian village. There were good houses and nice gardens, a church and a schoolhouse on a hill. This was a pleasant sight as it had been weeks since we had left civilization.

As we were quietly passing through the village, we were greeted by the booming of cannon and there sprang into view almost instantly a band of five hundred Indian warriors on horseback and armed with guns, bows and arrows, tomahawks and scalping knives. Our captain called a halt, and he and father went forward to learn the meaning of this battle array. The Indians had not attempted to molest us but the place was alive with them.

A white man came up to the captain and Father and said there was no occasion for alarm and that we could proceed on our way, that the Indians were friendly and belonged to the mission. They had been out fighting the Pawnees, been victorious and were returning with their trophies of war and prisoners. This display was to welcome them home.

Soon after leaving the village we encountered a stream of water at flood stage and had trouble in crossing it at the treacherous ford. One man was thrown from his wagon into the river and came near drowning. We consumed several hours in getting all the wagons and stock across, then pitched camp for the night as it was raining and there was plenty of good wood nearby and grass for the cattle.

The next morning we were early on our way and all went well for a few days when we had an accident. The captain's little boy fell from their wagon and, before the team could be stopped, a wheel had passed over his body and almost crushed him to death. He suffered terribly for days but finally recovered.

Shortly after this we camped near another Indian village. There was a nice church and schoolhouse, good dwellings, orchards, gardens and fields of corn. Some white families lived at this mission and the agent was a brother of an old friend of Father's. The agent said the Indians learned easily to be farmers and did well in school. He also told us that they would not steal. Our captain thought if they were so honest it would be unnecessary to put out sentries for the night. Next morning, when the cattle were driven into camp, a fine pair of oxen and a cow and calf were missing!

After searching for them and failing to find any trace of the missing stock, the agent was informed. He sent an Indian to help hunt but still the cattle were not found. At last one of my brothers tracked them to a lot in the woods some distance away, where the stock had been driven and bars put up to keep them inside. Brother drove the cattle towards the bars to let them out, when an Indian interfered and said the stock belonged to him. At that moment our captain rode up and ordered the Indian away, helped get the stock out and hurried them towards camp, as we had been detained several hours by the agent saying, "The Indians are honest!"

We experienced some heavy storms on the prairie. I recall one afternoon about three o'clock we were moving slowly along. The day had been warm but suddenly a cool breeze sprang up and a dark cloud covered the sun. This was very pleasant after the heat but in a few moments there were crashes of thunder and vivid streaks of lightning. The wind was terrific in its force.

The train ascended a bank to get on higher ground, as the place where we first halted was soon found to be a stream bed and we did not dare unhitch the teams there. If there was a deluge coming, we could not get out should the cattle stampede.

After arriving on higher ground and turning the wagons the best we could against the storm, every team and all the horses excepting one black pony were turned loose to try to find shelter for themselves, not thinking they would go very far away. All the men got into or under the wagons for shelter from the rain, which came down in torrents. As soon as the worst of the storm was over, the men rushed out after their teams and were dismayed to find them gone. The cattle had raced out across the prairie, trying to keep ahead of the storm. The men could not overtake the stock on foot and they did not know what to do as the horses had followed the cattle. Then someone thought of the black pony and quickly mounting him went after the run-away teams, which had gone several miles from camp but were all safe and soon brought back to us. The black pony, that had no doubt saved our teams from capture by Indians, lived to reach Oregon and for many years after.

Next morning, the weather was as warm as usual and we moved quietly on our way to the ford of the South Platte. It was the first day of June, 1851.

This was a large river, about two miles wide at the ford and deep and muddy. We either had to ford the river or make a boat from a wagon and ferry everything across—a slow process.

After consulting with two men who had been west before and were somewhat acquainted with the river, we decided to ford, but how we dreaded it! After making all the loads secure and taking every possible precaution, a stout-hearted young man who had crossed the river before volunteered to wade in and lead the way over.

At last the long train of wagons started into the stream and then it was our turn. Mother was on the wagon with us and a faithful man assisted our team to keep on the right track, for if we got off the ford we would go down in quicksand. We looked ahead and saw the leading team near the further shore, then another reached the bank. Father said, "Now they are across and we soon will be." It was necessary to cross the river in a half circle. We started in and went down stream and then came out safe on the other shore, but then [there was] an argument, the first since we left the east.

Some wanted to rest for the remainder of the day and others wanted to go on. Hot words were spoken and one man drew his gun to shoot another. The company disbanded. The captain rolled out on the road and said all who wished could follow him. Some others started and called to their friends. Several others went. Father did not go. Four families stayed with him. Those who had gone on insisted on traveling fast. Father and some others did not care to rush along and wear out their teams at the beginning of the journey. The fast travelers got to Oregon before we did but lost nearly all of their stock and had trouble different ways.

We now had the company we had at first planned coming with; a good man was elected captain of our new company, with Father as assistant and adviser. The families were all good and reasonable people. We were all from the same county and had known of each other before starting out. We had no quarrels or disagreements in our little band and were like one large family.

Father had four wagons and the other families a wagon apiece, making eight wagons in all. Eleven men were able to carry arms and fight if necessary. We usually camped near some other train for protection if we were in a dangerous part of the country.

One morning early we heard buffalo lowing some distance away. We were camped on a buffalo trail which led to a watering place in the nearby river. We rushed to get away as we heard the animals coming from beyond the hills nearby. The men hurried with the loose cattle for if they got into the buffalo herd they would stampede with them and be lost.

Everyone was on the lookout for the beasts. Their leaders were bellowing furiously as they had discovered us as quickly as we saw them, and here they came thundering towards us. Nothing would turn them from their path. Their heads were down and on they came. We did not know what to do for they seemed to be coming directly across our road and right through our wagons.

The captain was on horseback near us, watching the buffalo and we were waiting for him to say what to do. We were moving slowly when he called for us to halt. The buffalo went roaring past just in front of our lead wagon! We heard their heavy breathing and the earth trembled under their weight as they rushed by and disappeared over the hills.

Father was a good marksman and usually kept our little company supplied with fresh meat. One day we needed some broth for a sick woman and after making camp near a river the men began looking about for game of some kind. An antelope was spied across the river and pointed out to Father. All thought the animal too far away for a shot and the river too wide and deep to cross to bring home the antelope if he were successful in killing it. Father said he thought he could hit the animal. Then someone remarked that if he did they would get it if they had to swim! All the men and boys were out watching so Father picked up his best gun and walked off toward the river to be more alone. There was a sharp report and the antelope fell. When he saw the shot had brought down the game Father walked back to camp and said he had done his part. Now someone else could bring the meat home! Two men went over without trouble and brought the game to camp. It was very fine and we divided it among the company and all had a meal of tender fresh meat.

The journey, although a long one, was not all dreariness or hardships. We had a variety of diversions, or no doubt things would have been almost unbearable. We spent many happy evening hours around the camp fire, visiting with our neighbors, telling stories, singing and guessing conundrums. There were many amusing incidents always happening and we made much of everything, because we had no news or word from civilization and must originate our own news and mirth.

An Indian came to camp with buckskin trousers to sell. A teamster bought a pair and next day he looked all dressed up in cream colored trousers and a red blouse. Our road during that day led often across a muddy stream of water. One ford was very sticky and our man with the new suit drove into the ford with his team. They stuck in the mud and he could not get them to pull the wagon out. He had to get into that mud and urge the team forward. Each step carried them into the mire deeper and deeper but he came safely across. Those cream colored trousers, however, were ruined.

Early on the morning of June 14th, 1851, I was awakened by the wailing of a child. I asked mother whose babe was crying and she said it was hers. I kept quiet for a long time, fearing I might have to welcome another brother! Finally I was so anxious to know I asked, "Is it a little brother?" Imagine my joy when mother said, "It is a little sister." I hastily dressed and went to look at the baby. I thought Sarah Julia Gay was the sweetest little sister in all the world! This was in Nebraska teritory. . . . We all welcomed her with love and soon she was the pet of the entire company.

My greatest fear was the Indians. I thought they would want her and I asked our captain to set out more than one sentry at night to keep the savages from stealing my baby sister. We crossed the North Platte the 21st of June on a good ferry boat at the rate of three dollars per wagon. But we were glad to get across so easily and did not mind the price. We were met with a large train of emigrants known as the Illinois company with whom we traveled a great deal for the rest of the journey.

Wood and water were scarce at times. We had casks to carry water but wood suitable to take with us was hard to find. Sometimes we had no wood at all. Then we would pull grass and twist it into coils and burn it in our little stove to cook with. We would pull grass the night before to get breakfast with next morning. Thus we managed to get along, the weather being warm we needed only fuel for cooking. We had a guide book that informed us of all the good camping places, otherwise we would have fared much worse than we did.

Sometimes we had to travel after night to reach water and grass for the stock. It was considered a dangerous thing to do and it was only with great caution that we could undertake it. The Indians would conceal themselves in a ravine or near the road and wait for the train, then frighten our teams and cause us a great deal of trouble.

I remember one night we were driving slowly along. Father and the captain had gone on ahead of us to find a camping place when, very suddenly just as we were crossing a ravine, every team seemingly started at the same moment. They ran a short distance when my brother, whose team was in the lead, managed to get them stopped, and the next wagon locked wheels with his, and in this way all the teams were controlled excepting the last one which struck out across the country. The herd of cattle and horses came dashing up and added to the confusion. We expected to hear the war whoop every moment but were agreeably disappointed.

After getting the stock quieted and the runaway wagon back in line, we went on to camp and found the captain and Father wondering what had become of us, we had been so long on the road. When they heard of our stampede, they advised us all to be as quiet as possible and make no fires or lights. Sentries were posted and we spent the rest of the night in wakefulness as there was no other company near us and we had little hope of assistance if we were attacked. Fortunately we were not molested.

Next morning while we were preparing breakfast we were alarmed to see Indians skulking through the sagebrush toward the camp! They came slowly towards us and were the most degraded and savage looking specimens we had seen. They could not speak a word of English but made known that they wanted food, and as soon as they were fed, they disappeared. There were many warlike tribes in this section of the country and we had been warned to give no advantage and to be always ready to defend ourselves.

We arrived at a large stream with its banks thickly set with trees and underbrush, giving the foe a fine hiding place. Father and the captain were a short distance ahead of the train, noting every indication of danger, when they were suddenly confronted by five warriors decked out with paint and feathers. The chief grabbed the bridle of the captain's horse and said in English, "Stop, white man!"

The captain quietly signalled to the train to move up faster, knowing that the Indians would have killed him and Father instantly if the wagons had not been so close. There were Indians behind almost every tree waiting for a signal from the chief. The captain led the train to higher ground, expecting an attack every minute. When we got out of the woods on a slight elevation with the Indians still with us, the train was halted and the men ordered to be ready for fighting at a moment's notice.

While the teams were resting after their rush up the hill and the Indians more quiet, we ate our noonday lunch of cold meat and bread, offering some to our unwelcome visitors. They accepted the food but remained on their fine horses, which no doubt had been stolen from the whites. Their chief rode from one wagon to another, peering in to see if he could lay his hands on anything to steal. They were surly and would not talk to us but spoke among themselves.

The captain said they were talking about calling in their recruits and attacking us but our men looked too resolute and ready for them. The chief rode up to the wagon where Mother was sitting with my baby sister in her arms and made a grab for the child but his horse jumped and Mother screamed for Father who rushed to her.

The chief suddenly gave a signal to his men and they all dashed off towards the river. Just then we saw a long train of emigrants coming up behind us. No doubt their timely arrival had saved us from death. We heard a few days later that there had been three hundred warriors nearby and they attacked a train at the same place and massacred nearly all of the emigrants.

My oldest brother, James Woods Gay, kept a diary. One day just after we had crossed a river he missed his book which had been lying on the wagon seat near him. Of course he was sorry to lose the diary and asked the captain for permission to go back and look for it. He rode the black pony to where he thought he had lost the book and saw it lying on the ground. When he jumped down to pick it up he was alarmed to see Indian tracks in the sand where we had just crossed the river.

He knew the tracks had been made since we were there and he came back to camp as hard as the pony could run to tell us. Brother said he had not seen an Indian but we thought they might be numerous and intended following us, so we hurried forward to catch the train ahead of us, which was the Illinois band.

We crossed the Green River the Fourth of July. . . . There was a good ferry across the river and we crossed so quickly we scarcely realized it. Then we made camp and prepared to celebrate the Fourth the best we could under the circumstances. The ferry man had a violin and he favored us with some very good music. The boys fired a salute and Mother said we must have a good dinner, which she prepared and graced our table with a real cake!

The face of the country had now changed. . . . There were great mountains all around us. . . . The streams abounded in fish and we had fine sport catching them.

We met some fur traders near the Rocky Mountains with their great strong wagons loaded with pelts and drawn by six mules. The men were mountaineers of the true type, long shaggy hair and beards, leather clothing and fur caps. A brave hardy lot! Some of them would stop and talk, others would give us a wild look and pass on. One of the traders told Father that the Indians in that part of the country were warlike and savage—that we would not know they were around until they were in our midst.

In the afternoon of one dusty, sultry day we were moving cautiously along, hoping for some train to overtake us as we were expecting an attack any time. We reached our camping place just at sunset. We had to stop there for wood and water, but it was an unsafe location. We thought there were Indians in the brush and made things as secure as possible but we did not feel safe for the night as no other train had arrived. We rushed about and made as much noise as we could so the Indians would think there was a large company of us. The stock were allowed to graze near camp and after supper the team cattle were put in a corral which was made by running the wagons around in a circle. Then the orders were to let the fires die out and all keep quiet. Sentries were stationed and all was ready.

Father and the captain kept guard near the wagons to protect the families in them. There was no thought of sleeping, excepting the children, during that night of terror. Often during the watch Father would come to the wagon and whisper to Mother, telling her to keep awake for if the Indians did attack us we would have a better chance to escape if we were up and ready to fight.

Father came again and said they heard them and the cattle had given signs the foe was near and had tried to stampede but had been quieted. Every moment was now dread suspense. We almost feared to move or scarcely breathe, thinking we would hear the dreaded war whoop and then fall victims to the tomahawk and scalping knife.

Crossing the Big Horn River July 2, 1902.
Ray Baugh Collection, Lane County Museum.

All was once more quiet. Father left us and went towards the guard. It was now three o'clock. Hope began to rise. We waited, we listened, we prayed. A little bird sang, then another. Was it a sign of deliverance?

Father came again and said the Indians were leaving. They knew we were up, they heard us calling to the cattle. Streaks of morning light could be seen in the east. Was ever morn more welcome? Hearts grew lighter and soon the sentries came in and said the foe had gone.

Fires were built in a short time and the camp was all astir. The cattle were out grazing with some of the men guarding them and one cried, "Look at the arrows sticking in the backs of the cattle!" Sure enough, there were several arrows in the poor beasts' hides. They had been shot from a long distance to frighten the cattle and get them to run, knowing the men would follow and thus weaken our force at the camp.

I was aroused from my nap by my sister calling to me to wake up and see what was over my head. I at once opened my eyes and there was an arrow over my head, sticking in the wagon cover and another at my side. Moccasin tracks were in the road near our wagons. One or two Indians had crept up there during the night and for some cause, known only to themselves, had gone away again.

When we left, our road led up a hill and we could look back and see the Indians taking pos-

session of our camp ground. After that night of terror we always tried to keep near some other wagon train.

We had at last reached the western slope. The great Rockies were between us and other days and old friends and home. The trees were different, the animals and fowls not the same and we saw no more herds of buffalo.

In imagination we saw the beautiful Willamette Valley spread around us bordered by evergreen forests and cooled by the sea breeze, dotted over with happy homes, its waving grain fields and orchards loaded with fruit. Providence had protected us. We were thankful that all could answer at roll-call; not a death in our band since leaving our eastern home.

Our oxen were very thin and weak. Teams were doubled to enable them to get over the bad roads and up hills. We cast out everything we could spare and gave away the oversupply of provisions we had on hand, lightening the loads all we possibly could.

Everyone who was able walked most of the time as we could easily keep up with the train. Crowds of us would get out together from different trains and have jolly times, climbing the mountains and seeing what we could find. No doubt we were often in danger and did not know it.

My mother who had endured the hardships and privations of the journey bravely and uncomplainingly, had to give up. Tired nature called for rest. She hovered for days and weeks between life and death, and in her fevered delirium she would see her children carried off by the Indians or tortured by her side. Again, she would be wandering in scenes of the past, happy and at peace. We often begged her to let us stop so she could rest and gain strength, but she would say, "No, go on. I am afraid we will all perish in the mountains if we are late arriving there. It will be cold and stormy." She insisted on us going steadily forward. After making her as comfortable as we could, we did as she wanted us to do.

Friends came to help us and the dear kind women of the Illinois train did all they could to arouse mother from the lethargy into which she had fallen. They would take my baby sister and keep her for hours and bring dainty morsels of food for mother to try to eat. Finally mother showed signs of improvement and asked to sit by the campfire. After a time she recovered and how glad and thankful we were to have her with us!

Soon after mother recovered, a Mrs. Ross, one of our company, was stricken with fever and was very ill, but with good care was brought back to health. Those two cases were all the serious illness we had during the journey.

We traveled along the Snake River to Fort Boise. They told us it was not safe to ford at that point and advised us to use a large canoe to ferry our loads and families across. Some friendly Indians agreed to help get the stock and wagons over at a ford farther down the stream. . . . After leaving the Fort we traveled over a high sagebrush country for days. . . . There was bunch grass and our stock fared better. . . . We had some very rough, steep roads, and the weak, jaded teams made the ascent with difficulty.

We came to a famous hill on the old emigrant trail and from it descended into the Grand Ronde Valley. The hill was so very steep it was more than perpendicular, it curved under!

To make the descent safely, a tree with a brushy top was tied behind the wagon and the team taken off; then with long ropes or chains to hold the wagon upright, it was lowered to the foot of the hill. Then another, until all were landed in that pretty little valley, which we thought was a Paradise. It was not marred by buildings but just as Nature made it. Near the hill on the river we saw Indian wigwams and all over the valley were thousands of Indian ponies. This looked more like home to us after the dreary journey across the barren plains.

After leaving the mountains we came down into the Umatilla Valley and were so pleased with the country we were sorry to move on again, thinking we would not find another place so beautiful. Some Frenchmen had gardens and we bought potatoes from them and beef from a trader. We were glad to hear that we would soon be at our journey's end, having left the Snake River several days before, and were now traveling down the mighty Columbia.

We climbed a high hill to look down on a valley where there were great herds of ponies. One chief, who could speak English, was very kind to emigrants and thought we were wonderful people to come so far. He asked Father to go home with him and see his house and was greatly pleased when Father went. We could see the Indian cabin and did not feel afraid to have Father go. There had been whites in this part of Oregon for some time and the Indians were more civilized and not so war-like as the tribes of the plains and those about the Rockies and the Snake River. The Nez Perce were a tall, fine-looking tribe.

When we arrived at the Deschutes we camped and called a meeting to decide which route to take across the Cascade Mountains. Some wanted to cross by the Barlow route and other thought it better to go by The Dalles and down the river by flat boats. Here the company again separated.

Father and the captain concluded to take their families across the mountains. . . . While we were in camp on the Deschutes River the weather was quite cool and the first night clear and frosty. Here we witnessed a wonderful display of the Aurora Borealis. It stretched across the sky in broad red and white stripes—a magnificent sight.

We found many other emigrants at the Gate ready to start across. For several days we had been meeting people from the valley with strong teams going out to assist friends across the mountains. We asked them many questions about Oregon and they welcomed us to their beautiful land but gave a doleful account of the mountain road. With brave hearts and jaded teams we slowly ascended the eastern slope of the Cascades. Old and young were out in the rain storm, walking up the rugged mountain over rocks and fallen trees through mud and water.

There was a great deal of crowding and confusion. The road was so narrow and the huge trees so thick on either side no one could pass the teams ahead. Some were obliged to move slowly and others wished to hurry and could not do so, then they would complain. There could be no haste with the poor, tired oxen. Sometimes they fell in the mire to rise no more. Then others were put in their place. Thus we struggled on. One day the great train of us only moved a mile.

At last we reached the summit in a snow storm and then started down hill. At Laurel Hill

Camp on the trail, 1902.
Ray Baugh Collection, Lane County Museum

teams were again removed from the wagons, trees tied to the back as had been done before. The wagons were then slowly lowered down Laurel Hill. We found a good place to camp near the road, as the timber was not so heavy here. All who wished could pass on and thus we got rid of the troublemakers.

We camped one night in the road on Zig-Zag River, which was a crooked rapid stream, tearing along its way. Some of the children were standing on a high bank above the river fishing with thread lines and pin hooks. I went down the trail to get a bucket of water and was standing on a root of a tree holding to a limb with one hand and dipping up the water with the other, from a whirlpool, when one of the children fell over the bank into the pool at my side.

I dropped the pail and caught the boy as he came up and called for help. Someone ran to my assistance and pulled the child from the water and carried him up the trail to camp. He was nearly drowned and badly frightened, but recovered shortly and always said that I saved his life.

In September we arrived at Foster's [an established farm at the west end of the Barlow crossing of the Cascades where emigrants often stopped to rest, buy vegetables and take stock before beginning their search for land or friends who were here ahead of them] and camped at that haven of rest for the weary emigrants.

Martha Ann goes on to tell of settling near Albany. Martin Gay and the boys built a house and fenced corrals, fields and a garden. They made a place for chickens and plowed fields for the spring planting. Her father built a shop and made some nice furniture from Oregon maple.

By the spring of 1852 Martin decided to go further south to buy a stock ranch near the hills because the valley land would all be fenced soon. And so they came to the Gay Donation Land Claim.

In contrast to Martha Ann's vivid, detailed account of their trip, her brother James made very cryptic entries in the diary which he rescued from the river bank. Here are some sample entries:

May 16, 1851—We traveled 14 mils. camp on a branch of blue quick sand at the creek.

May 17—tr'd 18 mils to camp crossed 2 creeks seen antilope passed 13 wagons

June 2—12 mils to camp split in the company

June 14—wash day & rest & hunt killed black tailed deer and antilope sister juley bornd

July 11—today we layby on acount of sickness 2 antilop fans killed wagon left

July 16—tod 15 mils to camp on the fork. fine grass rich land indians at the camp buckskin pants baut with flour we met oregon packers.

July 17—10 mils to camp on river I killed antilope we passed the chimney rock it is formed of cley & is 3 mils from the road

July 20—to day 20 mils to camp at the foot of a big hill where there is plenty of wood and water and grass today there was rain around us cows leg broke

July 24—15 mils to camp on a creek we past the American falls they are nice we had some bad road this evening and not much grass tonight

July 30—20 mils to camp on rock creek good grass bad road this morning for 6 mils and then remainder was good, we had the unpleasant sight this evning of seeing the train of loos stock runaway and one wagon run 200 yards & 4 more started but was stoped one wagon t[ongue] broke.

August 6—today we crossed the river and camp on the bank for the day it is a da[n]geress ford it will average 3-feet for 400 hundred yards we crost right oposit to iselands we all got over safe after 6 hourers work 20 wagons crossed today & 43 more to cross tomorrow this river is fit for nothing from head to mouth only to give the indians fish and water

August 9—18 mils to camp on the plains this morning after leveing camp a few mils we came to a hot spring it biled up in several places it was to hot to hold your hand in 5 arrows found this morning 3 of them in stock they was in 30 steps of the wagons about 3 mils from the spring we come to a creek of good water and 7 or 8 mils from there we come to another one in a deep canon ruff road all day.

THE LEWIS RINEHART FAMILY

(From an unpublished manuscript entitled *The Rinehart Story* loaned by a descendant, Charles Wallace, after a Rinehart Family Reunion reported in the Eugene *Register Guard*.)

James was the oldest of the Rinehart sons to travel with the family to Oregon in 1853. One must suppose from the context that he wrote this account.

To me the whole trip across the plains was very interesting and entertaining. I was, as I have mentioned, in my 18th year, strong, healthy, and full of life. Here I got my first experience in culinary work. I was detailed at the start to assist my mother in cooking on the journey. When a man has cooked for five months, often without wood, and sometimes without water, he is fitted to meet any emergency in the culinary line. To eat off a tablecloth spread on the ground with nothing but ox yokes for seats and not enough of those to go around, would seem quite unpleasant to a traveling man nowadays, who is accustomed to ride in a pullman car and take his meals in a diner and to being waited on by colored gentlemen of African descent.

Father and mother with the seven youngest children, James H., Frank M., Henry, Lewis B., William E., Jasper N., and Sarah E., ranging in age from one to seventeen years, started from Iowa on the long trip across the "plains" April 7, 1854. They arrived at Eugene September 12, having been enroute five months and five days.

Our train on leaving Omaha consisted of thirty-one wagons; twenty-five were pulled by ox teams and six, horses. My father, Lewis Rinehart, was elected captain of the train which was henceforth known as the "Rinehart train." Thomas Edwards and George Duncan, husbands of my two sisters Barbara and Louisa, with their families were in our train.

In those days a train usually consisted of from ten to fifty wagons. The owners banded themselves together for mutual protection against the Indians who often created great disturbance. Often stock would be stolen and driven away at night, and at times war was made by day or night against the weary travelers. Their raids sometimes resulted in the massacre of a part or even the whole of a train, and the bones of man and beast would be left to bleach upon the prairie.

Our principal route of travel was up the north side of the Platte river and up the Sweetwater, through the present states of Nebraska and Wyoming, past the Independence Rock, and by way of the "Devils Gate" over the South Pass of the Rocky Mountains, by way of Soda Springs, where we were July 4th, across the Bear River Valley and down the Snake River through the present state of Idaho, by the Salmon Falls and American Falls continuing on the south side of the Snake River at all times until we arrived at the Malheur River where the town of Vale now stands. Before reaching this place our train had divided on account of the dust.

There was very little sickness in our train, and we had but little trouble with the Indians. Many persons in the Ward train were massacred that year by the Snake Indians on the Snake River east of the present site of Boise, Idaho. The last trains each year always suffered the most, as the Indians knew that these could not be reinforced from behind.

One day in the Sioux country we made a dry

camp on a level plain country to rest an hour at noon. While eating our dinners, ten large, brave-looking Sioux Indians came to our camp and made signs that they wanted two big cows as toll for allowing us to cross their country. Our train being full handed, we refused to turn the cows over to them. The braves looked desperately mad and made signs that they would shoot, but later, probably through respect to our forces, they went away from the road about a hundred yards and held council. We moved on and felt much relieved when they were out of sight.

When we had traveled about three miles a messenger came up to us at full speed and asked us to send back help to relieve his train of four wagons and eight men as the Indians had attacked them and shot down some of their loose cattle. Then and there we had our first Indian scare and prospect of battle with the redskins. The time was about three o'clock in the afternoon and as we were near a camping ground where there was water, the order was given to strike camp immediately.

Our thirty-one wagons were placed in a half circle for two purposes. First, they served as a protection against possible attacks from the Indians, and second, it served as an enclosure in which we could guard and hold our cattle at night, when there was great danger of the Indians creating a stampede by a sudden approach in the dark.

Immediately on the arrival of the messenger, ten men were detailed to go back and assist the attacked train. All others were ordered to remain in camp to protect our families and stock.

Everything was excitement. Men were busy hunting their guns and ammunition. Our weapons were Colt's revolvers and single-barrel rifles, all muzzle loaders and many of them flint locks, and Bowie knives. Then we used the powder horn with the charger to measure the powder, and melted bars of lead to mould our bullets by hand.

Of the relief party, six men started on horseback and four on foot, all anxious to kill Indians. All were in disorder and confusion. The first ready started first and soon the ten men were strung out in a train half a mile long. When a mile out on the road, two of the footmen lost their enthusiasm and thirst for the redman's blood and returned to camp. When about two miles from camp our six horsemen met the unfortunate train coming up the road and about a mile beyond they could see out on the broad, level prairie the ten Indians skinning the cattle they had killed. Three of the train men were detailed to move the wagons along to our camp and the other five men on horseback with our six horsemen and the two remaining footmen, now in sight, decided to give those In-

dians a big scare.

They all started in a full run, and the Indians, seeing them coming, quit their beef skinning and ran at all speed at right angles to the road, our boys after them. After running about a mile over the level prairie and when almost in gunshot the Indians disappeared over a bluff. When our boys arrived at the place where the redmen had disappeared, they looked down into the valley and saw a village of about one hundred "teepees" or more. At the same time there seemed to be at least a hundred warriors issuing from their habitations. Dropping their blankets and with guns and other weapons in hand, they started for the eleven horsemen on the bluff, sending forth a deafening "warwhoop" as they went.

The scale was now turned. The horsemen retreated at full speed, the Indians pursuing on foot. Our two foot soldiers, when they had seen the ten braves retreating and our cavalry giving full chase, had taken a short cut across the country that they might be in at the finish to mingle in the sport. When they saw the horsemen turn tail with at least a hundred Indians in hot chase, they, without even stopping for council of war to decide on future plans, also made tracks toward camp. One of the horsemen on passing took one on his horse and they easily made their escape. But the now lone footman, a boy of nineteen years, was soon overtaken and surrounded by Indians. After holding a little "pow-wow" they took the boy's coat, vest and neck-tie, and after relieving his pockets of a little cash and all his ammunition, they let him go. In his hurried flight he had dropped his old flint lock gun, but an old Indian, after him in the chase had picked it up and after firing it off, returned it to the lad. This boy had been ordered to remain in camp on that day, and not to go on the Indian chase on account of his youth, but go he must, and go he did. After that it took very little persuasion to cause him to remain in camp when there was an Indian scare at hand.

The Sioux were not making a great deal of trouble for the immigrants at that time, but they apparently wanted to levy a little tariff for tramping on the grass of their territory.

That night all the cattle, about 250 head, were guarded in the half circle formed by the wagons, and our tents were set on the outside of this circle and the horses were staked outside the tents. A double guard was placed on duty that night within the circle to guard the cattle and pickets were put outside to prevent a surprise attack by the Indians.

All excepting those on guard had retired by 9:30. The night was dark and rain was falling. Lightning was flashing from all points of the compass. The cattle were all quiet and were lying down to rest at about 10:30 p.m. Suddenly every animal of the cow kind was on its feet and away. A regular stampede was now on and the cry from every tent was "save your horses, boy, mount and follow the cattle, the Indians are upon us."

By the time a dozen of us were in our saddles, we could hear a distant rumble made by the hooves of those 250 head of cattle. It sounded above the roar of thunder as they raced out over the Platte River hills. We followed the sound and the lightning flashes helped to guide us on our way. But for the lightning the night was of the darkest kind. After speeding a few miles in the course of the rumbling sound, we passed a few head of our cattle revealed by the flashes, that had apparently gotten over their scare. We followed on and soon we passed a small bunch that were trailing slowly. Still we raced on, guided by the noise of the fleeing hooves of the main herd. Gradually we gained until we finally came up with the leaders that were yet pressing forward with all the power within them. Slowly we checked them and turned them back upon the trail by which they came, picking up the tired stragglers as we returned. At sunrise we arrived in camp after our long chase and strange to relate, not an ox was missing. No Indians had molested the camp that night and to this day we do not know what caused the cattle to stampede. We presume that the scent of Indians carried to them on the storm, or there may have been a few prowling in the near vicinity under cover of the darkness. It often happens in the Platte River country that whole teams and even whole trains of foot-sore emigrant cattle would catch the scent of Indians and would stampede and run away even in the daytime.

We did not take the old emigrant road through the Grand Ronde Valley, Pendleton and to Fosters. When we arrived at Vale on the Malheur, we were informed by what we called a "squaw man" that Thomas D. Edwards, my brother-in-law and a part of our original train consisting of twenty wagons, had been met there by a man by the name of Key who had proposed to pilot them through the Harney Valley, over the Ochoco country and down the Willamette River to Eugene. An 1853 train had been lost on this route and wandered hundreds of miles out of their way.

The Edwards train, in 1854, decided to trust the pilot who had met them at Vale and their journey was over an unknown country. The valleys and streams between the Malheur and Deschutes Rivers were not named at that time. Thomas D. Edwards, when he had decided to follow the pilot and "mash sagebrush" for four or five hundred miles, had left a letter with the "squaw man" stating his intentions and asking us to follow if we chose to do so. The letter was handed to father when our train arrived at the Malheur and we soon decided to follow the other train.

Our train at that time consisted of four wagons and thirteen persons, counting all ages, which is considered an unlucky number nowadays, but we were not so schooled at that time. There was father and mother and seven children of whom I, then in my eighteenth year, was the oldest, and George Duncan and wife, and two children, Surrilda and Emma, making the thirteen in all.

We started on the new trail about the 20th of July, just two days behind the Edwards train. For five weeks we never saw a human being on the way, not even an Indian and not until we arrived at the Deschutes [River] where we overtook the advance train resting after crossing a forty mile desert without water. Our course was up the Malheur and its tributaries for several days. One day while yet along this river, about mid-day, I saw a lone covered wagon pull suddenly from out the line of our train and make for a small grove on the bank of the stream nearby. Then I noticed that the oxen were unhitched from the wagon and allowed to graze on the beautiful bunch grass. Just then father instructed us to drive on a distance of about four miles and camp for the night. He and mother then went to the lone wagon at the grove where they remained for about five hours, and during those fleeting precious hours I was captain of the advance fraction of our train, with all the rights, powers and privileges appurtaining thereto, and as was customary for one holding that important office I rode on ahead to select a camping place, which I found along the banks of a beautiful mountain stream fringed with willows and alders. Just as the sun was disappearing along the western hills the lone covered wagon arrived in camp and when the roll was called that evening the "thirteen" superstition could no longer be applicable. Number fourteen had been born, and then and there they named him Warren Malheur Duncan.

We were traveling through the land of Indians who were unacquainted with the white man, and though we saw many moccasin and barefoot tracks in the dusty road made by the train ahead of us, we never saw an Indian between the Malheur River and the summit of the Cascade Mountains, a distance of about 400 miles. They were numerous all through that country at the time, but they were as yet unacquainted with fire-arms and were afraid of their pale-face brothers.

We followed one branch of the Malheur to its source and after crossing the divide we often had to travel long distances on lava rocks where wagon wheels had failed to make a mark that could be seen. Sometimes we lost our way for a while, but soon one would call out "here it is" and again there would be sufficient marks to enable us to follow the track of the train ahead of us.

Those ahead would often leave letters at their camps with information for those that might follow them, telling distances between watering places ahead and other facts of value to the traveler. These instructions they gained from their pilot who was quite well acquainted with the country through which they were passing. A stick would be driven into the ground near the camp-fire and the letter would be clamped in a split at the top. These letters were often of much value to us and saved us from much suffering on the dry parched prairies.

After leaving the table lands we descended into the Harney Valley and in one day's drive, about ten miles, we came to the edge of the lake, which was to our left. We traveled for about six miles along the margin of the lake and in leaving it crossed a beautiful silvery stream. After this we saw no more lakes but we ascended many long and very high hills for many miles. Sometimes we would cross a stream twenty times in an hour or two. Sometimes we traveled in the bed of the stream for hundreds of yards only to come out on the same side as that from which we entered. I have since been told that this was the Crooked River.

We again passed over a high and hilly country for a long way. Then we came to a long downgrade where again we had to tie trees to our wagons to hold them back. This time we descended into a deep canyon where a small amount of timber grew in the side gulches. I am told that this stream is what is now known as Bear Creek. We found water there and plenty of wood for camp use. We also found another letter in a "split stick" stating that it was forty miles to the next water, the Deschutes River.

Our train started from Bear Creek at seven in the morning, climbed a steep side gulch for about a mile and traveled over a nearly level plain to the Deschutes. At midnight the train rested four hours and then started again on the weary journey, arriving at the river at eleven the next morning. The time between the two watering places was twenty-eight hours. Here we came up with the advance portion of our train resting in camp.

As we left Bear Creek one of our best horses, running loose, strayed from the bunch, and scenting the trail of the other train two days ahead of us, started up the canyon on the run. We could hear him at intervals as he thundered up the gulch. As our train started from camp, I was detailed to try to overtake and catch the runaway. With a half gallon canteen of water secured to the horn of my saddle, and with two biscuits in my pocket, I started on the trail. I was riding a poor immigrant horse, so I doubted my ability to catch the loose animal in a short run. Accordingly, I said to mother as I started that in case I could not catch the horse within a reasonable distance, I would not return to meet on the desert, but would go directly across to the Deschutes alone, and if I overtook the leading train there I would send back fresh water to them. I reached the other camp at seven o'clock in the evening after a twelve-hour ride and that night at midnight three men started on the back trail with canteens full of fresh cool water from the Deschutes River for the dry and weary people in our train.

From here the entire train followed up the Deschutes and its tributaries to the summit of the Cascade Mountains. Then we went down the Willamette River to Eugene where we arrived without further incident worthy of mention, on September 12, 1854.

THE JONATHAN AND NICK TOLL FAMILIES

(From an unpublished manuscript entitled *Nicholas Barnett Toll* by his grandson, Lester Swaggart.)

Over a century ago (1863) my grandather crossed the great plains into the far west at the age of six years. His parents' wagon was part of a train of more than forty, drawn by ox teams. Over the years he shared memories of the trip with his family.

Nicholas Barnett Toll, who homesteaded 160 acres on Fox Hollow Road in Lane County in 1883, was born near Pittsfield, Pike County, Illinois. His father Jonathan Toll ran a sawmill there on Painters Creek in the ground floor of a grist mill managed by Nick's Grandfather Barney.

The Barney and Toll families had never owned slaves, and when Civil War tensions reached their border area of Illinois, trade at the mill began to fall away. Feelings both for and against slavery ran high. The mill became a place of loud quarreling and often vicious fighting between customers, who used guns, stones, clubs and knives as weapons. People were bruised, cut, and occasionally critically injured in their persistent dispute.

Barney and Toll tried to remain neutral, but both factions pressed them to take sides. Skirmishes between soldiers developed in the vicinity. Some plundering had been reported. So the families decided to sell the mill and move to California.

Jonathan Toll.
Nettie Lyons

Since crossing the river into Missouri was restricted, people were traveling up-river and crossing into Iowa. Determined to start west before it was too late, one morning in 1862 Jonathan Toll loaded his family and goods into a wagon and hurried north to join a group that was rumored to be nearly ready to leave.

When he reached the Iowa ferry landing he found the boat loaded with big hogs on their way to market. Fearful of missing the emigrants, Jonathan talked the ferry operator into letting him on board anyway.

"All right. Move on, if you can find any room," the ferryman said. Jonathan crowded his team and wagon onto the deck. The horses bumped and bruised the hogs. The wagon moved right over some of the big critters and they lifted and tossed the wagon around on their backs. Hogs squealed. Horses snorted, stomped and kicked, and the boatman shouted and complained.

As soon as the ferry reached the opposite shore, the Tolls were asked to move out in a hurry. If the owners of the hogs saw the situation, there might be trouble for all concerned. So Jonathan drove out fast and kept going.

When the Toll family made connections with the gathering train the wagonmaster refused to allow them to join the group on the grounds that they were ill-prepared for the long hard trip. It was planting time, and Tolls didn't want to go back to Illinois. They found a place to live which had tillable land. Jonathan planted a

large field of corn. The crop grew well and harvest time neared. Meanwhile word came from the family in Illinois that the wagontrain there was still in preparation. Toll tried to sell his crop to the landlord, who didn't want to buy, but eventually gave him twenty dollars for it.

Back at the Illinois ferry the operator told them, "I have orders to refuse crossing into Illinois. Soldiers are expected any time and there may be a battle here. I have a peach orchard just down the river. You can hide there if you like." So Jonathan and his family stayed in the orchard for about two weeks. The soldiers passed through but no battle took place.

When [the] Tolls reached Pittsfield they learned that Grandpa Barney had not found a buyer for the mill yet, and the trip was postponed again. But eventually they were off, made connections with the Missouri contingent near Kansas City, and headed west. More than forty wagons rumbled along. Each family had one or more extra cattle. Eighteen responsible looking young men, probably deserters from the war, had been hired as guards, and doubtless were also pressed into service to keep the extra stock on the trail.

During the early part of the trip Indians often appeared. The travelers understood that if none showed up they were probably in hostile Indian country. Nicholas remembered one Indian boy who rode alongside the wagons saying, "I want a bisikit. I want to bite a horseshoe." He meant that after he had taken a bite from a biscuit the remaining part would be the shape of a horse-shoe. One evening Jonathan shot a couple of ducks and brought them to camp to clean for dinner. Two young Indians were sitting nearby on the grass. When the entrails fell to the ground those boys grabbed them and tossed them into the fire. When they had cooked a bit, the boys drew them out and ate them.

Another time the train made camp in a timbered area. Soon a group of soldiers rode up. It was hostile Indian country, but the military captain said part of the men could go berry picking if the rest stayed to guard the camp. Jonathan got carried away with his picking and moved farther into the berry patch. There he came upon a pile of partly burned logs. Among the charred timbers he saw human bodies. Hurrying back to camp he reported his discovery to the captain who cautioned him not to tell anybody what he'd found. Orders were given to pull camp and the train moved into more open country to spend the night.

About eight hundred miles across Iowa and Nebraska the train camped on the bank of the Platte River. This was real "Indian country." Wagons were pulled into a circle when they made camp. After being watered the cattle were driven inside the circle for the night. Campfires were built around the outside and supper prepared. Guards were posted as folks settled for the night.

Just before dawn on a moonless night a cow-brute let out an agonized bawl, and the whole herd was instantly on its feet milling around and around. Some wagons were upset by the plunging animals and part of the stock got out and ran away. Indians had crept through the tall grass and shot arrows into the enclosure. One had hit a vital spot and the prowlers accomplished their goal of stampeding the herd.

The Toll's wagon overturned, shaking up the family. The wagon contents were scattered and trampled, including sacks of flour which had been packed on the wagonbed. Nicholas' mother was pinned underneath and couldn't get up till the men had partly lifted the wagon.

At daybreak some men set out to look for the lost stock. After two days of searching someone found tracks at a river crossing upstream. Some of the cattle were found penned in an enclosure in a patch of timber across from the camp. An old Frenchman in charge and a bunch of Indians claimed they had found the cattle out on the prairie, which was true in a sense. They wanted five dollars a head for any stock claimed by the travelers.

The Toll's cattle were not in the stockade. Jonathan and another man whose cattle were still missing went looking some more. As they stood by the road a stage coach came along. The driver pulled up his teams and said, "You fellows are risking your lives out here by yourselves. There's a lot of real treacherous Indians around and they would just as soon kill you." The other man boarded the coach and rode back to safety while Jonathan continued his search. It was hot and dry. Heat waves danced before him as he strained his eyes for some glimpse of the missing animals. Thinking he saw them, he chased a mirage for some distance before returning to camp. Next day he went back. While trying to decide whether hoof prints he'd found were those of cattle or buffalo he heard clattering hoofs. There came three Indians on horseback in hot pursuit of a buffalo. Jonathan dodged under nearby brush. The hunters passed very close, but fortunately did not spot Mr. Toll. He said the Indians rode bent over their horses, trying to hamstring the animal with their tomahawks.

When the riders were out of sight he moved on. Soon he saw cattle grazing in the distance. When he called they recognized his voice and came running. He got them back to camp with little trouble and his family was glad to see both man and beasts.

The folks at camp were still conferring about their cattle in the stockade across the river. They decided on a plan. The wagonmaster directed the travelers to break camp and move their wagons down to the river ford. He posted armed men at the ford, then took other men with him to the Frenchman's hideout. There they dickered with the outlaw, pretending to try to talk the price down. After bargaining a while the wagonmaster said, "All right, men. We'll meet their terms. Take down the bars and drive the cattle out."

The stock was counted as it came out. The leader paused to figure what he owed, appearing to have trouble arriving at the amount. After hesitating a spell, he jumped on his horse and galloped away after the cattle. Some of the Indians fumbled with their ponies for a few minutes and pursued. By the time the Indians caught up with them, the cattle and drovers were crossing the ford. When the braves saw the armed men on the opposite bank they knew they'd been tricked. Rather than risk getting shot they retreated.

The wagonmaster had sent a guard ahead to an army fort a few miles beyond camp to report the trouble with the Frenchman. It seems he was also wanted on previous charges. Some years later they learned from records on file in Nebraska that the soldiers had caught and hung the Frenchman.

The train camped at Fort Bridger in Wyoming for a few days. Supplies were purchased and necessary repairs made. While at the Fort a child which did not live was born to the Toll family. The infant was buried there in an unmarked grave.

From Fort Bridger the travelers bore slightly south, following the Mormon trail down from the Great Divide. Fifteen years behind the '49ers, the track they followed was well-travelled. When they reached the Mormon settlement at Salt Lake the people were friendly. The immigrants were able to buy flour, bacon, lard, dried fruit and the like, and refill their straw ticks from new straw stacks.

Nick Toll used to tell the following story about that stop. The family came to Salt Lake City one evening. They inquired at a large white farm house, asking permission to camp for the night. The women wanted to get new straw for their bed ticks, since they had been on the road for a good while, and the straw was in need of replacing. There was a fresh new pile of straw at the farm where they spent the night.

The next morning when Jonathan went to the door to ask about straw, the resident Mormon farmer admired the good milk cow the Tolls had with them. He obviously wanted the cow, and his method of approaching the topic, observed by a six-year-old boy and recalled in later years went like this.

"Mr. Toll, I have two wives, and they fight all the time. I want to get rid of one of them. I will give one to you in exchange for that cow." The boy remembered that his father responded, "I have one wife already, and that is all I want."

There was a dinner bell hanging by the door of the farmhouse. The cook rang that bell for breakfast while the Tolls were there, and the visiting campers were amazed to see what seemed like dozens of children of both sexes and all sizes crawling out of the new straw pile in various stages of undress and hiking for breakast inside the farmhouse.

Some of the immigrants followed the Oregon trail into the northwest, but the Toll family went toward California. By this time it was November. The Tolls and some of the others stopped at Rich Gulch Flats, Nevada, for the winter.

The Tolls went on to California the next summer. They tried several locations there over the next few years. More children arrived. In 1876 Nick made an exploratory trip to Eugene with his dad and others. Here he found a job herding sheep for Mr. Judkins in the Spencer Butte area for a few months, after which his family returned to California.

In 1882 several of the family members came back again to Oregon. Nicholas and his wife went to work for a Junction City farmer. In 1883 Jonathan Toll bought about 85 acres from Keeler Farrington on Fox Hollow Road. Nicholas then took up a 160-acre homestead adjoining his dad's property on the south.

Jonathan Butler.
Lane County Museum

JONATHAN BUTLER

(From a family genealogical study prepared by Fern Conners of Columbia Falls, Montana, and others.)

Jonathan Butler's mother, Sarah Morgan Butler, was born in West Virginia in 1785. Her family moved to Ohio, then on to Indiana in 1835 where her husband died in 1851.

Several of Sarah's brothers also lived on the Indiana border where they defended the settlements against the Indians. Malaria caused unrest. . . . Isaac Butler's daughter [Isaac was eldest of Sarah's children] Elizabeth wrote: They began to talk about going west. They had heard about the fertile soil and healthful climate in Oregon. Indiana was full of malaria and no one seemed to escape it, many dying. The Butlers and Morgans invested in land and had comfortable homes, but wanted to leave.

Daniel Webster Butler, son of Isaac and Anna Butler, a boy of 18, grandson of Sarah Morgan Butler, was restless to move, Dan and Jonathan Butler were anxious to leave. Isaac Butler agreed to fit them out for the trip to Oregon. No sooner had he agreed to do this than grandmother Sarah, 67 years of age, declared her intention of going. Jonathan, her youngest child, could not be induced to stay and she would not

Mary Ann Butler.
Lane County Museum

let him go without her. Her children tried in vain to persuade her to stay until Jonathan and the others could go and prepare a home for her, but her faithful heart would not give up.

Two of Sarah's children married Blachys, and their families came to Oregon in the next few years. Much of the following report appears to have been written by a Blachly granddaughter.

My father did all he could to make the trip as easy as possible for her. He got a fine strong horse and covered carriage, which was made so slats could be laid across the box for her feather bed with its blue and white covers placed on it, that she had made. It took over a year of work to get ready. Everything had to be made by hand—wagons, chains, ox yokes, wagon covers, clothing enough to last 3 years, and provisions for 6 months. Father was overseer in packing provisions and did it with a lavish hand. There were "lots of pokes" as grandmother called them, with herbs of many kinds. She expected to prescribe and care for the sick, which she did to the fullest extent of her ability.

Our folks started with 10 yoke of oxen [and] some cows were broken to drive like oxen. Grandmother and Jonathan started a few days in advance so she could visit her children in Valparaiso, Indiana. She worried for fear the ox caravan would not stop for her, but in due time the long line of dry land schooners showed up. They started near Plymouth, Indiana with a farewell April 2, 1852. I was the little girl 9 or 10. Dan was the last to leave and he was the finest looking man that ever was. He was always Danny to us and fine and tender.

All went well with the travelers until they reached Des Moines, Iowa. They thought all danger of storms was over, but they encountered a terrible snow storm. It was only a stopping place for emigrant trains. Many cattle died, but they bought more at high prices, and hay too, [and] then started on. Near Salt Lake City they saw an emigrant train destroyed by Indians. They were advised to fort up and wait for a large train that was coming. This they did and took up the march again.

After leaving Utah many in the train took Mountain Fever (typhoid) and some of the strongest were buried by the wayside. Three sons of the Brayton family were left in that lonely country. Grandmother was everywhere helping with her skill. I doubt if she ever thought of contagion, and if she did she scorned the idea. She would walk miles, letting someone sick ride on her feather bed. At night she would lie on the ground (at age 67). She even cared for sick Indians too. She endured the trip better than many. She was always cheerful and helpful. The oxen were so worn out that some died or were left to die. Grandmother's horse died. Wagons and clothing had to be left; provisions were scarce; they suffered for water and feared Indians. All were footsore and ready to give up. They forted up in The Dalles in October for winter. In the spring of 1853 they went on to the Willamette Valley (via Barlow Road) to file on homesteads and farm.

Sarah Morgan Butler lived 10 years on a beautiful farm near Junction City. Eliza Blachly January was a 13-year-old girl in 1852 when they came across the plains and she said, "Grandmother stayed one night at our house in Valparaiso before she left. The chief desire of my grandmother in coming to Oregon was to take up land in her own right. . . . Her claim near Junction City was 80 acres where she built a cabin and planted trees; but she lost her holdings. . . . When [she] lost her homestead she lived with her son Jonathan Butler."□

CHAPTER 3

The Big Ranches

Most of the homesteaders in the Spencer Butte area left their homesteads within a few years, often selling out as soon as they had met the homesteading requirements and gained title to the claim. In general these requirements consisted of living on the land and cultivating a portion of it for a set period of time, usually five years. As the land became available several adjoining homesteads were bought up by enterprising ranchers who raised beef, sheep and dairy cattle. One of these ranchers was Alexander Osburn who lived on the George Rinehart Donation Land Claim and ran his cattle over nearly 2,000 acres. His story, prepared by the author, is reprinted here from the *Lane County Historian*, Vol. 23, pp. 39-42. (See map on page 122.)

A. M. OSBURN SPENCER BUTTE DIARY
1866-1894

The Christensen Brothers Rodeo Ranch south of Spencer Butte now occupies land which formerly was the site of a large dairy and cheese-making business. The valley was originally homesteaded by George W. Rinehart of Adams County, Illinois, who settled on his claim January 1, 1854. Rinehart sold the claim to Joseph L. Brumley in 1860 and moved to Creswell.

Alexander M. Osburn, a music and mathematics professor from Allegheny College, Meadville, Pennsylvania, bought the Brumley ranch south of Spencer Butte in December 1866 at a sheriff's sale. The deal included 1,000 acres which sold for $3,805. In addition to Rinehart's Donation Land Claim, Brumley transferred title to the John Blanton, Garnett Riggs and George Ritchie claims.

Osburn's granddaughter recalled that his first wife died while crossing the plains. After he had "located his land" he returned to Pennsylvania and married Sarah J. Ring. He brought his new wife west by way of the Isthmus of Panama where her bridal trousseau was stolen during the mule portage.

Once settled in their valley, the Osburns apparently lost no time establishing themselves in the cattle and dairy business. They added the Washington Jewett, William Renshaw and Jonathan Riggs Donation Land Claims to their holdings during the next few years, bringing their total acreage to 1,993.52 acres. The ranch stretched from what is now South Willamette Street on the west to the Dillard family place on the east, and south from Spencer Butte to Camas Swale.

When Preston surveyed the area in 1853 he described the terrain as rolling prairie country with oak openings here and there, brush in the bottoms under balm of Gilead and ash trees, and occasional clumps of fir or yellow pine. Alex Osburn hired some of his neighbors, including Charlie Swaggart and Nick Toll, to keep his pasture clear by cutting out seedling oak and cedar trees which tried to get a start.

Rattlesnakes and Horse Thieves

Life wasn't all a bed of roses. Sarah Osburn had to kill an occasional rattlesnake. The Eugene City *Guard* of December 5, 1868, reported on horse thieves as follows:

Our citizens should be careful in purchasing horses from strangers just now, as it appears that quite a lively business in the way of stealing horses has been recently going on in the valley. Our sheriff has received several telegrams making inquiry of horses stolen from below. Mr. Chichester purchased a horse at auction during court week, which was claimed and taken from him. *Mr. A. M. Osburn* found an animal in Salem which was stolen from his pasture on the Brumley ranch a few weeks ago. Mr. Graves had one he purchased some three months since, proved and taken from him. A stranger left one at Mathew Wallis to be pastured which is claimed by a gentleman in Salem. It seems that their mode of doing business has been to steal horses below, bring them up the river, sell them, and steal another to ride back to dispose of below.

In spite of these and other hardships Osburns moved ahead with their business. Again the Eugene City *Guard*, July 10, 1869, carried a clue.

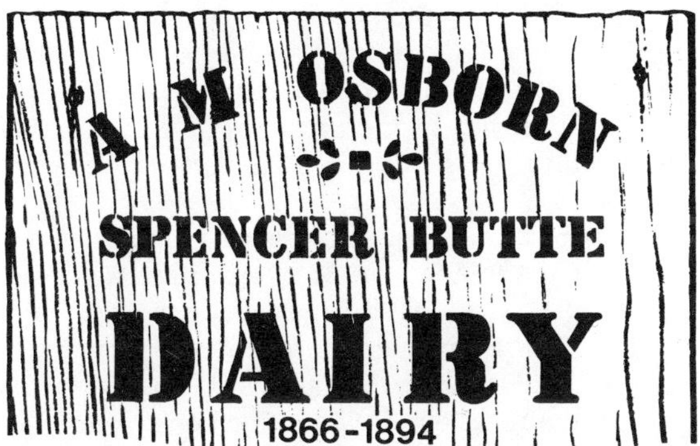

This stencil pattern was found on a piece of lumber in an Osburn outbuilding torn down by Christensens a few years ago. It may have been used to identify Osburn cheeses.
QLB graphics

Mr. Killingsworth of the Star Bakery has shown us a magnificent lot of chees (sic) which he has just purchased from the dairy of *Mr. A. M. Osburn*, and which he is offering to sell cheap for cash. We have not tasted them, but have been informed by those who have that they are very fine.

Alexander and Sarah had seven children. George Chester, the oldest, took a wagon load of cheese to Medford, traveling alone over 300 miles roundtrip when he was fifteen years old. He also helped with barn chores regularly, milking twenty cows every day for years. Another hired hand, probably the German-speaking Swiss immigrant neighbor named Ziniker, taught Chester a few German words which he remembered and used in later years. Chester became an accountant, working most of his life with Bell Telephone Company.

Other Osburn children were Paul who went into real estate in Portland; Morris who died at seventeen; Albert who established a store in Roseburg; Wade who became county assessor at Newport; Ruth, a secretary, who settled in Bend; and Guy, who was a commercial fisherman on the Columbia.

Ruth, the sixth child and the first girl born to them, brought such joy to her father that he rode clear in to Eugene City to tell all his friends he had a girl child at last, according to granddaughter Helen Meador of Portland.

Charlie Swaggart told his family the Osburn kids used the cheeses that "went bad" as wagon wheels by fixing an axle between two cheeses. These worked fine till the cheeses got wet.

A Bull Story

Leonard Ziniker of Creswell said his father worked for Osburn. He tells this story about an Osburn bull:

My father and another hired man were sent on the Butte to bring home the Holstein bull. He had a ring in his nose. A rope for each man was tied to the ring as they started to lead him home.

"This isn't going to be too simple," my father said. "This bull is going to take a lunge for one of us sooner or later, and when he does, for goodness sake hang on."

Presently the bull lunged for Albert Ziniker and the other fellow lost his hold on the rope. There were no trees nearby around which to snub the rope, but there was a ditch. Albert fell into the ditch. The bull fell too, but a little distance away. So they had the bull down in the ditch and the fellow got ahold of his rope again.

Albert said, "Next time he's not going for me because he thinks I put him in the ditch." By this time they were into a grove of scrub oak trees. Sure enough the next lunge was for the other fellow, but he was able to wrap the rope around a tree and hold the bull.

About that time a gravel wagon came along, running empty, with a tub of dishes sitting on the gravel bed. The driver offered to hitch the bull to the wagon and let the horses pull him along. Ziniker warned, "Now listen. This bull is pretty mean. Don't ever stop, 'cause if you do, he'll get his horn in the wheel and upset the wagon."

They went along and pretty soon something happened that made the driver stop. The bull went right for that rear wheel and upset the wagon and the dishes. There wasn't a whole dish left in the bunch.

Life wasn't all work on the ranch. Another Eugene City *Guard* story dated August 8, 1887, refers to the Osburns. The paper had been damaged so that some words were incomplete. With those blanks the story reads as follows:

____ester Osburn has returned from Port____ where he has been since the excursion. ____ understand that a sister of Mrs. Os____ is visiting at the Dairy. She hails from ____ and ____r. Alexander of Scotland who has been ____ing cheese for Mr. Osburn this summer ____ed for New Zealand the for[sic] part of the ____.

A second news item on December 27, 1887, is datelined:

Alexander and Sarah Osburn.
Helen Meador

Spencer Butte—The Spencer Butte literary society meets Monday evenings at 7 and speeches made by some of the young people are wonderful indeed. At an election held last Monday the following persons were elected to hold office for the next four years: Pres. L. Parker; V. Pres. W. W. Dillard; Sec. *Bert Osburn;* Journalist, Theodore Renshaw; Asst. Journalist, W. W. Dillard.

Like many of their neighbors and other valley cattlemen, the Osburns pastured cattle in eastern Oregon during the summer months. The November 15, 1890, Eugene City *Guard* notes, "Mr. Osburn brought his cattle in last week. The greater number are in better condition than the average cattle of the valley. He lost several head on the road and Johnny Hampton has gone after them for him."

Harry Taylor and his mother went to work on the Osburn ranch in 1893. Mrs. Taylor helped with the milking and cheese making. Harry, a boy of fourteen, split rails for fence, then brought in the milk cows in time for evening chores. According to him, Osburn pastured about 400 head.

A Wild Pig Story
Harry told about the time he helped Osburn trap a wild pig:

This sow was runnin' loose, part of the stock that had got away from the early settlers and run wild for years. They lived on acorns and bracken root. We seen she was with pig, so we made a tight pole corral right about there where the barn sets (on the Riggs Donation Land Claim). We baited the trap with corn. She'd sneak in and eat the corn when nobody was around. After about a week we was able to slip up and drop the gate and then we had her. We loaded her into a spring wagon with high sides on it and hauled her over to the Osburn place. We'd made a pen there and dumped a couple wagon loads of oak leaves in for bedding. When we turned her loose in that pen she dived in under them leaves and we never seen her for about two weeks, but every morning the whey was gone. She had a nice litter of little porkers after a while and that bacon sure came in handy, 'cause that was a mighty hard winter—'93."

On July 28, 1894, Mr. Osburn, aged about sixty-five, sold his entire ranch to C. L. Roper for $34,000 plus mortgages due to Mary Walker. He lived out his years in the Troutdale area east of Portland. His wife celebrated her eighty-eighth birthday there May 15, 1930, according to the *Oregon Historical Quarterly,* No. 3, p. 214.

Four of Alexander Osburn's brothers also settled in Oregon. They were Billy, whose son Frank was the Osburn of Osburn and Delano Drug Store in Eugene; John, who donated the land where Oregon State University was built; Ed, who was employed in the Lane County Post Office; and Alfred, who settled near Albany.

The ranch south of Spencer Butte changed hands eight times in the next few years, then was broken into forty-acre lots and dedicated as Porter Acres Subdivision in 1912. A Charles Sexton mortgaged the land to the Alliance Trust Company in Dundee, Scotland, for "$4,000 in gold coin to him in hand paid with interest at 10 per cent" in 1900. Terms of the mortgage required that he "keep improvements in good repair and the present buildings insured against fire for $500."

About 25 years later Lawrence and Molly Christensen arranged to rent 300 acres from Eugene bankers Chambers and Snodgrass. After renting for seven years they bought the first of many parcels, gradually enlarging their holdings to exceed the acreage of the Osburn dairy which flourished from 1866 to 1894 on the sunny side of Spencer Butte.

Lawrence Christensen was born in Denver but moved to Eugene by the time he was grown. He spent his early years logging. He and Mollie were married in 1911. Mollie said about those early years:

> I never knew his dad. After our marriage I stayed with his mother and he went to work in the woods. He worked for Booth Kelly for a while. His mother was a widow woman when I stayed with her—it was a little over a year. Henry was born while I lived there, but Bobby was born over on Lake Creek. I have a clock in there that still keeps good time. My husband broke log jams in Lake Creek for that clock—one day's work for that clock.
>
> We rented this place in 1921. He quit logging and he was no rancher, and it was pretty hard to convince him that you could make a dollar any other way but logging. He finally adjusted to it. His brother, George, was in partners with us for a few years. Then we bought him out.

Above: First Christensen Brothers rodeo (late 1920s). Osburn buildings in the background. Note spectators in car.
Patricia Christensen

Opposite: Henry Christensen about 1945.
Patricia Christensen

"Henry was eighteen when the rodeo started; Bobby about fifteen," Molly continued.

"We got started in rodeoing right here on the ranch," Henry Christensen said. "Earl Hutchinson who owns a bicycle shop in Eugene led a troop of bicyclers up here each spring to watch the branding. One year he suggested we have a little rodeo for the kids. We did, now we've been going ever since."

THE MARTIN BAKER GAY STOCK RANCH

Martin Gay stayed on his homestead until his death, adding acres from the surrounding territory as he had opportunity until he had two thousand acres under fence besides open range pasturage in the surrounding foothills. Martha Ann Gay Masterson continued her reminiscences in *The Sunset Trail* to include the years on the ranch up to the time of her father's death. The following account prepared by the author is reprinted from the *Lane County Historian*, Vol. 24, No. 2, pp. 30-37.

> Just about this time, in 1852, father decided to go farther south and buy a stock ranch near the hills as the valley land would soon all be fenced.
>
> Our friend the captain, father and my oldest brother went to Lane County and also to the Umpqua Valley. They returned well-pleased with the former place, sold their homes and moved up the valley and settled south of Eugene, taking up a donation claim.
>
> We found some of the Illinois company living there and they were well pleased to have us near them. Our ranch was in the hills and we did not like the place very well. We had settled in the valley when we first arrived and were satisfied with our home and its surroundings. We felt lonely and isolated back in the hills.
>
> Father put up a camp temporarily for a kitchen which was constructed by placing four posts in the ground to support the roof. The wagon boxes were set off the wagons and served as bedrooms. We put up shelves for our cooking utensils and had things quite convenient.
>
> One afternoon, just as we had finished washing the dishes and had all the milk pans on a shelf with buckets and cups hanging from the eaves of the roof, we were surprised to see a man riding toward the camp. He dismounted and spoke to us and as the posts of the kitchen were convenient, he tied his horse to one of them. We recognized him as Mamie's would-be beau! The man we had first met where the big stove was left (along the trail east of the Cascades). He was glad to see us again and said that he had located a donation claim on the McKenzie River.

While he was busy talking with Mamie his horse became frightened and tried to pull loose, but instead, to our dismay, the horse pulled down our kitchen! Pots, kettles and pans fell with a crash!

Our visitor was much chagrined and tried to help us rebuild our kitchen. In after years we often reminded him of the catastrophe.

We had been in camp a short time when we discovered it was a rattlesnake district. We would see them all about us; there were hundreds of them. We could not walk about the place to explore our new ranch because of the numerous reptiles. Father felt so badly about it. He was now building us a log house as there was no saw mill near and logs were plentiful. Also we saw small bands of Indians around us and we thought a log house better protection if the savages molested us.

In 1852 the summer weather was good for our building operations and before long we had a comfortable house to move into, with large rooms and an extra nice stone fireplace. We built near a spring of water, so had no need for a well.

Our nearest neighbor was a mile away; the next, five miles away. We were lonely but knew there would soon be other settlers as there were frequent inquiries for land. The married brother, James Woods Gay, built near us and our captain settled in the Siuslaw Valley, several miles away.

Our house was near a hill and at the edge of the little vale with a nice view, and I think we should have liked it if it had not been for the snakes. Mamie and I were out walking one morning when suddenly she cried out, "Oh, here is a rattler!" I jumped back and said, "Here is another." Then Mamie said, "Here are several more." We had walked right into the mouth of a rattlesnake den. We killed five and as many more got away. We told the boys about finding the den, so they watched and killed several large rattlers.

Mamie told me one day soon after moving into our new house in 1852 that she was intending to leave us and go to a home of her own. I suspected as much as her adorer had been very attentive of late. Preparations for the wedding were in progress and a trip to Portland for Mamie's outfit and other supplies must be made. At that time Portland was a village of 1000 people. Father started out with two wagons and one of the boys to help with the driving. Mamie made a list of her wedding outfit needs which father gave to the merchant in Portland and told him to fill it just as it was ordered.

Father was gone about 10 days. Ox teams were slow but sure and we were all proud of the nice articles he brought us from Portland. Ma-

Mollie Almasie Christensen.
Patricia Christensen

mie's wedding dress and all her other clothes were quite beautiful, but I shed tears over them because I realized she was to leave us soon. How could I give up my dear sister who had been with me all my life? I had no one else for company. She was next to my mother, with me!

Many families had moved into our neighborhood during the last few months. New houses were all over the country, three families of our old company among others.

The rainy season was here again. The storm clouds gathered in the distance and the wild geese were going south. The wind was sighing among the fir trees and found a sad echo in my heart for Mamie would soon leave us as the wedding day was drawing near.

Some old friends came fifty miles on horseback to attend the wedding. The great day arrived in a rainstorm and the groom and his attendants and the minister were late. At last all were assembled and the great room was filled with the guests. The bridal party entered from a side door. Mamie and her attendants in white made a charming picture. The wedding ceremony was short but impressive (Oct. 22, 1852, Mary Frances Gay and John Cogswell). Friends gathered around with good wishes and congratulations, then all repaired to the dining room where an old style wedding supper was waiting. During the evening old time games were played and old songs sung.

Lawrence Christensen.
Patricia Christensen

Next day, being fair, all we young folks went for a horseback ride, coming home late, tired and hungry. The following day Mamie went to her new home on horseback, as there was not a carriage in this part of the country at that time.

Mamie came back to see us in a couple of weeks and was well pleased with her cosy white cottage under some great oak trees on the bank of the beautiful McKenzie River.

Since Mamie left home I had become more interested than ever in my baby sister, Julia, who was a charming little girl a year and a half old. She talked quite plainly and tried to sing. Mamie wanted to take her and mother said, "No, we can't spare the baby."

Father and the boys again fenced land for grain and gardens, plowed and sowed, reaped and mowed, with a good will. We had a fine crop of wheat, oats, corn and potatoes and a good garden. We liked our new home now and father said he would never move again.

Nearly all the Indians had gone to other parts of the country but those that were left were very quarrelsome and considered dangerous. One day mother had gone to visit a neighbor and left me to get dinner and look after the younger children. Father and the boys were down in the field at work a half mile from the house. I was busy setting the table when one of the children ran in and said, "Shut the doors quick. I saw three Indians coming into the yard!" I ran to the door and told them to stay out, closed and barred the door. In the meantime they had gone to the kitchen door and walked in before I could get to it. I told the Indians to go away but they said, "No, give us dinner." Then I said no. They went to the stove and raised the lids from the kettles, then to the cupboards and looked over the shelves.

They saw that I was afraid of them and told me so! I took the children into the front room and left the Indians in possession of the kitchen. One of the little boys was looking out of a window and said, "I see father coming!" The Indians heard him and got out in a hurry and went to their ponies.

Father followed them and threatened them with a long stick that he had in his hand. He scolded them for entering the house when I had told them not to come in. He had seen them coming and knew that mother was away so hurried home thinking the Indians would frighten us and take a lot of provisions. Father told the Indians to leave and not to come here again. As they were riding off, one of them said in good English, "The old man is mad!" Father said, "Yes, I am mad and if you ever come back here I shall thrash you!" We always treated the Indians kindly when they came in peace but when they persisted in entering the house after being told to stay away they were ordered out in a hurry.

A short time before the three Indians came to the house our horses had all been driven away twenty miles. We laid it to them, as we had seen them pass the evening before and they had ridden round the horses and looked them over. The next morning our horses were gone. One of the boys followed their trail and fortunately overtook them. The Indians saw that they were being followed so they ran off and left our horses. Father said he thought the Indians ran off the horses just to give us trouble because we would not leave their country to them. Brother was gone so long we thought the Indians had wounded him and were much relieved to see him coming home with all the horses.

Our first crop of wheat was cut by hand with an old-style scythe and then stacked in the field around a level spot of ground which had been selected, then scraped off smooth for a thrashing floor. The sheaves of wheat were untied and scattered over the floor evenly, then several pairs of oxen were driven around over it, tramping out the ripe grains of wheat.

We thought the flour made from that grain of our own raising was of an extra quality and I suppose it was, as the wheat came from a choice variety which was quite expensive in those days. I remember one sale my father made of five bushels of wheat for twenty-five dollars. He did not like to ask such a price but it was customary and he did not wish to lower the price for others who had wheat to sell and besides money was very plentiful with all. Before another crop was ripe father had a good large barn to store it in with a thrashing floor and bins for the grain. We raised poultry by the hundred and it was my work to care for them. I was much intersted in this line of industry and delighted with my success, often rising before the sun and going out to feed the flock.

Mother came home from a visit one evening and told us we had a niece over at my oldest brother's. Father was very proud of his first grandchild and she was given the name of Suzanne. And over at Mamie's house soon after came a black-eyed little girl whom they named Mary Anne. So there were two "Annes" and father said he felt quite an old man now to be called grandfather by two little girls!

We found many places of interest on our big ranch as we explored it year by year. Two miles from the house over a rough road was a huge pile of great octagonal columns (similar to those recently dug out of Skinner's Butte). This pile of stone resembled the ruins of a castle and there were great trees growing among the rocks. No doubt a geologist could tell the origin of the stones—if an avalanche was accountable for them or if they came in the ice age. [This was a columnar basalt out-cropping just west of the crest of what came to be called Gay Hill on Fox Hollow Road. Emory Pruett told me in 1978 that his first job away from home was working with a portable rock crusher, making road gravel from the basalt outcroping. —L.B.]

There was much wild fruit on our place—strawberries, blackberries, cherries and crabapples. Cold, clear springs of water and magnificent fir trees.

Eugene was now quite a village and one brother went there to live and two other brothers left for the California gold mines. Soon after they went, the Rogue River Indian War broke out and we were much worrie ¹, thinking they would be killed. After some time we heard from them and they had safely passed through the danger zone. Volunteers were sent to fight the Indians and soon there was a battle and many were killed. The trouble lasted several months but finally the Indians were overcome and sent north to a reservation.

There were good schools in Eugene now and I boarded in town and attended the classes during the winter months. When spring came how glad I was to be at home with Mother and my little sister! I enjoyed tramping over the hills, gathering wild flowers and watching the white lambs playing in the sunshine, then working in the dairy making the golden butter into pound patties, hunting for eggs, in the barns and sheds and caring for the cunning baby chicks! Happy childhood days!

Father and the boys had made many improvements on the ranch and we had a splendid home with all the comforts of life and many of its luxuries. We were happy, well and prosperous in the large house father built for us. The old log house we had at first was pulled down and moved away to the hills for wood houses and farm machinery. We had great hay barns, grain barns, shops and a tannery, all together making quite a village.

Emma Ziniker described the Gay house in a letter written April 1, 1979:

It is a pleasure to write about the beautiful house the Martin Gay family built on the big cattle ranch the Ruegger family and my father John Ziniker bought.

There were four entrances to the house. One through the porch on the east side, one on the west side, one on the north side, entering a large parlor and one entering the kitchen. There was a fireplace and a hanging kerosene lamp in the parlor. Other rooms had the lamps. There were copies of famous paintings hanging in the parlor. There was another large room on the west side and a bedroom. There was a stairway upstairs from the beautiful porch. The porch was like a room open on one side, with beautiful house plants. You could eat your lunch on the porch. You could enter the dining room from the parlor or different parts of the house. The kitchen was next to the dining room. There was another stairway from the parlor to a bedroom.

There were large bushes of roses and honeysuckle and other flowers around the house. There were many fruit trees—apples, pears, plums and other fruit.

Martha Ann Gay Masterson continues:

Father bought land at different times until he had two thousand acres under fence besides thousands of acres of range in the foothills.

And now a brother had returned from California mines and was to be married to an Albany girl. Some of us went fifty miles on horseback to be present at the wedding, then visited our old neighbors a few days before returning. The bride and groom made their wedding trip on horseback as the river steamers were slow and not always on time.

Another little daughter, Florilla, had come to Mamie's home to keep Mary Anne company but not for long as they both sickened and died and were buried in one grave on the hill near where they had played. They were taken ill with scarlet fever while on a visit to our home.

This was our first deep sorrow and it fell heavily upon us. My sister was broken-hearted

Gay's house as it was when Zinikers lived there.
Marie Erdmann

over her loss. She grieved so much that father advised a change for her. They planned a trip east to visit Mamie's new relatives and were to be gone a year. It was a dangerous trip in those days, down the coast by ocean, across Panama on muleback, across the Gulf of Mexico and then up the Mississippi River. They made the journey safely and how glad we were to see them home again.

Two older brothers went to the gold mines in Idaho, so our family was not very large. But there were several grandchildren to come and visit us. Pink was a young lady now and fond of music. She played nicely on the beautiful melodeon given her by one of the older brothers. I was very fond of horseback riding and often rode ten miles to church Sunday morning, remaining for afternoon services and home before dark.

In 1866 we had now spent fourteen happy years in our home and it had been a haven of rest for many others. We cared for the sick, aged and the needy. No one in distress ever came to my father in vain. Those whose hearts were heavy with sorrow found in him a true friend: the wanderer was given food and shelter. The people all loved father for his warmhearted southern hospitality.

But father was growing old now and often spoke of the absent members of his family and wished that he might see them once more. It was ten years since we all met at the dear old home. Father's birthday, October 24, was drawing near and a younger brother and I thought of a happy surprise we would give father on that day. We told mother our secret and she thought it a fine plan and said she would help us. We prepared for a family reunion and sent invitations to all the ones absent and they accepted. We had a busy time and took Pink into our plot and she was delighted to be trusted with grown-up affairs.

The day arrived and all was in readiness to receive our company. Some came the night before; some the next day, until all were present except one family. I wondered if they would complete the circle. It was dark now so we illuminated the house and waited and listened. At last we heard them calling to us and we rushed to the door and answered. They were soon in the warm bright room and the whole family was now at home and what a house full! Father looked on the group with pleasure and our eldest brother said, "Here we are, Father and Mother, all of us." We were gathered in mother's large sitting room and father said, "I am so glad to see you all once more. Who got up this surprise for me?" We told him we children did it with mother to help us. Then father told us all to stand up in a line and circle around the large room. We did so and asked father and mother to head the procession.

After all had partaken of the evening meal the children were shown into a large room where they could play and romp without disturbing the older people who were planning the arrangements for the following day. Next morning we all congratulated father on his birthday. He would not have been considered old for these days, but his head had been white for years.

We told him that we had arranged for a family group picture and wanted him to go to Eugene with us. We had engaged a photographer for the day and ordered a dinner at the principal hotel for the family party. We started out from home a happy crowd, leaving friends to prepare supper for us and care for the house during our absence. We spent a happy day with many friends coming in to see us and congratulate father and mother on the reunion of their large family.

We arrived at the right time for supper and found our friends and the feast awaiting us. After breakfast the next morning some prepared to leave and father said, "Shall we ever meet again on earth?" They kissed him goodbye and a shadow seemed to pass over the group as they left us behind.

In a few days they were all gone to their homes and how we missed them. The house was so still. How quietly we moved about and how lonely we were. Pink looked sad and father talked but little. He walked out on the farm and returned weary. Friends called to see father but he seemed too quiet for him. The photographs were brought home and father had one sent to each child.

We were busy about our work, getting ready for winter which was approaching. The rain clouds were hovering over the distant mountains and most of the birds had started south. A sadness settled down over our once-happy home because we could see that father was failing. He said that his time was nearly over. We tried to cheer him but he said we had best understand from the first that he was soon to leave us. He told me of the improvements he wished made about the house and on the farm.

Father grew weaker and took [to] his bed. We called a physician and sent for absent brothers and sister. They came to see him for the last time. He called us around the bed, then looked at the family circle with mother near him and said faintly, "All here but one." We told father we hoped the absent brother would soon be with us but he did not come. Our telegram did not reach him.

Father talked to us and told us where to bury him and to take care of mother and our baby sister and to live as he had taught us to live; not to grieve for him. His race had been run on earth and he was ready to cross over. So, calmly, his great and noble soul passed on March 17, 1867. We laid father away on the hillside which he had given long ago for a family and neighborhood burial ground, and then sadly returned to our lonely home. Mother was disconsolate. For forty years she and father had shared life's shadows and sunshine, its dangers and joys. Often she started to meet him when she heard approaching footsteps, then remembered he would never come again.

The sister Julia contracted tuberculosis in the spring of 1870 and was buried on the hillside near her father. Mother, Ann Gay, continued to live on the old homestead until she died. In January, 1874, she was laid to rest beside her husband, Martin Baker Gay, on the hillside in their family cemetery now known as the Gay-Cogswell Pioneer Cemetery.

James Gay sold his donation land claim to

Martin and Ann Gay.
Dr. Eva Johnson

his brother John in 1859 and moved to Fall Creek where he operated a sawmill for some years before moving to a small farm near Brownsville where he lived till his death in 1903. The homestead remained in the family until 1878 when it was sold to Ira Hawley.

James made irregular entries in his trail diary through 1855 commenting on daily events and the weather. Each entry is dated, mentions what day of the week it is and often includes some weather report. The following entries prepared by the author are reprinted from the *Lane County Historian*, Vol. 24, pp. 27-29.

April, 1852

1 fair we went to Mr Stoels to preaching I begun to set my apples [sic] trees in the northwest corner I run east south and west the first one is a Rambo, the 2 a golden-sweet. 3 Amer. Pipin. 4 Winter Queen. 5 golden ruset, 6 yelowbelflour 7 2 Waxens 8 fall Beauty 9 Esophiaspitsburg I begun in the northwest corner of my garden and run east and then back again. [No further entries except weather information until January, 1854]

2 fair to day I helped Mr. Killingworth stake off his claim in the forenoon the remainder I worked in my shop [James was a cabinetmaker. There is another page which records income from making "chares," tables, bureau, two coffins, sette, book case, 4 chicken coops, and 6 "troves" during early 1852 for a total cash income of $220.25.]

3 rain I worked in my shop light showers I killed a fine goos on my wheat today

4 snow at home it snowed some little this has been the coldest day that we have had this winter we went to father's today ice 5/8 thick

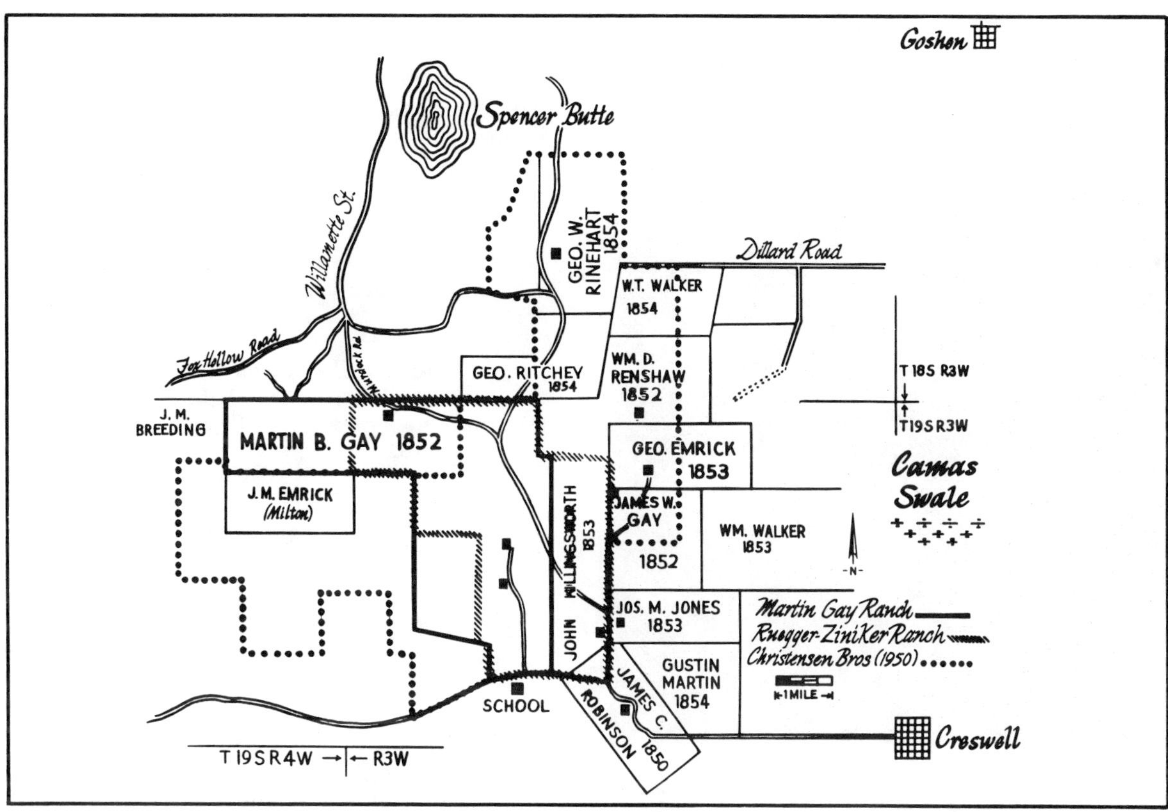

Martin Baker Gay Ranch. Roads and buildings as they appear on a 1921 topographical map. Homesteads of neighbors mentioned in James Gay diary, with year they "settled" on the land. QLB Graphics

January, 1855

1 it is fogy and cold today I hauld wood and cleaned wheat to carry to mill

2 it is snowing this morning I went to mill and just as I got to the river there blue up astorm of rain and snow I bought 6 sacks $3.36

3 it has ben raining and snowing ever cince yesterday evoning and is still at it I got home from mill just at dark

4 there fell a snow 6 inches deep last night and it is still snowing

5 it fill an 1¼ inches deep last night I went out and killed a deer today

6 it has ben raining to day the snow is melting of to day on the botoms I killed a goose

7 It has ben showery to day and cool the snow is still melting off sloe. Baker was hear today [his brother].

8 I went to town today there was some rain to day. I bought some salt and sugar and other things to the amount of $11.00 killed a crane

9 I worked in my shop and killed a pig and went to papa

10 I have ben choping wood to day and fixing up my pig and calf house father was hear to-day and Mr richia was to borow a sadle rain

11 I went to fathers to get the wagon to hawl wood but could not find the oxen it rained to day I worked in my shop the remainder of the day Mr Read was hear.

12 I went to town to day after apples trees I bought arope today $1.27¼ Mr kilingsworth was hear Br John was hear and stayed all night

13 I have been diging holes to set my trees sold beets $100 I was at papa to day Mr. emrick was hear Mr jones children was hear after beets it has ben fair I was at Mr emrich

14 Milton Emrick was hear to day

15 Thomas walker was hear to day at work inn shop Brise staard [Stewart?] was hear I sold 2 plans [planes?] $6.00

16 Mr & Mrs. Richia was hear to day and mary Mcmury Mr. Walker and Mr emrick I hauled wood to day I was at papa to day

17 I have ben at work in my shop Mr emrick was hear to d papa was to d

18 Francis Cogswell was hear to day I have

James Gay Family. Back row, from left: Ed, Annie, George. Front row, from left: James, Lincoln, Mollie (Frances).
Arthur Sperling

been at work

19 francis Cogswell sister Mary & Martha was hear Mary & Martha stayed all night there was some snow today with the rain it is warm and has been so for some time

20 Brother good was hear today there has ben some snow to day I have ben at work in shop

21 Mr emrick was hear it is warm the snow will be off of the mts in a few days

22 it has ben warm today I was at papa to day thomas Walker was hear to day

23 Mr. T. Walker was hear I was at Mr Richias this morning and out to hunt my cow I killed asquirl and seen a deer

24 I went out and found my cow. at my work and them Mr. emrick & Mr renshaw was hear Mr. emrick killed the largest fowl on the swail that I ever seen it weied 28 lbs & was 8 feet across the wing B Roberson was hear today

26 I went to town bought four yds of domestic it has ben coll today

27 Mr jones sonwas tohear killingsworth Mr Reed, Brother green, Mr ward, Brother john & Baker I went on the swail to kill geese

28 Brother evan, was hear to day fair and warm

29 Mr emrick, was hear I was at Mr killingsworth four doors & 60 light of sash finished $35.00

30 I went to papas for the wagon I did not get it

31 Mother was hear tod & Kely was hear I was at m emricks

February, 1855

1 Mr Walker & B caldwell & William Renshaw was hear I was at Mr Kilingsworth and at fathers twice I cleaned wheat

2 $1.95 I went to town to day sold 7½ doz eggs $2.87½ Brother john and martha was hear Mary r emrick was hear

3 I was at Mr joneses and fathers T Walker and Mrs kilingsworth was hear I got a letter from M M gott [father in law].

4 it is warm and has ben for seval days

5 I was at fathers for the oxens W. Walker was hear to cut a screw

6 Brother green was hear to drive the I was at Mr jones to get the plow

7 I went out to hunt my cow and to try and kill a deer I shot but missed Mr emrick was hear

8 Mr Roberes was hear it is warm

9 has ben raining all day I have ben at work in my shop one plain made $4.00

10 I was at fathers to get help to kill a hog Brother john was hear and help me kill it mr emrick was hear

11 at home and alone

12 W. Walker, father Mr. emrick mr. walkers son, W. Renshas and Brother Evans was hear

13 I went to town today sister Martha was hear I bought ahat soap sugar and tin cup tethor sold 12 doz eggs. $4.22½ $13.00 [for purchases?]

14 father was hear to make a sadle

15 I went to fathers to day to help him start his beef cattle to the mins Mr Mankin S. Martha, B. green, Martha walker, and mary emrick was hear

16 I went to Mr emricks after a cettle Mr. Dabney Dade was hear I have not seen for near four years he is from california hear

17 Mr jones was hear twice today a gentleman bought the harrow home Mr Dade left for town I have ben making soap today and yesterday

18 it is some cooler to day than it has ben for several days

Albert and Rosena Ruegger, Emma, Edward and Rose (the baby).
Marie Erdmann

19 I have ben haling to day I was at fathers to day to get the catle and wagon it snowed on the hills W. Walker was hear today

20 I have ben choping wood today W Walkers son was hear to day Mr Marten was hear the Mts is white to day with snow

21 I was at father Mr emrick was hear twice today

22 I went to Mr Breeding today Mother was hear to day Mr emrick was hear

23 I was at Mr. emricks Mrs. & miss emrick was hear Brother evans and green was hear Mr walkers son was hear

24 Mr emrick and milton & b john was hear it has ben cold for 3 days

25 Baker was hear today

26 I went to Mr Breedings to day Mother was hear I went to Mr steards [Stewart?] and R Renshas Mrs Br was hear

27 I was at Mr Martins today

28 I was at fathers to day W. Walker and Miss M emrick was hear

March, 1855

1 Mother was hear Brother john, and green was hear $1.50

2 B john and goode was hear Mrs emrick was hear $2.50

3 I was at fathers last night Mother was here L. Greenwoode was here mrs Emerick was here

4 S. Martha was here to day Mother was here

5 Mother and Sister Martha was here

6 Martha was hear I killed an Eagle

7 Mother and Martha was hear thunder Showers in the morning

8 Martha was hear R. Renshaw was too I was at W. Renshaws and papas to day

9 I went to town to day sister Martha Bro baker was hear I shot at a deer

10 I was at the school house to day to organize the school district. I was at Mr. emricks to day. B. john, Bro green, sister martha and Mrs. emrick was hear it snowed on the mts last night

11 Mother was hear to day

12 I was at fathers to day Bro green Bro. Baker sister martha and Miss M emrick I killed a crow 120 yds.

The next entry is dated December 1, 1861, and was written after the move to Fall Creek.

RUEGGER AND ZINIKER
Successors to the Martin Gay Family

Prepared by the author and reprinted from the *Lane County Historian*, Vol. XXIII, pp. 3-30, Vol. XXIV, pp. 40-44.

After his mother's death Evan Gay bought out the other heirs' interests in the Gay estate and held the ranch for about three years. In 1878 Albert Ruegger and John Ziniker, Swiss immigrants, bought 1,750 acres of that land which they held as a partnership for several years. Ruegger was Ziniker's uncle.

Albert and Rosena Ruegger arrived in the United States with two children. They spent their first year at Trenton, Ohio, moved from there to Nebraska for nine months, then farmed for about two years in Kansas. They rented a farm for three years along the Columbia just east of Portland which is now the site of the present International Airport. Their landlord was unwilling to sell that place, so they moved to the Gay holdings in Lane County.

An entry in *Portrait and Biographical Record of the Willamette Valley, Oregon* states that

Ruegger and Ziniker carried on a large prosperous stock ranch and added dairying and cheese-making. Interviews with descendants of these early ranchers have disclosed interesting details of their life.

John Ziniker's daughter, Emma, wrote in a letter in 1979 of her memories of her childhood home.

> There was a well a few yards from the house. It was paved with concrete. The water came from a natural spring. There were troughs for the cows and horses to drink from. There was a creek running through the ranch.
>
> My father built a small pond on a sloping hillside. A short distance downhill we had a big garden. They built troughs to the pond to get water to the garden. My father put a stopper on a long rod to open the plug when we irrigated the garden. There were pipes to the garden.
>
> There were two large barns. The very large one my father and the Rueggers built with stalls to milk the cows by hand. They stored the hay in the barns. In the fall the thrashers would come to thrash the wheat and oats. There was a granary to store the wheat and oats. The Rueggers and my father built a cheese house. The Rueggers made round cheese about the size of a dinner plate, a few inches high. Some larger and some smaller.
>
> They butchered the pigs and smoked their own ham and bacon. There was a smoke house and a store house for the potatoes, apples and other things from the harvest. They made a barrel of sauerkraut. We had a bean garden for dried beans. There was a chicken coop. We had lots of chickens. There was a work shop and a hot house. We had a large herd of cattle. My father used to take train loads of beef cattle to the stockyards in Portland. We also had horses. It was an ideal dairy ranch.
>
> The Ruegger family and my father John Ziniker lived in Switzerland. They decided to come to America to buy a dairy ranch to make a fortune by making cheese and selling milk and beef cattle. They found an ideal place for a dairy ranch in Lane County.
>
> My father was fourteen when he came with his uncle and family. About ten years later he wrote to a girl he went to school with in Switzerland and asked her to come to marry him. I have the photograph of my mother she sent to him. She came and they were married June 11, 1884. My father and mother lived in the house the Martin Gays built with the Ruegger family for some years. When the family got larger they built a large house on a hill. The Rueggers moved in there. That was the big white house. It burned some years ago.
>
> When my father's uncle passed away his two grown sons, Edward and Ernest Ruegger decided to go on their own. The surveyors came to make two ranches out of the big one and the Rueggers decided to move back to the Martin Gay house. We went to live in the big white house. A few years later my father sold his ranch and we moved to the state of Washington. . . .
>
> Sincerely,
> *Emma Ziniker*

John Ziniker had quite a reputation as a "wild driver". His method of breaking horses was to hitch one that had never worn a harness to the wagon with an older, steadier animal. He'd get on board, say "get up" and off they'd go. The wagon would likely be broken before

White house built by Rueggers which John Ziniker family eventually moved into, 1900. Children, from left: Lilly, Laura, Frieda, Emma, Lena, Albert (the baby), and John.
Mrs. William Alexander

John and Vrena Ziniker. These are the pictures exchanged by Vrena Siegerist and John Ziniker before she came to America to be his bride.
Emma Ziniker

the end of the drive. He hardly went anyplace without having a runaway in those early years.

One story tells of the family council wherein John's wife was selected. They sat around a table examining pictures of girls back in Switzerland. Which one should become the bride? One was pretty. Another had money. One was chosen and sent for. When she came into Creswell John went to meet her. She was "pretty dressed up" for the trip, including a big picture hat. John had, as usual, hitched up a wild horse. A lot of people along the route home remembered seeing them pass. The bride-to-be was hanging on to her hat with one hand and the wagon with the other. Before they reached the ranch, so the story goes, she was off the seat and down in the wagon box.

Ralph Ruegger of Gresham has his grandfather's family account book detailing income and expenses from 1878 to 1909. Beginning entries in the book are in old-fashioned German script, since German was the native tongue of the Ruegger family. Over the years entries were made in "hybrid" German-English words and later almost entirely in English.

We learn from the account book that Ruegger sold hundreds of pounds of cheese per year, often in 100 pound lots, to merchants all over Oregon as well as to neighbors such as Thurston Goodpasture. One entry even mentions a sale to a Chees Haus in Pennsylvania. For some time he supplied the St. Charles Hotel in Eugene City with a weekly shipment of 70 to 80 pounds of butter, quantities of cheese, potatoes, a 40 to 50 pound pig, in addition to other goods in season.

Ruegger brought a good Holstein bull from the east to improve his dairy herd, and the book contains some record of bull service to neighbors' cows.

A penciled draft of a personal letter, possibly to the folks back in Switzerland, appears on ledger page 47 below entries dated 1896. The following translation shows that the U.S. election system and politics were getting their share of blame for hard times even in those days:

Dear Lina,

We received your card and letter. We are fine, but we had a very dry spring. Since May it has rained only once, but we had a lot of hay which is worth a lot to us. Only cattle is very low in price. All together business is not very good. This is to blame on the election of a new president. When that is over things will get better again.

We are expecting Ida from Portland in a few days. She was away for a year, but then everybody will be at home again. The (fall-death) of such a young woman as Mrs. Albert Rundgins is sad. It is hard to understand why these people eat horse meat. They did not write to us yet.

We wished you could come and visit us once, but I don't know if you would like it now, since everything is dry and yellow. But plums, apples and pears and potatoes are growing only not as plenty.

We have now sold our land. We kept the part on which Hans Ziniker lives. That is the better land, better than the one we live on.

Please don't be angry with Edmund, that he did not wrote. He and Ernest have to do Birnbaum's work. They are building a big barn all by themselves, and have a lot of work to do, and it is very hot here.

In 1887 Albert Ruegger and John Ziniker sent passage money to Switzerland for John's younger brother Edward to come. He was a boy of sixteen when he came. Went to work for

Ziniker's "German castle."
Elsie Sutton

Ruegger ranch buildings in 1910.
Edward Ziniker Jr.

his uncle earning fifty cents a day. He helped build farm buildings among other things. Edward eventually married Emma Ruegger and they had ten children. The oldest son Paul, when he grew old enough to go to school, went to board with his grandparents the Rueggers through the week to attend school with the Ruegger children since it was 5 miles from his home to the school—too far for a six-year-old to walk alone every day through the woods.

Paul described the Ruegger cheese house as he remembered it: "There was a large vat. I don't know how many gallons it held. It seemed to me it was about ten feet long, maybe four or five wide, eighteen inches deep down to the main part where the pipe was that heated it. They built a fire in that round pipe underneath at one end, and the other end went out through the wall. Had to build a little fire to warm the milk."

The cheese house was a wooden outbuilding, divided in the middle, with a shop in one end and the cheese-making equipment and storage in the other. They bought a little gas engine to run the milk separators, a one-horse engine purchased in 1908 according to an entry in the Ruegger account book. The men made a shaft through the whole building. The engine was in the workshop end. A pulley on the shaft ran the milk separator. A small feed mill in the shop was also run off that shaft. One of the girls once got her long hair caught in the pulley and made quite a stir.

Cheese-making was an early summer activity. The milk cows freshened in the spring, and when the grass came the milk would be plentiful. By the time the grass dried up in late July or early August milk flow was dropping off as well.

Ruegger followed the practice of other valley stockmen of the period and pastured the beef animals in Eastern Oregon during the summer months. According to family recollection those same beef animals were favored during the winter. There usually wasn't enough feed in the barns to keep all the animals, so the milk cows had to forage for themselves. When pastures were poor some of the milk cows just about starved. One grandchild remembers her mama telling how in the winter they would chop down oak trees so those hungry cows could eat the moss:

"Mama had a sort of horror of cattle because they used to have to tail 'em up," she explained. "In the spring after the calves were born and before the grass came on good the cows would get down—weak and thin as they were—and couldn't get up. The men would grab their tails and pull up to help get them to their feet again." A grandson recalled, "Years later when I had cows out here Mama always told me, 'Now don't get too many of 'em'."

Whereas Martin Gay *drove* cattle to the mines, Ruegger *shipped by train*. An entry in the family account book notes receipts for "1 carload Beef 19,650 lbs. @ 3¼¢ per lb. = $635.70 – freight $50." This was in 1887. There are numerous entires of a similar nature; e.g., "June 9, 1899, check from Zimmerman for one carload of cattle $818.87."

Albert Ruegger passed away in 1907. His wife, who lived until 1931, continued to operate the ranch for a time with the help of her sons, but a division of the land was made, giving John Ziniker title to one half. *Portrait and Biographical Record of the Willamette Valley, Oregon* tells us John, in partnership with his aunt "has about two hundred acres under cultivation, but his principal source of income is Durham cattle, which are raised in large numbers, as are also a variety of other kinds of stock."

A listing of items divided at the time the partnership was dissolved includes the following:

Charles (horse)	87.50	one comforter	3.00
one saddle	5.00	poncho	1.25
one washbucket	1.50	wineglasses	.35
waterbottles	.50	1½ doz. milkpans	4.50
2 beds	5.00	one cider barrel	3.00
cider	12.50	one wall clock	5.00
planing screw	1.75	1 knife and bowl	1.00
milk strainer	1.00	2 lanterns	2.50

Other items included 18 cows, 8 calves, one machine and rake, one spring wagon, 2 harnesses, saw, shovel, mousetraps, curry brush, yoke, wagon blanket, nails, 2 boxes wagon oil, broom, chairs, stove, table, cheese kettle, anchor, kitchen cabinet, grinding wheel, salt shaker, hay fork and stove pipe.

According to records at the county courthouse the division of property between John Ziniker and Albert Ruegger's heirs took place June 23, 1908. In September of that year John Ziniker sold his 847.09 acres to Richard Newhall. Six years later Rosa Ruegger gave a quitclaim deed to her sons for the remaining 847.09 acres, and Ernest sold his interest to his brother Edward the following December. Edward and his wife Mary continued to operate the farm, including the dairy and cheese making business until 1920, when they sold out to W. J. Butler and moved to Gresham. Mr. Butler was unable to keep up with the taxes through the Depression and the property went back to the Rueggers after a sheriff's sale in 1938. In 1945 they sold to Sher Khan. The land is now part of the Christensen Brothers ranch.

THE ONION KING
(Prepared by the author and reprinted from *Lane County Historian*, Vol. XXIV, pp.67-71.)

The Sunday *Oregonian* of July 25, 1915, carried a story about Edward Ziniker, onion grower under the headline **THREE ACRES AND ONIONS MAKE A FAMILY WEALTHY.** Recent interviews with some of his children and former neighbors have uncovered interesting details about Ziniker's rise to "fame and fortune."

Edward Ziniker, then sixteen years old, came to the Spencer Butte area from the German border of Switzerland in 1887 with financial help from his uncle and two brothers who had preceded him by a few years. At first he hired out as a day laborer. Ziniker became a landowner when he purchased his first fifty acres from Albert Ruegger by working out the purchase price at 50¢ a day (about $3.00 an acre).

In 1890, when he was twenty years old, Ed married Emma Ruegger in Creswell, borrowing money to buy the marriage license, according to the *Oregonian* article. By 1915 they had ten children and owned 350 acres of land. Their son Paul says 100 acres of that was bottom land in what is now known as the Christensen Valley, and may have been partly beaver meadow.

Quoting from the *Oregonian* article:

"I worked hard those first years," said Mr. Ziniker. "I had no money to buy horses or tools with. I did everything myself in the hardest way." Two acres he planted to prunes. Three acres he planted to onions. [Paul said he spaded the onion field those first years.] On these five acres he concentrated his efforts. During the many years

Ziniker family gathering onions.
Marie Erdmann

that he has been at the business, Mr. Ziniker has raised on that three-acre tract at Spencer Butte 1,500,000 pounds of onions. He has grown approximately $25,000 worth of onions. This year [1915] he has three and a half acres. He expects a yield of 50 tons. This is the average annual yield.

The *Oregonian* goes on to say that for nine successive years the prunes bore heavily without a single crop failure, and that he has planted six more acres which "will soon be bearing."

"Speaking of the Spencer Butte country," the *Oregonian* quoted Mr. Ziniker, "you'd hardly expect a man to make more than a living there. It's hard to do that raising general crops. I have made everything I've got by cultivating just a few acres."

One secret of the onion field's productivity was undoubtedly a liberal dressing of chicken manure. The Zinikers kept 300-400 laying hens. They had an incubator and brooder and raised their own replacement flocks. The old hens were sold live for meat when they passed productivity.

His children remember with pride the "handy" way their dad fixed the chicken house to make care and feeding of the flock easy for mother. Wheat storage bins were upstairs in the barn, with a built-in chute and a trap door at the bottom so grain could be drawn into a bucket right in the room where the chickens ate. A clean-out bin, accessible from the outside, had been built under the roosts, so raking out the manure was as simple as possible. All the convenience didn't make the job any less smelly, however. And that was work the boys "got to do."

Edward Ziniker was known in the Spencer Butte area as the Onion King. The title may have been earned in part by the "castle" he built to house his growing family. The work was done by Ziniker and his sons without outside architectural or carpentering help, at a cost of $4,000. Mrs. Florence Murdock, who lived in the house after Zinikers moved to town, said the interior was all beautifully finished with first-grade tongue-and-groove paneling—walls, ceiling and floors. The living room was large enough to accommodate three sets of square dancers and was used for community dances during the '20s when neighbors would come from miles around by horse and wagon to dance all night. Old-timers in the area still refer to the building as the "German castle." Unfortunately it burned to the ground nearly fifty years ago.

The house, completed about 1910, had an

*Above: Edward and Emma Ziniker,
Paul, Otto and Helen, 1895.*
Paul Ziniker

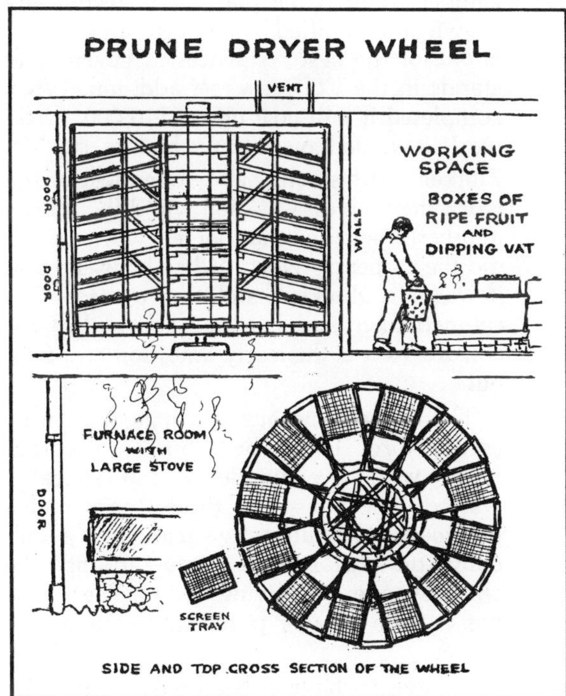

Swaggart prune dryer purchased from Ziniker.
Lester Swaggart drawings

Opposite: May Duke cherries from the Ed
Ziniker orchard.
Lane County Museum

acetylene light plant which provided good illumination through gas lights in each room. There was a bathtub upstairs and hot and cold water. "Oh, we were modern out there," said Edward, Jr. "We had running water in the house—except the toilet. It was a three or four-holer out there over the creek."

Marie Ziniker Erdmann recalls with pleasure the evenings of singing around the fire in their home. Both parents were yodelers. Her mother had special skill. The children learned Swiss yodeling songs from them and from neighbors who often came to sing with the family.

Nephew Leonard Ziniker of Creswell remembered his Uncle Edward as something of a mechanical wizard—with an inventive turn of mind. He designed and built a unique fruit dryer—a wheel dryer. The drying trays were stacked around a revolving central post within a circular shaft having the furnace at the bottom, instead of the usual slanting tunnel arrangement. A door into the upper part of the shaft allowed trays to be moved to lower shelves as the fruit dried. The first such dryer Ziniker built was sold to his neighbor Charles Swaggart. In the summer of 1976 Elsie Swaggart Sutton and I counted room for about seventy trays in that dryer. According to the Ziniker children the second one built by their father was larger. The family dried prunes for neighbors as well as their own crop.

Ziniker's garden and orchards flourished

The Ziniker family town house, 29th and Portland Streets.
Lane County Museum

with minimal irrigation because they practiced dust-mulching. Farmers of that period in the Spencer Butte area raised successful dry-land commercial crops of strawberries, sweet corn and tomatoes using this technique.

"It used to rain more in the summer time," Edward, Jr. told me. "Every time it rained dad would make us stir the topsoil in the orchard with the harrow to break up the crust. We even had to hoe the potatoes the same way." "I used to didn't see any sense in hoeing when there was no weeds," Marie said of the mulching operation.

The onions took more water. Ziniker purchased water rights from some of his neighbors to augment his supply. He built a tank in which spring water was collected above the orchard and then released down a homemade wooden flume to flood-irrigate the first onion patch near the house. Later when the beaver meadow in the valley was developed into an onion field the irrigation system was more complicated. Harry Taylor, Jr. explained the set-up. "Ziniker laid a line of field tile under the ground every four feet or so. He stood one tile on end at the beginning of each line. Then he'd fill all those tile with water to sub-irrigate." "He must have had a small fortune in 2-inch galvanized pipe," Lester Swaggart said.

"A lot of the springs dried up when the timber was cut off," Edward Jr. remembered. "Used to be a lot of fish in that creek down by the onion field. Used to be big pools there, and my goodness we used to catch lard pails full of trout. And there was two-three nice swimming holes too."

After he moved to Eugene, Mr. Ziniker and some of his sons became brick masons. By the time he had retired in the late '20s they had more than 700 fireplaces to their credit, including the one in the farmhouse where this writer lives, not far from the former "onion kingdom."

The *Oregonian* article concludes with a description of the new house which was located at 29th and Portland Streets in Eugene.

The house in town was designed by Mr. Ziniker, though the plans were technically drawn and modified by a Eugene architect. It is one of the best residences in Eugene and stands in the College Crest addition. When completed it will cost about $10,000. Ordinarily it would have cost much more, but Mr. Ziniker and his sons have done most of the work themselves. One son wired the house, another supervised the concrete work and all did the carpentry work. When he was a boy it was Mr. Ziniker's ambition to become a cabinetmaker and his love and ability for construction is this early ambition cropping out.

The house is unique and ingenious in its architecture. Every bedroom is a corner room with five windows. No space is wasted. The house has three stories and a basement. One attractive feature is a balcony on the second story around the chimney over the living room. The house has a wide area of porch and contains 14 rooms.

"I have to have a big house," said Mr. Ziniker. "I have a big family." So he has. Ten children, five boys and five girls. . . . Mr. Ziniker has moved his family to town so his children will have better educational opportunities.

The older boys will look after the farm which now consists of 320 acres, the original 50 having long since been paid for and added to. Mr. Ziniker will devote his time to the two acres of black onion land which he has at his town house in Eugene. "I expect those two acres to make me a living," he said.

Mr. Ziniker is only 45 years old and has no intention of forsaking the onion for some time yet.

Ed Ziniker's farm property is now known as Christmas Tree Land and is located on Murdock Road, an extension of South Willamette Street south of Spencer Butte. Unfortunately, both of the Ziniker homes eventually burned.

HARRY TAYLOR

Chronologically, the next large landholder to get a start in this area was Harry Taylor.

James Taylor and his family settled on a "brush ranch" between Spencer Creek and Fox Hollow in 1895. His son, Harry, eventually took over that place and later bought about 900 acres, including the Jonathan Riggs and Garnett Riggs homesteads directly south of Spencer Butte. Here is the Taylor story, from "The Story of My Father—J.O. Taylor," written by Harry Taylor before his death in 1959.

My father was born in Aug. 1833, in the State of Illinois, 16 miles s. of Wisconsin line. He was the youngest of 9 brothers and two sisters. In the spring of 1850 his father and mother and family went on the road to California. Father has told me many stories of the hardships of the trip, and lack of water, loss of stock and sickness made the going very hard.

Father never mentioned meeting the Latter Day Saints when he came through Utah although I have read that they were on the move at that time.

The Taylors settled on the Cosumnus River and set out 40 acres of apples. In 1853 Father went to mining at Michigan Bar, and from 1853 to 1862 he worked mining, hauling freight and farming. Some time in '62 father volunteered [for the] U.S. Cavalry in Co. C of Calif. and he served in the Eastern States until peace was declared. In 1872 Father was married to Fanny Jane McKee. His first born was a daughter, Mary Taylor. Two years later a son who died at 2 yr. old.

In 1876 the family moved to Oregon and spent the winter of '76 near Ashland and in '77 moved to a homestead on Bear Creek 20 mi. S. of Prineville, Oreg.

Four years later, in May 17, 1881, I was born at Prineville.

Owing to the cold winters in 1890 Father and Mother moved to Springfield, Oregon, living there 1 year, then to Fairmount. We lived at

Harry and May Taylor circa 1950.
Harry Taylor Jr.

Fairmount 4½ years and in 1895 we traded for a brush ranch on Spencer Creek. I was married to Miss Belle Blanton in 1905. My Mother passed away three years later. Then my father lived with my family for 20 years, being 95 years of age.

My Father was a very mild man by nature, never spoke disparingly [sic] of his neighbors. He was loved by the family and all his friends.

This story was written in response to Harry's involvement with the Church of Latter Day Saints. He used to tell of a dream or vision he once had wherein he looked out the window of his home on the Riggs Donation Land Claim to see an arm in the sky pointing upward. He understood the significance of this sight to be that he should "make his peace with God." The next day two Mormon missionaries came to his door, and he connected their visit with his dream and joined their church. Some years later, after we [the author's family] had provided weekly transportation to his LDS church each Sunday for a good while, Harry began to attend the Friends Meeting with us. He was put off by the LDS emphasis on what he termed "ancestor worship" to the point of changing his religious affiliation.

The "brush ranch" for which the Taylors traded their Fairmount property was 160 acres. As the years went by they bought eighty acres here, 120 there, two and one-half from a widowed neighbor and so on until they had a large operation centered on the hilltop now accessible by LeBleu Road. There they raised commercial crops of strawberries, grapes and raspberries. They pastured a flock of Angora goats which were clipped each year for the mohair. Sale of the mohair paid annual taxes on many a property in the area through those years.

Several folks remembered incidents involving the Taylors from those years. His children, Jane and Harry Jr., filled in details, as did former neighbors Lester Swaggart, Bertha Toll, Florence Murdock and others.

James and Fanny Taylor lived down the southwest slope of the hill mentioned above. Harry's home was up on top. Sometime between 1900 and 1910 Harry became part-owner of a sawmill with Mahlon Hill. The mill was located on Hill's place until the timber was nearly all harvested there. Then Harry bought out Hill's interest and moved the mill, possibly in 1919 or 1920. Jane remembered when he had the sawmill and that the school teacher, Charlie Dawson, helped him in the mill in the summertime.

"They logged the logs in, in the winter time, and then sawed them in the summer after the crops were planted and everything. It was easier to log in the winter because the ground was slippery and the logs pulled easier," Harry Jr. said. "Before he had his own sawmill he had oxen and he logged for other people. He logged for Booth Kelly over at Saginaw, and he logged at Wendling." Other neighbors said that Harry would be gone for several months in the wintertime with his logging team, and his father looked after things at home for him.

Taylor and Hill sold their lumber mostly to farmers or local people for farm buildings. John Gimpl bought some of it, and in 1981 Irene Albro still lived in a house which was built from lumber sawed by that mill. They got

This house, home of Irene Carson Albro, was built of lumber from Taylor's mill.
Irene Albro

around $10 a thousand board feet at the mill. The farmers came and got what they needed and hauled it away.

The older children attended the Fox Hollow School for several years, but then Taylors moved down over the hill on the Spencer Creek side, to be nearer the mill. They went out to Lorane Road across what is now known as Chezem Road, and that was the usual route to town during dry weather; but in the winter while mud prevailed the flats were so deep as to be practically impassable and the Taylors had to go "up over Spencer Butte" to get out. The road they used is the present South Willamette route.

Bertha Toll recalled a time when the Toll horses died from the "staggers."

"We had to have somebody to do the work until we could get horses again. We had grain to take over to Trunnel's mill, over at Creswell, the flour mill. In those days everybody

Taylor children circa 1910.
Harry Taylor Jr.

took their wheat and had it ground into flour. So this particular day I remember Harry (Taylor) yelling at the oxen 'Gee! Haw!' coming up the ridge. Each ox was named: Whitey, Blackie, Buck . . . I think he had four. Anyway, I could hear him comin' way long up there on the ridge. 'Course at that time nobody lived up there but the Taylors. I could hear him coming way round up there. So he came in his wagon. Mrs. Taylor and the children, Rosie and Jane, stayed here. He pulled the dead horses back up over the hill so we didn't have to smell them. Then he went to Creswell. It was dark, of course, when he came home. Mrs. Taylor, she got all excited when he come back. Didn't want to keep him waiting. They were hurrying down the front steps, and Rosie stubbed her toe and away she went, head over heels. Her dress clear up over her head, just a crying. Jane was the baby. I remember them going down and gettin' in the wagon."

Merl Albro told of a time when Harry brought his ox team and pulled an abandoned cabin off the next ridge and down to the Albro's so they could use it for a store room. Harry still had a team of oxen that he drove in the Trail to Rail Pageant one year in the 1930s.

In a taped interview, Harry Jr. talked about the farm on the hill: "That whole ridge was farmed. About an acre and a half of grape vineyard up there. They raised wheat and we had our own wheat flour mill. At first we hauled it in to Eugene to the old Warnick's feed mill and had it ground, and later we traded wheat for flour. Then during the war there when you couldn't buy any—everybody was so hard up and you couldn't buy flour—Dad had a grain mill, and he just ground it and we used the coarse flour. Did that during the Depression too.

"We raised strawberries. Had a big berry field over there by the grape vineyard. At one time almost that whole field was in strawberries. We picked strawberries all day, and Dad would be gone with them. He'd get up early in the morning and take them in . . . they sold most of them at Ax Billy's store in Eugene, and he would go back and forth with them in the daytime while we were picking, and Tolls and Swaggarts and Kindts, and several families come and helped pick strawberries—for money you know, to earn their [school clothes

Belle Taylor, her sister and Rose, Jane and Isaac. George Knox Album

Harry Taylor and his ox team pulling a stump. George Knox Album

Shearing goats. Fred Knox working the clippers. George Knox Album

and books]." Ed Ziniker remembered seeing Harry pass their home on Murdock Road with a wagon load of strawberries drawn by an ox team.

"We always had a herd of Angora goats," Harry continued. "We'd get them in and shear 'em once a year and we got enough money off that to pay the taxes on the property. Dad always paid the taxes with goat's hair.

"It was quite a job to shear them. They had the old thing they had to crank by hand in those days. It was a regular clipper just like a hair clipper, only it had a long arm, a flexible shaft on it. It was a killing job, I tell you. Somebody had to stand there and turn that crank that made the knives go back and forth. A good goat would give up to sixteen pounds of mohair and it generally run twenty-five to thirty cents a pound. We had all the way from forty to 120 head. It would usually take about three days to shear them by the time you went and rounded 'em up and got 'em in the corral and sheared 'em. We did that in the springtime. And then they got the idea that if you sheared 'em twice a year why you'd get more hair off of 'em. But it didn't prove out at all.

The theory was that if you sheared 'em at the right time why then the hair would grow real fast to get ready for winter, but that wasn't so. It was just twice as much work for the same amount of hair."

Lester Swaggart told about a bear hunt which took the hunting party to Taylor's place: "We tramped along the road till we came to the 'lower garden' on the Taylor place. Suddenly the dogs took off on a hot trail in that direction. Soon I came to a high, sturdy woven wire fence with two strands of barbed wire on top. In the fence stood a large body fir tree which Mr. Taylor had used as a post. To my amazement I saw a lot of large scratches on the bark of that tree. They'd been made by the bear. He was climbing up a few feet and then hitching his way around above the fence. When he reached the other side he backed down to the ground. Pretty smart bear, I thought. The dogs were still barking on ahead. When I got through the brush to a clearing I saw the dogs running all around, sniffing here and there. They were nosing the bare soil under some large trees which stood on a level spot. This was apparently a goats' bedding ground. All over the area lay the remains of goat carcasses. Some appeared to be old but others were fresh kills. I was surprised to find the goats at this place. Mr. Taylor kept the herd to kill the unwanted brush and because they produced mohair. Judging by the number of kills I doubted if the rancher had many animals left in his herd."

Lester told another story about Harry and his father: "Harry Taylor's father, he was a war veteran. He got a pension. A dollar was a dollar in those days. And his dad bought him a big gasoline engine. And the McBeths, they had the separator (threshing machine), so they went together and the crew followed around threshing out the neighbor's grain. And so George Toll and I, we were hauling the grain to the granary. That was our job. So we came toward the place and we looked up and there and all around the gasoline engine it was on fire. And Harry Taylor says, 'Everybody run! Look out!' he says. 'It might blow up.' Grand-pap Goodpasture, he was hard of hearing, you know, and he didn't know what was going on and he looked up there and he saw the fire and so he just grabbed his shovel and he just goes

James Taylor with Harry Jr. and Loretta. Harry Taylor Jr.

up there and he just threw dirt all over. First thing I know, the fire was all out. He saved the day. Otherwise it would have burned up the separator and the grain and everything. We saw that happen down on Spencer Creek where the Snorrenbergs were one time. That was the First World War. I was working on the Caterpillar Smith place. I looked over there where they was threshing and it had caught fire. It was in a grove of timber, and oh, it made a big fire. It just went to the tops of those trees and clear up on beyond the meadow. It was a huge fire and everything burnt up. I'll never forget that."

Harry's father, James Taylor, was hard of hearing too. Irene Albro told this story about James:

"Taylors came to buy some cattle of my folks. It was a cold morning and so Harry brought his daddy in by the fireplace. My daddy always had a big fire in the fireplace. So my dad sat down to talk to Mr. Taylor. He tried to talk to him and pretty soon dad just got up and scooted back his chair. He said, 'If you don't want to talk you don't have to.' He went outside and left James sitting there. Of course Mr. Taylor hadn't heard a word. Dad felt real bad about it afterward. 'I could'a made signs,' he said when he learned that Mr. Taylor was hard of hearing."

George Knox said, "This old boy [James Taylor] was deaf as a fence post, and he had long white whiskers. He wasn't so hardy [as in this picture] when I knew him. He used to work at digging out stumps up there on the hill where their place used to be. He'd get tired and lay down to sleep and the goats would come in and they'd eat his shirt off. The kids used to joke and say they'd eat his whiskers. I don't know whether they did, but they chewed on his shirt, I guess. He'd sleep right through it."

Sometime before World War I Harry worked at Parson's Mill down on Camas Swale. He owned half a dozen oxen and used them to yard logs from the donkey engine to the skid road into the mill pond. Harry came over and stayed at the bunkhouse for a week or two, then took his oxen and went over the hill to home while the mill was shut down.

John Napper and his brothers used to stand and watch the logs slide down the skid and splash into the pond. There was a big stump at the top of the slide. As the ox team passed above the stump the log would begin sliding down toward the pond. The stump tripped some kind of release to loosen the chain and away the log went, leaving the team free to go for another.

Emory Pruett said, "I can remember when Harry Taylor had his little sawmill set up right there where the Attneaves live. In fact, he's got a little old corral in there yet where they kept their horses. It was a real small mill. They sawed the wood and put the slab on a piece of chain and then tied it up and hauled it down the hill with horses. There were slab piles stacked all around. Part of them are lying there yet, scattered all through the brush."

Every year Harry would make a trek to tidewater at Mapleton for a wagon load of salmon to put away for the winter. The trip with the team and wagon was an overnight trip. Harry Jr. says he never got to go because the trip was made in September when the salmon were running and he was always in school.

"But I remember the salmon," he said. "They'd buy about 600 pounds and we'd get them for three cents a pound. We'd bring 'em home and we'd make these trays out of wire and we'd hang 'em up in the smokehouse. We'd cut that salmon all up and smoke it and it was delicious. Smoked with vine maple, mostly. Apple wood was good too."

Harry's son Lee remembered making the

Harry Taylor and two Barton children circa 1956. Harry made a hay crop, piled it on the site, then built a barn over it.
Lois Barton

trip with him once in an old Ford truck. They went by Route F when it was little more than a mountain trail. Lee remembered passing one cliff where the outer wheel of the truck had only a flat-hewn log for a track. When they reached Mapleton, the farmer who was to have the fish ready for them wasn't on hand. His place was across the river and Harry is reported to have dived in and swum across to check things out. They put a fern frond inside each fish to keep the flies from blowing them on the return trip, and they rubbed them with salt to help preserve them.

There were eleven children in Harry's family. As the sons grew older their father deeded eighty acres to each of them from his holdings, leaving about 350 acres to one younger son who was to "look after him in his old age." We [the Barton family] bought that 350 acres in 1951 and Harry lived here on the place most of the time helping with chores, repairing fences, planting and harvesting hay crops and gardens in cooperation with us until his death in 1960.

THE KNOX FAMILY

Shortly after the Taylors moved onto their "brush ranch" above Fox Hollow Road, another family of relative newcomers to the area began to establish their place in the history of Fox Hollow.

Frederick Vivian and Georgeanna Mary Bampfylde Knox came to Lane County about 1900. They originally acquired property in the

Fred V. and Georgeann Knox.
David Knox Album

River Road area. That eleven acres was under water two or three times during those first winters, so in 1903 F. V. Knox traded for 600 acres in Fox Hollow. This was land which had been homesteaded by Ernest and Charles Knoop about 1893.

Fred V. Knox was an Episcopal minister who served in India as a chaplain in the East India Company. The three oldest of their children were born there. He was a Latin scholar whose father also was an Episcopal minister. After his service in India and before coming to America, he was the headmaster of the Limpsfield School for Boys in England. Georgeanna Knox was from an aristocratic English family and maintained the family practice of "dressing" for dinner each evening, even after they were established in Fox Hollow.

Fred V. Knox occasionally taught Latin at the University of Oregon. John Pipes, also a Latin scholar, became close friends with Fred V. His wife Susie Pipes was an accomplished violinist who "used to give concerts all over the state," according to cousin and nonagenarian Mary Skipworth Corum. The Knox girls took violin lessons from her, and the Pipes family often used a cabin on the Knox place for weekend outings.

According to descendants, it was because Fred V. wanted something for his three sons to do that they came to America. The oldest son, Charles, was married to Eva Hudson and they set up housekeeping in an old cabin on the Taylor place nearby. Fred V. and his family moved into the Charles Knoop house which was built from lumber sawed by Knoop in his sawmill. The house is said to have been largely constructed of rough lumber inside and out, but granddaughter Gertrude Knox Albro said it was the only house in Fox Hollow that had a bathroom in it when she was a child. That bathroom did not have a flush toilet, but in later years there was hot running water piped to the tub. At first water was heated in the reservoir at the back of the kitchen stove and carried to the tub.

The Knoop house was three muddy miles up Fox Hollow from the Lorane Road. Knoop always said Knox never would have made the trade, which was practically completed by phone, if he'd been out there in the winter time, because there was no bottom in that road. Years later when grandson George rode in a buggy to Fox Hollow School, he said, "The mud used to get almost axle-deep on the buggy. It was just an old dirt trail for years and years and years."

The cabin Charles and Eva Knox moved into was old and dirt sifted down over everything, so Eva papered the inside with newspapers to help keep some of it out. This was probably the cabin that James and Fanny Taylor had lived in, near the "lower garden" on the Taylor place. Some of the Taylor children used to come down to see Eva. Mrs. Taylor had a big family and couldn't always give them as much attention as they would like, and they enjoyed the "mothering" they got from Eva

The Knox Family.
George Knox Album

Knox. Harry's son Lee said Harry helped Charlie Knox build a house of sawed lumber and that Charlie worked for the Taylors. Charlie helped the Taylors tend their berry crop in the lower garden during the years before he joined the Canadian Army and went off to war. Charlie never came back from World War I and his younger brother Guy later married his widow.

There was a pond on top of the hill above the former Knoop house where the kids often went swimming. It had been scooped out by a team with a big scoop and was filled with water piped from a strong spring. The family album has pictures of family and guests at water's edge. All the swimming stirred up the mud so what came down for irrigation and watering the stock was pretty muddy sometimes.

Fred V. Knox eventually divided what had accumulated to more than 1,100 acres between his sons Fred G. and Guy. Fred inherited the acreage down on the Lorane Road, leaving the homeplace—including the muddy road—to Guy. This was something of a sore point with him in later years.

Charles and Eva Knox's son George kept rabbits in the loft of the old Knoop homestead cabin which was used partly as a storage shed near the "new" house. It was a building constructed of logs and a split shake roof.

George remembered, 'There was another log barn down below this house, down over the hill. It had been the flailing barn, and it had two stories in it and the top story instead of being floored, it had split cedar rails laid, and of course they couldn't get them tight enough together, so they would lay the straw on these rails, and down below they had a sawed tight floor, and they'd get up there and they'd beat the grain with flails on those rails and the grain would rattle down through and they'd sweep it up on the tight floor below."

Guy Knox was a farmer who stayed on the land. He ran cattle, mostly milk cows as his daughter Gertrude remembered it, maybe fourteen or fifteen head.

Gertrude recalled, "It was a pretty wonderful life when you stop to think back on it. We had our chores . . . we milked cows and sold a little cream. That's where our income came from. And every year Mother would raise turkeys and ducks. We fed the skim milk to pigs. Then when the pig was ready to butcher, why you butchered it and sold it. We always butchered a calf or two and sold that meat. We didn't have any way of keeping it. Mother would maybe can a quarter of beef or something like that—a front quarter. But we lived pretty much on canned venison. And we'd catch a few fish. Both creeks were real good fishing. Early in the spring when the water was cool the fish came up in there. And we always had lovely gardens."

Guy Knox also kept sheep and raised hay.

Eva Knox carried the mail for a Star Route for a time. Her sister-in-law, Aslaug [Norwegian for Elsie] Knox had the post of-

Knox ranch from the bluffs.
David Knox Album

fice in her home on Fox Hollow Road from November 27, 1922, till September 1, 1924. The Star Route is reported to have been operational a bit longer and there were other carriers after Eva until Route 3 from Eugene was extended to include that route. Eva carried what they called "bag mail." It was put in a bag and hung on a nail on a post at the people's houses. In the wintertime she delivered with a horse and buggy which was really a kind of two-wheeled cart. In the summer she drove an old Model T Ford. The route went from Lorane Road clear through to the Spencer Creek schoolhouse and on up to the Alder Street road.

The Guy Knox family boarded the schoolteacher, Janet Bell, for a time. Young George and his teacher got to school by horse and buggy part of the time, but she remembered walking the three miles part of the time.

Before the Guy Knox home burned in 1925 or 1926 Eva used to have dances for the whole community. "She'd tear out all the rugs, linoleum rugs. She'd take them all out and roll them up. Then they'd have the dance and it would be four o'clock in the morning before people would go home. 'Course us kids would always crawl onto a bed someplace amongst all the coats and go to sleep. We had banjo music. Svarveruds over here played the banjo, Melvin and Clarence Svarverud. We had a piano in later years. Nick Toll played the fiddle. So there was fiddles, guitar and banjo. Danced all night," Gertrude remembered.

In the mid-twenties a community club was organized and a clubhouse built on land donated by Charlie Swaggart just up Gay Hill from Murdock Road. Gertrude Knox told about that too:

"We used to have a dance up there every other week or so. People in the neighborhood played for it. Everybody would take a cake or sandwiches or something. The clubhouse was never quite finished. It was always just a big hall with two-by-fours that were going to be partitioned off but it never did get finished.

Guy Knox home.
David Knox Album

*Fred and Guy Knox
with load of hay on
Fox Hollow ranch.
David Knox*

There was an old barrel stove in it and they would start a fire. Tables for food. We used to have Sunday School there. I can remember going to Sunday School picnics there, and there was the tents and the restrooms. Breedings and McBeths and Tolls, Kindts. . . . There was just a certain group that always came to the same things. Westropes was another family. I was about eight years old. . . . I can remember many a time going to a dance in the middle of winter up there. Mother and Dad would put us in the back of the hack, on a blanket, and the road would be so rough. We'd cry and fuss about it, and they'd sing at the top of their voices to cover our fussin'. We had a wonderful time after we got there. They'd dance till midnight, then eat, and we'd have that long drive back home."

Guy Knox sold his Fox Hollow farm in 1937 and moved to Coburg where he farmed until his death in 1952.

In contrast to his brother Guy, Fred Knox became very much involved in activities outside his farming over the years. Like Guy, he kept sheep and goats, made hay and carried on general farming. A Eugene *Register-Guard* story at the time of his death in April, 1964, has these details of his public works:

. . . Charter member of the Extension Advisory Council for Lane County; president of the County Agricultural Council for 10 years; representative of agriculture on the State War Board; Lane County chairman of the Willamette Basin Commission from 1946 until it was reorganized and then was the chairman of the Flood Control Commitee for the Basin Project Advisory Committee.

Knox was also an organizer of the Lane Electric Cooperative; was chairman of the Natural Resources Committee for Pomona Grange and the Willakenzie Grange; Chairman of the McKenzie Water Control District No. 1 from 1946 until his death; member of the LeBleu School District board for 25 years; chairman of the Natural Resources Committee of the Oregan Farm Bureau; member of the planning committee for the Lane County Courthouse; member of the committee for promoting bonds for Lane County roads in the early twenties; member of the advisory committee for the Willamette National Forest; Director of the Willakenzie Fire Control District; grange master of several granges; a long time member of the Lane County Water Resources Advisory Committee; president of the Lane County Livestock Assn.; and held several offices in the Eugene Chamber of Commerce. In addition to these activities he managed the Lane County Fair from about 1940 to 1945, and was at one time master of the old public market at the southeast corner of Broadway and Charnelton Street.

Fred G. Knox always spoke of himself as "just a farmer." He married Aslaug Thorp in Coos Bay in 1914. During the years that they lived in Fox Hollow he did some logging of his acreage.

Walter Kindt who worked for him several years told about that:

"I drove team for Fred Knox, yarding with horses most of the time. I logged that whole thing off there from where he used to live clear back. The logs went to Hyland who used to have a little sawmill down there. We took the

*Fred Knox
residence on
Fox Hollow.
David Knox*

logs to his mill on Model A trucks. Loaded them from a rollway using a peavey. Bill Snorrenberg and Bill Howard was loggin'—had the trucks there. They hauled the logs down to Hyland and I think they got three dollars a thousand [board feet]. Those trucks could haul sixteen-foot logs.

"In the wintertime—I had a loggin' team and it got so slick goin' down the hill, I'd just throw the lines to the side and let the team go down the hill. They'd run all the way down to keep the log from hittin' them. Then they'd got to go around to the rollway. They'd always stop down there. They knew what to do. I'd just throw the lines. Oh, that was slick! One time Ernest Josin was a fallin' or buckin' or something. Anyway a log came down the hill toward him. Luckily it stopped just before it hit him. It would have killed him if it hit him. Boy, that was close! Never will forget that—

how scared I was. You know, a guy's so helpless. You couldn't do a thing! No, sir. That's one thing I won't forget!

"When I worked for Fred Knox he had somebody else to come in and shear the goats. He sheared his own sheep. I don't know why he didn't shear the goats. Some sheep shearer come in and did it. I've turned that old hand crank to shear the sheep when he was shearing, and then we'd get the goats down and somebody else would do it.

"Boy, them goats sure could jump. They'd get up there on top of Round Mountain. They had a bedding ground there. And one time there come a big snow and we couldn't get the goats home, so we went up there with a saw and axe and we felled a bunch of trees for them to feed off of. That's the only way we could keep them alive. There was about two feet of snow." □

CHAPTER 4

Family Farm Life

The families whose stories appear in this chapter lived in the Spencer Butte area after the turn of the century. The memories are those of people who were living when research for this book was under way. The homestead maps, pages 122 and 123, will show where most of them lived. The emphasis in this chapter is more on the land—how it was utilized and how it supported the settlers—than on the details of family life. Unfortunately, it is simply impossible to include the names of all the family members who resided in the area 1900-1950. By retelling the stories about the crops, the "critters," the trapping and some of the social activities, the attempt is to provide a composite picture of what life on the farm was like.

When the original homesteaders settled this area, some of the land was open prairie country. But by the turn of the century, forests had grown and had to be cleared to make fields for the numerous farmers who were trying to eke out a living for their families. The Zinikers, the Tolls, the Kindts and others speak of felling and burning trees to make way for wheat and orchards. The trees were dropped in a line or a pile so they could be burned together as much as possible. The fallers burned the slash when they got them down, then sowed wheat among the stumps and logs, and later harvested it with cradles (a special scythe with carriers for the grain stalks). One report noted that a single sowing would raise two or three annual crops because enough grain shattered while they were harvesting to seed the ground for another year.

The soil in this hill country wasn't—and still isn't—very good. It would raise grain for two or three years when first cultivated, but then got stickier and harder to work—clay soil that stuck to the spade so badly it was unmanageable. Then they would turn that field into pasture and often "goat weed" took over for a few years.

Zinikers used to burn it in the winter time to destroy some of the seed and the dead tops. They told about a big fire one year. When the slash got good and dry in August they'd set it on fire. Ed Jr. recalled: "Oh, it would just *burn!* Uncle John went around with a torch and set the whole thing on fire, and it got away! Got over into Osburn's place. Sparks flew so far! And it made a terrible noise. The wind was blowing. There was no way to stop it. We had to let it go until it burned out. The pastures at Osburn's were pretty short—not enough grass there to burn which really slowed it down."

WHAT THEY GREW

Bill Kindt gave this account of what early farming was like:

"They farmed some of that country up there on the hill. It's all grown back to timber now. It wasn't too bad. They had some fairly good crops up there. They raised oats and wheat. Some livestock. Not a great lot. Enough for milk and sold the cream. We had three or four cows we'd milk. . . . We always had some calves and a steer or two around there to butcher. . . . We usually raised two or three hogs every year to butcher. We smoked part of them and they were salted down in an oak barrel. We raised most of our living there actually. Dry beans and potatoes. That was part of my job when I was a kid—hoeing the garden. We didn't water much—we had plenty of water for use, but not enough for irrigating.

The wells weren't that good. We had two of them and various springs around the place for the stock to water. We grew some corn. Dad would plant corn—oh maybe a couple or three acres to feed to the stock. It didn't mature too well out there. Corn needs warm nights to ripen as it should. We had chickens and would sell a few eggs, but for our own use too. Had chickens to eat, fryers. We cut wood a lot for a living and hauled it into Eugene with a team of horses and wagon. A cord of wood to a load. Sell it to anybody looking for wood. George Toll did too. He hauled wood with a team and wagon."

Irene Carson Albro recalled:

"When company came Mother would send me to the garden to get something for dinner, 'cause we always had a good garden. One was down here where the barn is, and then we had another garden out in the corner of the field. It dried up early—it was a spring garden. We planted early and then it went early—such things as peas and lettuce and radishes that you could raise real quick. We raised most of our own potatoes and we used to raise an awful lot of squashes—winter squashes—then put them away. Dad had a cellar and we always put [away] the apples and the squashes and the pears, a lot of times, and parsnips was always put away for winter. We had apples to last all winter long. And Dad used to raise cabbage, winter cabbage he called them, and he would pull 'em up by the roots and then he'd bury them in dirt and then throw straw over them. He'd pull up the whole thing and turn the leaves all around them good on the ground in the cellar. And then we'd dig those out and peel them out and they would be just as white as snow. They'd be so good and crisp."

Irene Albro also remembered butchering time:

"We always butchered in the fall of the year. Rendered the lard. That was such a job. You couldn't have it in the house. You always rendered it outside. Dad would fix a place in the woodshed. We had one of them great big iron kettles. That's what we rendered the lard in. We always liked the cracklings. Elmer [her son] said to me just this fall when he was here, 'Oh, I'd love to have some cracklin's.'"

Maggie Kindt Toll spoke of their crops:

"George raised a good home garden. He

Gay Hill road, 1912.
David Knox

raised corn to fatten the hogs with. Two or three acres of corn. Part of it was field corn, part was sweet corn. What we couldn't eat he just snapped off. I canned a lot of it, and I canned beans and peas, and then when we killed the hogs I canned some backbone—tenderloin. We made sausage and we made sauerkraut. We used up our own garden and our own wheat. I had lard, plenty of lard. We raised potatoes and cabbage and everything we needed.

"Oscar Taylor, Harry's boy, planted a nice cherry orchard. The people that bought the place from him said folks would come in there when they were away and break off the limbs and swipe the cherries. So this man cut the trees down. I sure hated that."

Candis Haley Harris spoke of their neighbors:

"Jim Breeding raised wheat and I guess he had a few cattle. He made a living for him and his wife. There was just the two of them. They had chickens too.

"Goodpastures were nice neighbors. They were pretty old," Candis remembered.

Elsie Sutton also remembered the Goodpastures:

"Grandpa Goodpasture raised tobacco up here on the hill. He'd dry it in the house up there and crush it by hand."

THRESHING

Before the advent of mechanical threshing machines several families built special threshing floors. Martin Gay threshed his first wheat crop right on the ground. By the next season he had a "good large barn . . . with a threshing floor and bins for the grain," according to Elsie Sutton.

"We had built a place onto the goat barn that dad used as a tramping-out-grain floor. It was usually wheat for the chickens or hogs. We had two teams of horses and a couple of riding horses which we would have go around and around tramping on the wheat they would throw in there from off the hay wagon. A couple of fellows would stand in the center and turn the wheat until it was all off the straw, and out of the heads. Then they would drive the horses off and let them rest till the straw was all thrown into the goat barn, then they would throw in more to be trodden on by the horses.

"Sometimes we would do this all day long till it was all thrashed out. The wheat would all be put in sacks and taken down to the barn and put into the grain bins. Later on there was someone in the neighborhood who purchased a thresher and went from place to place threshing people's grain for them. When they came to Grandpa Goodpasture's my dad would haul his wheat and oats there to be threshed. It would come out so nice and clean. The other way we would have to use Grandpa's fanning mill to clean enough to plant the next year."

Merl Albro also recalled the wheat harvest:

"We cut the wheat with a binder and shocked it, and then we took it in and stacked it in big stacks. Then the thrashing machine would come through. The first thrashing machine that ever came through was an old steamer, and it was run by a fellow named Crow—Oral Crow. Come from Lorane. Would come through here and you'd gather wood for several days beforehand so you could run this old steam thrashing machine. And they'd back in with a separator and it would be two, three fellows with the traveling thrashing crew. And they'd climb these stacks. These stacks were—oh, they'd go up twenty feet high. It was quite an art. My dad was real good at it—at building those. And they'd be here maybe a day—day and a half, thrashing. You'd get wheat and you'd thrash oats, white oats mostly and some gray, and then you had the big straw stack. That was a great thing, you know. You'd fence that and then let the cattle in and let 'em eat on that during the winter."

People who had big enough barns put the straw inside. Howard McBeth told me:

"The first machinery we had to thrash with didn't have a blower on it. It was just a conveyor belt and the barns were made so the conveyor could go up in there, then you had to get back in there and stack that stuff back. The dust was terrible. The blowers were worse than the conveyor because it blew more dirt. Knox's machine had a conveyor too."

Mrs. Nancy Breeding,
1911.
David Knox

Below: Mr. and Mrs. Thurston Good-
pasture.
Elsie Sutton

Knox's threshing outfit at work.
David Knox

Another threshing job was the dry beans. Bill Kindt explained:

"We raised all our dry beans. Thrashed them out. We pulled them—bunch beans—and we put them in the barn where it was dry. We had a big square box that was six or eight feet high and about ten long. We'd hit the beans against the side to knock them out—or beat them with a pitchfork. Then dad had a little fanning mill which he used to clean the grain—various size screens and stuff. We'd run the beans through there to get the chaff out."

If you didn't have a fanning mill, then you needed a windy day. You'd spread a tarp or an old blanket outside where there was a good wind blowing. Then you'd take a dishpan or tub full of beans up a stepladder on the windward side of the tarp and slowly pour the beans onto the tarp. The wind would carry the chaff beyond the tarp, while the beans dropped nearly straight down. After a couple of repetitions only the heaviest sections of stem remained to be picked out by the cook, plus any small pebbles or clods of dirt which were heavy enough to fall with the beans.

"CRITTERS"

Life on the farm usually involved dealing with livestock. Anything could happen with stock and often did. When Tom Gates lived where Halbergs now do, near the end of South Willamette, his milk cow disappeared. He hunted for nearly a week, and checked with all the neighbors. At the end of that time he hap-pened to look in an empty house in the meadow where Maxsons have recently built a new home. The cow had gone inside and the wind had apparently blown the door shut behind her, leaving her trapped without feed or water for all that time. Another day or two and her rescue would have come too late.

Emory Pruett talked about open-range pasture on Spencer Butte:

"I can remember the cattle used to have quite a bit of pasture on this flat up above the house. It's just solid timber now. That field was all clear west of the road too. There used to be a real good spring up in the park. When we moved here there was about a two-inch piece of pipe there in that spring and a wooden trough there for stock. That run a good stream of ice-cold water. The spring had been dug out. It was probably six feet across and maybe three or four feet deep. The water run down hill, gravity feed, to the trough. One time a bunch of Christensen's goats got in it and drowned. I suppose they was buttin' each other, actin' a fool. We pulled out half a dozen of them. Then we put a fence around the spring so the goats wouldn't get in. They could drink out of the trough."

Elsie Sutton told this story humorously:

"Grandma had a white Leghorn rooster that was always spurring you if you wasn't watching. Carl and Lester were walking ahead of Bertha and I. We saw this rooster spur Carl. It made him so mad he picked up a stick and threw it at the rooster and hit him in the head, knocking him cold. He aimed to scare the rooster, not hit him. The boys thought he was dead and wondered what they should do. They picked him up and took him down to a big brush pile and threw him in. Then came walking up the hill worrying about what Grandma would say. Bertha and I was watching all this. When their back was turned the rooster moved, jerked and shook his head. He got off the pile and shook his feathers and started following the boys up the hill. It all seemed so funny to Bertha and me we began laughing. They looked at us with disgust. We told them to look behind them. They both looked back and there was that rooster alive. Then they could see the joke."

Mollie Christensen told me:

"We always had cattle. We milked thirty to forty cows right out there in the corral with an overcoat or a gunny sack over our shoulders when the weather was bad. Rather than run them all in the barn and stanchion 'em—go to all that trouble and pack the milk back to the house—we had a little corral right out there and we milked 'em right out in the corral. If one kicked you over why you just got up and went at it again. They weren't particularly dairy cows, just anything that gave milk. We sold the cream."

Elsie Sutton told about riding a horse to school:

"Somehow he got a'straddle a telephone wire that was down, and he backed up instead of going forward. The wire got tighter and tighter and tighter under him and then pretty soon he began to buck. Well, I couldn't hardly stay on him and I couldn't get off. Finally he did go forward and I got off, and I'm tellin' you there's a time my knee caps shook and shook."

George Knox told about getting in a fight with a goose:

"I was about three feet high and I had a red cap with a knot on the top that Grandma Knox had brought out from England. [We had] great big gray geese that Dad had brought out from England. He had them imported. There was a gander in there that stood about twice as high as I did. That damned goose would see me out there playing in the yard and would git my hat. He'd come over and grab that hat with the red knob on top. I was just a little boy about 4

Knox's geese.
David Knox

or 5, I guess. I got a board and took off after the gander. We met somewhere out there in the yard, and I wasn't doin' so good and Carl Toll came along and rescued me. This old gander was as old as the hills and he was really mean, a son-of-a-gun. That rescue is Carl's favorite story."

A good many people raised turkeys. They did pretty well for a while, Bertha Toll remembered. Then the ground got contaminated and they got a liver disease. "Mother was treating a sick turkey. It wouldn't eat and she was stuffing food in. Disgustedly she commented, 'I'll either kill or cure you.' The turkey died."

Mollie Christensen was possibly the first woman in the area to raise turkeys commercially. She bought a good looking tom at a fair somewhere for twenty-five dollars. She didn't remember where she got a start of hens, but she eventually sold brood hens to other folks. She raised as many as 1,500 in a year. The kids would find the hidden nests and bring in the eggs to keep for a setting. When four or five hens got broody she set them in coops where she could keep an eye on them until the broods were hatched. After the poults were started they were turned loose to forage for themselves. They wandered all over the area—as far as Tolls.

There is more than one story about conflicts over ownership because the turkeys ran loose all summer. At butchering time one family had rounded up their flock and killed about half of them—as many as they thought they could get plucked and cleaned that morning.

Toll homestead in winter.
George Knox Album

There were perhaps seventy-five left in the field for the next operation. It was a cold, rainy November day, miserable for working with the wet birds, and the whole family was out there slogging through an unpleasant task. When they finished and went to get the rest of the birds they discovered that the neighbors had come with horses and driven them over the hill. The tracks of horses and birds clearly led into the next valley. When they got to the neighbors' farm seeking the rest of their flock, they learned that the birds had that very day been loaded into crates and delivered to market by the neighbor as his birds. The turkeys made it to Thanksgiving tables but who knows whether their rightful owners were thankful for the income from their sale?

Another story says, "I lost my only turkey and all her brood because my neighbor turned his out and when he collected 'em he had to have a certain number. I'm sure mine were in it. You don't always get back exactly what you turn out. The coyotes and foxes always get some of them."

The calves were usually dehorned to prevent them from injuring each other, or the folks who worked with them, as they got older. "When you cut too deep, removing the budding horn, you used spider web to stop the bleeding," Elsie Sutton explained.

The livestock weren't always the instigators of unusual goings-on. Elsie continued: "When Sam and Will [Toll] came home on vacation from school [School for the Deaf in Salem] we spent a lot of time down there visiting. Some way or another they found out how to wire a battery and charge the chicken's water trough. They was showing us how the chickens would squawk and fly and cackle when they charged it. The boys thought it was real funny, but the chickens wouldn't go back for a long time."

OTHER FOOD SOURCES

People weren't limited to what they could grow. The streams were full of trout in the spring when the water was cold. The boys trapped squirrels and coons and gray diggers to roast. There was always venison, of course. Elsie Sutton shared this recipe with me, and we gathered and shared wild lettuce for several springs:

"In the spring of the year in the burned-over land, wild lettuce would come up and we gathered it to eat. It was a slender-stemmed plant with a dish-like top that was cupped and the blossoms would come when the plant got to maturity. We always got this plant when it was young and my mother would fix shortening, sugar, vinegar and thick cream dressing, heated and then poured over the lettuce which had been washed clean and some green onions added. Then let it stand to wilt. We all loved this wild lettuce and [was] anxious for the time to come to gather it."

Wild lettuce.
Lester Swaggart drawing.

Waterwheel that ran Swaggart's sawmill.
Elsie Sutton

Ed Ziniker recalled that "there used to be lots of fish in that creek that goes down east from Murdock Road. Used to be big ponds next to the onion patch down there, and my goodness, we used to catch lard pails full of trout. And there was two, three nice swimming holes there."

"MODERN" CONVENIENCES

People didn't lack ingenuity when it came to tackling everyday needs. The Tolls had "running water" on their back porch. They brought it down the hill from a spring back of the house, but their conveyor was no pipe from the hardware store. They took a round pole and used a u-shaped or v-shaped angle iron to cut a trough in one side of the pole. Then they'd lay the poles end to end with the upper one feeding into the section below. The cutting was done by hammering on the angle iron placed against the end of the pole along one side so that it cut a trough clear to the other end. All this was done by hand.

Kindts had a well on the hill above the house. They dispensed with a pump by siphoning the water. Bill Kindt explained:

"The well was some thirty feet deep, but it was quite a'ways above the house and we siphoned water down to the house. As long as the pipes were in good condition and didn't get any air in them, we just opened the faucet and it would siphon. As long as the lower end of your pipe is lower than the water level in the well, it will run after you get it started. You have to put a pump on it to get it started. Then the flow down the hill pulls it up out of the well. We had water in the house and piped down to the barn. Later the pipes kind of rusted through and we couldn't keep the vacuum."

Lester Swaggart talked about his father's turbine sawmill:

"He had a little mill across from where Sutton lives, on the creek. First a large water wheel, then he bought a turbine from the flour mill. Made a penstock, you know. They could only run it when there was really a hard rain. It took a lot of water to make it run right. One time, the last time it was ever in operation, it wound it up. There was a real hard rain, and he had a lot o' flumes up the creek. Well, the water was so heavy it just broke the flumes all down. He didn't fix 'em up any more. That was the last of his mill and sawing. That was along about 1920. I was going to high school, and I came out there one day with him. We went over and saw what happened after the hard rain at night. The water was just teeming every place. The weight of the water had just took most of the flumes down." Elsie Sutton said her father sawed all the lumber for their farm buildings with that sawmill. They'd get the logs together during the summer and then make lumber when the winter rains came.

Ed Ziniker built a reservoir for water storage. The boys used to swim in it. His son Paul described it:

"It was made out of wood, stood on end. The earth floor was dug out and there was banks on the outside to hold the wood in place. The planks were put there to keep the bank from caving in. Water came into the reservoir in a wooden trough made from poles shaped with an ax. When the trough plugged up with leaves or debris someone had to clear it out. The water was piped in, and all they had to do was to pull the plug. The water would run through a ditch and flood-irrigate the onion patch below."

Oak hinges.
Dorothy George

Spreading gravel was a cinch even before dump trucks. All you needed was a gravel bed on your wagon.

Leonard Ziniker explained: "A gravel bed is built by standing two-by-fours on edge one right after the other. One end of the two-by-fours was shaved off so it had more or less of a handle to lift. You started out by taking out your end gate, and then wherever you wanted to dump this gravel you lifted up the middle two-by-four and some of the gravel fell through. Then you'd lift the one next to it, and so forth, until you were out of gravel."

People had to be resourceful to meet their needs, especially in hard times when cash was scarce. Or when the size of their families put an extra strain on what cash was available. Harry Taylor was one who made just about everything. The barn door hinges he cut out of oak limbs with the knot end left on are still sturdy and functional. One squared-up limb about four feet long was bolted to the door. The other, of a similar length, to the wall of the barn. The rounded knotty ends overlapped and were held together by a wooden pin about an inch across. No hardware store item could do a better job.

Another of Harry's ingenious devices served for many years to fence chickens in a yard which had a wet-weather creek running through it. It is virtually impossible to stretch woven wire fence across a creek bed in such a way that it will fence the channel clear to the bottom. Chickens will use pretty small openings to get outside their yard and a dry creek bed would have been as good as a freeway. Harry made a section of "floating" fence below the wire fence to fill the creek channel. He accomplished this by nailing broad boards perpendicularly to a log which lay across the channel. The ends of the log were anchored in small fitted forms which held them in place but did not prevent their turning as needed. When winter rains brought high water down the channel a stationary fence would either have washed away or collected debris until the whole channel clogged and water spread to do damage beyond it. Because the boards nailed to the "floating" log were graduated in length to completely fill the channel when it was dry, but would float on the water, turning the log up to a quarter turn in its sockets as needed, the stream would glide freely under with little ill effect. As the stream subsided, the fence settled back to its former perpendicular position.

CASH CROPS

Money was often hard to come by. There were some cash crops. Prunes, for example. A good many prune orchards "paid the taxes" over the years. Ingenuity came into the prune picture too, for an example, with the wheel dryer that Ed Ziniker designed and built. (See description in Chapter 3.)

Prunes were the main crop on the McBeth place. Howard McBeth remembered:

"There was an old dryer on the place when we moved there. Later years we built a bigger one in the orchard area so we wouldn't have so far to move the fruit. A big crop would be around 14 tons of dried fruit. . . . We run the dryer pretty much by ourselves and once we started it, it was a twenty-four hour job. We cut the wood ready before picking season came. It was cut in four-foot lengths. The dryer was built in a concrete room and had two furnaces in it. The pipe would go clear around the room underneath these tunnels and then out the chimney to get all the heat out of it we could, and sometimes those pipes would be red hot clear around that room. The fire danger was terrific, and we had

McBeth orchard in bloom. Prune dryer in the middle.
Ruth Svarverud

no way to fight it. There was a terrific draft up through the tunnels just like the wind was blowing, it was so strong. It created itself. Sometimes we'd hire help to watch it at night. Sometimes we'd watch it ourselves. Set an alarm clock so we could get up and feed the furnace and check the fruit. It was a nice warm place to sleep. This one had, I believe, six tunnels wide enough for one tray. At the upper end of the tunnel we had a big vat with a fire under it, filled it with water and we'd dip the prunes in there, just for a minute, to check the skin. And with the lye-water it would just make them all rough and the skin wouldn't part and fall off. When you split them wide open why that spoiled 'em for the market be-

cause they didn't look good, see? They looked all rough and wrinkled when they were dipped in lye-water, and they dry better than these do when they are cut in two.

'Taylors used to have quite a lot of grapes. One fall we tried dryin' some for them. It didn't work out so good. About all they had left was just a shell. Too much temperature, apparently, for them. If I remember, on the finish end it was right around 180 degrees. It was hot enough to burn if you was pullin' trays and got ahold of a nailhead. Where the prunes started in it was much cooler. They go in one end and out the other, and it was slightly downgrade. It took about twenty-four hours for trays to go through. Every three or four hours you'd remove what was ready, and then it would take two to line the trays up again; one on the upper end pushing, and one on the lower end telling him which ones to push down. There was no way to tell which ones when you was up above. You'd hold a stick against them at the bottom so they wouldn't go too far, cause you couldn't back them up.

'We cultivated the orchard and then just before picking time we'd run over it with a clod masher and make it just as smooth as we could possibly get it. It was often wet when the

Prune scalding vat in Swaggart's dryer, 1978.
Brick firebox below vat to heat water. Elsie Sutton holds the dipping bucket.
Lois Barton

*Charles Swaggart with a
load of cord wood.
Goat shed and tramping
floor in background.*
Elsie Sutton

prunes fell and they'd be muddy, but dipping them in the vat would take that off, and then we rinsed the lye off, and they were clean. Someone spread them one layer deep on the tray and they started shrinking right away."

McBeths bought from Lombard, and Lester Swaggart recalled a story his mother used to tell. Mrs. Lombard had passed away. Mr. Lombard worked in town and was gone much of the time. The kids had to shift for themselves a good bit and sometimes they got hungry. In Lester's words:

". . . they had the prune orchard and dried prunes. The kids had quite a time getting themselves anything much to eat, and they'd eat a lot of prunes. The prunes were stored in boxes and he'd get cranky if they ate too many of them, so they took a box or two and hid 'em out in the brush. So my mother told me. They made up a game to cover their secret. They'd 'go to New York'—go outside and get prunes to eat. The dogs found those hidden boxes and chewed the fruit all up. The kids worried that their dad would find out about it."

The making and selling of cheese, a source of income, was described in the Osburn and Ruegger stories in the previous chapter. Another cash crop was wool. Elsie Sutton told how her father rented a flock of sheep one time, an undertaking that didn't turn out too

well. The sheep were diseased and many of them died. To help save his investment Mr. Swaggart set the children to pulling the wool off the carcasses as soon as they had decayed enough to loosen it. "That was a smelly job," Elsie said.

A good many folks kept Angora goats for the mohair. They were sheared just like sheep. Elsie Sutton recalled how her brothers played with the half-grown goats and tried to teach them to pull the wagon:

"These were stock goats we raised for mohair and once every year we sheared them. That was another job for us, taking turns turning the crank for the shears. They was like a big hair-clipper, and the crank made them go back and forth. They was on a kind of arm and the shearer would move it over the animal while we kids kept the crank going."

Another source of cash income was wood products. People cut cordwood and hauled it to town, and they split shakes for roofing. Walter Kindt recalled:

Fred Knox's goats circa 1912.
George Knox Album

"I hauled wood from out there [on Fox Hollow Road] for a couple of years—team and wagon—hauled it to town for firewood. Fir wood. We sold it to anybody that wanted to buy it. In them days, people would see you hauling wood, they'd come over and order some wood. I hauled a hundred and twelve cord the first year. I hauled wood to Eugene with a team of horses. I could haul one cord per trip. It was all dirt road. In the summertime it was good, but in the wintertime we had an awful time. You couldn't really haul in winter. Most of the wood was four-foot long when we delivered it. They had a buzz saw come and cut it up. People had buzz saws around town then, you know. We got $3.00 a cord. We cut wood in the wintertime and hauled it in the summer."

Shortly after the turn of the century people began to realize they could get more for their timber than from working the poor fields. "Everybody began to sell their timber," Bertha Toll said. 'The farmer could get so much more in the lumber business they forgot all about farming." By World War II the fields that had been cleared in the hill country began to go back to woodland.

ANIMAL MARAUDERS

Along with the usual hazards of weather and domestic livestock losses, early farmers lived with wild animal depredations. Bears got into the fruit orchards, breaking down the tree limbs when they climbed for fruit. Rattlesnakes and wild hogs helped themselves to young chickens and the grain crops respectively. A cougar might down your prize heifer.

One of the Ziniker boys killed a bear in the prune orchard one night. Ziniker remembered it was moonlight: 'He got him right through the head with a thirty-two special. It was during the prune time when we was drying. Later we took that bear to Creswell in the wagon to show him off. On the way home the horse got a whiff of him and we couldn't hardly hold him from runnin' away. This was about 1906 or 1907. I was about fifteen at the time and my brother who shot him was younger than me."

Lester Swaggart said, "One day we were going home from town—up the Willamette Hill,

and there where Pruetts live we saw the folks out in the road. They were gathered around a dog that was just kicking and breathing his last. When we asked about it we learned that there'd been a big rattlesnake had come down to the chicken coop where a hen had a bunch of chickens, and the rattlesnake had bit the hen. She'd died, then the dog went barkin' at it, and the dog, just a pup, wasn't so shy and the snake bit *him*. He died in a little bit."

From left: Forest Hadsell, Louis Kindt and Lester Swaggart killed a bear. Lester had good bear dogs and was on call to rid local farmers of marauding bear.
Elsie Sutton

Another of Lester's stories: "Along about the first of the century or just a little after, when my dad was about twenty years old, why the wild hogs were just about to take the country. They'd root the ground all up and cause lots of damage that way. Actually, they was tame hogs gone wild. They had strayed off from different neighbors out there and started multiplying. They tell about one instance when my father had this big black dog, Jack. He'd round up the hogs, get 'em all corraled into a space by a tree or someplace. Once Grandpap Goodpasture, who was quite a good shot, was shooting one after another in a bunch Jack had rounded up. He shot one and the bullet glanced off its tough snout and went into the flank of dad's dog. Jack eventually died from that wound. Quite a blow to my father.

'Those hogs were so tough they'd just leave 'em lay where they were shot. They were trying hard to get rid of them so they wouldn't tear up the fields so bad. People had tried to eat them. They tried fattening some for the market one time. It didn't work too well. All the feed they gave them and they just wouldn't fatten. They made about thirty cents apiece on them—not much return for all that work.

"Grandpa Toll had a little more experience with wild hogs than most anybody. He, one time, when the dogs bayed three right up against a small tree, he took his belt off and while the dog was barking out in front of 'em, he got around behind and tied their feet—their legs—to this tree. Three young porkers. Then he went home and got help. They weren't very large hogs, so the men got 'em home. Another time he tells about, he and his brother Layt were out someplace and came on an old sow with pigs. She was pretty vicious-acting, so they took to the trees, and the tree that Layt went up was a small one and when he went too high why it bent clear over—down to where the sow could reach him. I don't know just how he come out of it, but he lived to tell the story and never forgot it either."

Jane Taylor Puett told about a bunch of their hogs that got away from the home area and hung out in a swampy place below the road. They got so they attacked anyone who went through. Neighbors reported the problem to Harry who knew where his hogs were but hadn't got around to bringing them home again. He went and rounded them up and brought them all home: 'They had great tusks. When they run wild the tusks grew out from the side of their mouths and they really looked like wild hogs. This one old sow was in the barn yard and some of the goats come up. Dad hadn't taken the precaution to pen her up, and she just tackled a goat and ripped its belly right open. She started eating it and dad had to come and shoot her. We kids weren't allowed to go into the barnyard when those hogs were there."

"Grandpap Goodpasture had a good many cattle on his place," Lester Swaggart said. "One day they heard quite a disturbance among the cattle. They wondered what it was all about—heard 'em bawling. Anyway a little later here comes a young fellow over the hill to see Grandpap. He said, 'My dogs have treed a big cougar over there and I'm afraid to shoot it.' The fellow was Sat Calloway. He was a little on the simple side, but he had three good hounds. He said the cougar was up in a big fork in the tree and that it was huge. The dogs ran him off a two-year-old cow he'd just killed,' he said. So they all walked up there,

Lester and Elmer Swaggart with skins.
Elsie Sutton

grandpap and my dad and his younger brother, Frank, and grandmother. The cougar was still up the tree, standing broadside on the big limb. That tree was known for a long time as the 'cougar tree.' The dogs was still ravin' and jumpin'. And grandpap was sorta winded from the long walk. He said to Sat, 'Can I rest my gun on your shoulder?' Sat says, 'No. Nothing doing.' So grandpap took an offhand aim, and he hit the cougar right between the eyes. He dropped out of the tree and the dogs, o' course, jumped onto him. Sat grabbed his gun and ran down there and shot it three times when the dogs was right in there chewing him up. The cougar measured nine feet from the end of his nose to the tip of his tail. Calloway lived over on Spencer Creek. He'd been trailin' that cat a good ways."

Jane Taylor Puett said, "We saw a cougar walking the fence one time right above our house. Mother called us out and showed it to us and warned us that we was to be careful about those things."

TRAPPING

For many people the wild animals weren't a dead loss. Trappers often paid their school expenses by selling furs from the skunks, beaver, foxes and other small wild creatures they were able to trap. Jim Breeding taught Lester Swaggart trapping:

"I went with him and got acquainted with the trapping game. In those days there were quite a lot of skunks and they were in dens. There were mink along the streams. Bobcat and coon were just most anyplace. Jim's trap line went down the creek—back of where Duckworth's nursery is now. I had a line down east from our place to the onion patch area, and then up to Spencer Butte and clear over to what they called Shepherd Hollow. That was west from Pruetts. They call it Spencer Creek now. I came back up Sockeye Creek to home."

According to Elsie, her brother Lester put himself through school trapping skunk, coon and mink. Bill Kindt spoke of beaver in Sockeye Creek. He used to trap them to get spending money. Elsie told about an expedition to get some skunk skins:

"Lester found a skunk nest that he knew would have several skunks in it, so he made a bargain with Elmer and me. If we would help him dig out the skunks he would give us a third apiece. One evening we got ready to go. We took the dogs. There were three of them and our old Indian horse. Dad and mother decided to go with us. Lester took some gunny sacks to put the skunks in after they were killed as he knew it would be dark before we got back home. Dad said we should take both lanterns. This den was a mile from home on the back side of Grandpap Goodpasture's place. It was a place where some large rocks had to be moved and Lester said he didn't know how deep the den was. We began to roll those rocks and dig the dirt as we had a shovel and axe along. Lester let the dogs dig too. One of the dogs got ahold of a skunk and pulled it out and then one of the other dogs got another until we had four of them killed. By this time the smell was getting dense. The dogs would roll and sneeze and we would put our handkerchiefs over our noses. There was more yet and there had to be more digging. Three more skunks was pulled out one by one. In the lantern light the air was yellow by now. It was hard to take but we made a good haul and was happy in spite of the horrible smell. Lester put the skunks in the sacks. Papa helped him tie them on the horse and we went home tired and all smelly. Lester said we had to help him skin them the next morning. When they were all skinned they had to be stretched on boards to dry. If there was too much fat we had to scrape them. After they were dry he bundled them up and sent them off and later a check would come in the mail.

"Another day, when our whole family was at Grandpa's, Lester and Carl went coon hunting. Bertha and I wanted to go but they told us we couldn't. They were gone a long time. Finally Lester came back alone and said he came after the axe. We asked him what he would do with it, but he said, 'Never mind.' After a while they both came back, looking secretive, but with no comment. Every once in a while they would laugh and we asked, 'What's the joke?' They never told us, but years later Lester told me what had happened. They found a hollow tree and Carl got his head caught in the hole when he looked down in it to see if there would be a 'coon. Lester had to cut the hole bigger so he could get his head out.

"Another time Carl caught a bobcat in one of his traps and had killed it by hitting it on the head. He told us girls he had caught one and thrown it in the shed till he could skin it. . . . I'd never seen a bobcat so I went out to look at it. I opened the door and there was that animal sitting up with a lopsided head and blood all over. I slammed the door real quick and ran to tell Carl it was still alive."

Marvin Swaggart, another of Elsie's brothers, and Emory Pruett used to work Marvin's trap line together. "We caught mostly skunks," Emory said. "We weren't very popular in school those days. We had seats all to ourselves. We used to trap up what they called the Dug Road between Swaggarts and Murdocks, [the] road that went through toward Camas Swale. We used to trap all through that and down what they called the Cedars on the other side. Went past Goodpastures. That road was dug out by hand through there."

GRAPE ROOT AND CHITTIM BARK

The Portland *Oregonian* of February 21, 1894, reported: 'There is an industry in Oregon which has reached quite a proportion but is little thought of—the trade in Grape root. This ad appears in up-valley papers: 10,000 pounds wanted @ $30 per ton. Roots must be cut in 2-4 inch length. Free from pith & of good

Andrew Hedger (seated in doorway) was teacher at Fox Hollow in 1917-1918.
Elsie Sutton

color. Lg. roots growing on the bottoms preferred."

"We used to dig Oregon Grape root," Elsie Sutton said. "This was an awful hard job. It was unpleasant to dig as it was so sticky. Another thing we did, Lester and I and Elmer when he wanted to, would be to take the Indian pony and go with a sled down in the timber and hunt chittim [cascara] trees. We took gunny sacks with us and peeled the chittim bark. We'd find big trees maybe twenty-five inches around. In the spring when the sap was coming up it would be easy to peel and we'd spread this bark on the barn floor where the hay was mostly off by now. When it was dry we'd break it up. Dad fixed a prune box with handles. One of us would hold the bark, sometimes it would be great long strips, and the other would come up and down on it with this box to break it. Had to be in about three-inch pieces. Seems to me we got two or three cents a pound for it. The farther you went down in the ground the thicker the bark. It was thickest on the roots. It was a big job on big trees because we'd peel the twigs as small as my little finger so we didn't waste any. Might take all day to peel a big tree. We had a hoe or something with us to scrape the dirt away from the roots."

Both of these plants were used in medicinal preparations.

BAKING BREAD

Bill Kindt told me, "My mother used to bake bread for some of the neighbors. She always baked our bread. I didn't know what store bread was till I was about grown. The neighbors would buy the flour—they'd ask what kind of flour she wanted, and then she'd bake for them. She didn't charge them very much. She baked for Mr. Hedger all the time. He was an old bachelor—maybe a widower. Had a boy—two boys that lived with him part of the time."

WORKING AWAY FROM HOME

Another scheme for buying school clothes was put to use by most families one time or another. Irene Albro remembered:

"We always went to the hop fields every fall. Dad seldom ever went. He stayed home, taking care of the stock and everything. It would be mother and us children that would go and pick hops. A lot of times my brother didn't go. See, I lost several brothers when I was just a little girl. This one brother stayed home lots of times. He'd farm and work out for other people. Us girls went with mother to pick hops. We went up to Goshen to Edmundson's yard. We took our tent and our eats. They furnished plenty of fruit and lots of times they'd have vegetable gardens that you could pick from. You could always keep bacon and we'd take some of that along. Usually mother cooked up some meat to take and when that was gone we'd go over to Goshen and buy more. Then we'd take flour and sugar and the staples. Lots of times they just put the calf back with the cow at home while we were away, to use the milk. We were usually gone ten days. That was the whole season. They had quite a lot of hop yards, big ones. And they had quite a lot of pickers too. But they always prepared a good place for you to camp, and there was always plenty of apples and prunes and lots of times we had berries we could pick. Mother always took jellies and some canned fruit.

"Mother had a little stove that we taken and fixed up, because she baked biscuits a lot of times for breakfast. I remember the little stove. It was just a little one that set up on legs. And then they put it up on blocks so it was higher. Wood stove. Edmondsons furnished all the wood you wanted. The stove had an oven with a door that opened and closed. It had four lids, but I don't think it was more than about two feet and a half [high]. And of course mother always had her coffee pot and her tea kettle along. We used to put on about three joints of stovepipe so we could run the smoke so it wouldn't bother and it would make a better draft.

Strawberry picking on Riggs Donation Land Claim circa 1955.
Lois Barton

Hop pickers' camp.
Lane County Museum

"Our cousins, the Calloways that lived down on lower Spencer Creek, went too. We always camped together. They had their little stove too. There was a big granary there at Edmondsons with a shed on each side, and we always had one of those sheds to be under. We had tarps or something we put up at the side to be sheltered. Hop picking was hard work. We didn't make much money was the trouble of it.

"My brother usually taken us in the wagon and got us all straightened up, and then he brought the team and wagon back home. It taken about a day to get our things loaded in the wagon and then go and get up there and get your tent and everything put up. We'd go toward Eugene and then take the old road up by Judkins Point and go over to Goshen. Followed the river all the way. When we were through picking we could send a note, or

somebody would come back home and then the homefolks could come and get us."

Harry Taylor raised a lot of berries and Candis Haley was one of the neighbors who helped with the picking. She said, "I used to help Belle with the children. I picked berries and looked after kids. Sit down on the ground and pick berries. Scoot along and hold a baby and pick berries. The babies got so they wouldn't bother the berries. I started helping her out with the kids when Oscar was just a baby. Just in berry season. Belle didn't pay me for helping with the children—just what I could earn picking berries. We got a penny a box for picking quart boxes."

Bill Kindt reported that the Kindt kids picked prunes for McBeth and for Murdocks.

Emory Pruett recalled, "The first public job I ever had was working on a rock-crusher right there this side of George Toll's house. Actually right behind Smith's house now. There was a little quarry there on that hill. Carl Holmes and Company operated it. There was three Swedes. They called them 'the Swedes.' Didn't call them Carl Holmes and Co. My brother worked for them for years. He worked there the same time I did. I just worked long enough to find out I didn't like to do that. There was Carl Holm and Pete Hanson. He lives up at Mohawk, and I think Ollie Meason is dead. . . . They crushed for Lane County. See, Lane County didn't have their own crusher. These Swedes just went all over the county."

Charlie Swaggart used to shoe horses for the neighbors. He also broke horses on occasion.

McBeth's prune picking crew at former J. L. Lombard house. Elsie Sutton

NEIGHBORING

Neighboring was an important part of life in an earlier day. People depended on each other for help in emergencies and for social life beyond the family. Even after the advent of the telephone, the time lapse between the call and the arrival of the doctor was substantial. The baby could very well arrive on the scene before the doctor could make it.

Howard McBeth told of having to go get the doctor when babies came at their house. He'd take an extra horse and meet the doctor over on Spencer Butte. The road ended at the Pruetts during the winter months as far as passage of a vehicle was concerned.

"My grandma was a midwife," he said. "I remember one time Harry Taylor came to get her for Belle. There was snow on the ground at the time. Maybe it was when Harry Jr. was born. He had the ox team hitched to the sled to take her over to their place in."

A number of the local women were midwives in the Fox Hollow area. Candis Haley Harris's mother, Mary, was one of them.

Candis told me, "She always went when people needed help. She learned what she knew from a country doctor in Michigan before she came west. When he'd get a case and nobody to help with it, he'd always call her. That's all she ever did learn about nursing from anybody."

Elsie Sutton said Mrs. Haley was midwife

to her mother when she was born and "I had the cord wrapped around my neck! Think how intelligent those midwives had to be in those days."

Another way neighbors worked together for their mutual satisfaction was in providing religious services for the neighborhood. The trip to town to attend established church services was impractical as a regular thing. Churches were eventually established and buildings erected in the neighborhood, but for years preaching was limited to the visits of circuit riders. Sunday Schools were organized and taught by residents. Edith Knox taught Sunday School at Fox Hollow School for several years. Elsie Sutton had attendance cards from that Sunday School in her scrap book. The Knoxes were Episcopalians.

Elsie Sutton recalled: "Our first experience of Pentacost was through the Haleys. Vernon had been injured in an accident and he was in a wheelchair. Some people down on Lorane Highway told the Haleys that Vernon could be healed through prayer. People up through this neighborhood was very skeptical. My dad said that there wasn't anything to it—that when the apostles died, healing and such was did away with. He was a Presbyterian. I didn't know anything about the church teachings then. You see we just lived up here and only went to Sunday School when this circuit rider came through. That was at the Fox Hollow School

Rock Crusher in Fox Hollow.
David Knox

when I was little and LeBleu when I was older. But when Charlie Price came through here—but I'm getting ahead of my story. The Haleys took Vernon down to this place where they was holdin' services and he got healed. You never in your life heard such a commotion among the neighbors up here. Oh, they had arguments. I remember them comin' here and settin' in front of the fireplace and just arguing and talking about how it was the work of the devil and all. Why, those Haleys had just lost their minds! But Vernon was out of his wheelchair—walking. It was too much for the neighbors—they could not understand it.

"I was just little and in those days a child was to be seen and not heard, but I thought to myself, if healing was the work of the devil I wasn't going to go near that kind of place. But years later we went down to hear Charlie Price and my mother got healed and then she took me. She was facing an operation to take out her kidney stones, and then she got healed. I had acute indigestion and she took me forward and I got healed. And you just can't imagine my father! He said that they was crazy, and that it was hypnotism and just everything. Later when mother and I decided to be baptized he went along too. But for a long time when we talked about getting baptized he'd say, 'Oh, I don't need to be baptized. I was sprinkled when I was a baby.'

"I never will forget those times earlier when all those men sat around jawing and carrying on. There was Jim Breeding and Thurston

Edith Knox's annual Christmas party, circa 1912.
George Knox.

Haley children.
George Knox.

Church group at Twin Oaks School.
Lane County Museum

Goodpasture and my dad and Uncle Abe and all these men folks, and they all chewed tobacco, or smoked, and they'd spit toward that fireplace. Sometimes they would miss and the spit would go up around the jamb. When we cleaned house it was my job to wash that off. I thought to myself then, 'If I ever get married, I'll sure never marry a man that smokes or chews or spits tobacco—." And she didn't!

A Spencer Butte Community Club was organized on June 4, 1921. The following clipping from Bertha Toll's scrapbook gives the particulars. (Source is not identified.)

June 4, 1921—A new organization to be known as Spencer Butte Progressive Community Club was formed last Sunday at the home of J. L. Murdocks, when about fifty people who make their home near Spencer Butte gathered for dinner and a social day. Officers for the club were elected as follows: J. L. Murdock, President; W. H. McBeth, Vice President; Louis Kindt, Secretary; Lester Swaggart, Assistant Secretary. A committee was elected to draft rules and bylaws, consisting of Mrs. Bertha Westrope, Thomas Hedger and W. H. McBeth.

On June 12 the club will meet at the home of W. H. McBeth. Those present for the day were W. H. McBeth and family, Walter Butler and George Butler, Charles Swaggart and family, Charles Westrope and family, Charles Dawson, Harry Taylor and family, Tobe Thornton and family, William Lindley, Nicholas Toll and family, George Toll and family, William Kindt and family, Elmer Roberts, Thomas Hedger, Fritz Woolschlauger and Thurston Goodpasture.

Club members gathered in homes for social events for a while. Florence Murdock told about Saturday night dances in their home, the "German Castle," built by Ed Ziniker: "People came from all around with their lanterns and their boots, even from Creswell. The living room was big enough for three squares at one time. Charlie Westrope was one of the fiddlers. Some of the Swaggarts used to play for the dances. Then the Swaggarts got saved and didn't go to dances any more."

Elsie Sutton confirmed this story and added, "When we got converted they had to hire someone else to play for the dances."

Later Charlie Swaggart donated an acre of land for the club's use and the neighborhood group started a clubhouse. The building was used for Sunday School classes and other functions, as well as the club's dances and social events.

Ralph Toll and his mother described the clubhouse as they remembered it: "It was a forty-by-sixty-foot building and it had a division for the kitchen. They never did finish that building. The two-by-four studding was framed in, and a bedroom the same way. They put a bed in there for the little kids. They had benches all the way around the main room and they danced in the middle. They had a big stove on the north end. It was a wood-heating stove. They used to stick me under the benches while they were dancing, and all I could see was ankles."

Ralph's mother Maggie corrected him, saying, "There was a long table stretched out there, eight or ten feet long. I put him back under the table—fixed a bed under there. He wasn't the only one. There was a whole bunch of kids under there. The Christensens' little girl was about four or five."

Ralph continued. "The kitchen was framed in on the north and the bedroom or lounge was on the other side. There was a door that faced toward the Sisters [mountain peaks in the Cascade Range] that would have been east. That was a double door, and the kitchen was on the right as you come in and across the alleyway was the bedroom. The alleyway was about ten feet wide and the framed-in bedroom was about eight by twenty as I remember it. There was twenty-one windows around the building. That east entrance was the main one. There was a single door over in the northwest, and then a single door came into the kitchen on the north. The stove set right off the kitchen on that north side.

"It was built with a triple floor. It was framed for a second story, but they never did do anything up there. It would have been right nice if we'd ever got it finished. They had shelves across the east side of the kitchen and a big cook stove in there with one of those warming ovens. I got the job of fillin' the reservoir."

Maggie interjected here, "Well, you *helped.* You was too little to do much but you took your little bucket and carried what you could."

Ralph went on. "Roy [Toll] and Marvin [Swaggart] and Bill [Kindt] and Orin and Kenneth Westrope brought the water in but they let me help. They had a pump, a pitcher pump, just outside the kitchen door. If I remember right it was about an eight-foot well. Jim Breeding dug that well. . . .'"

Later on someone tore the building down for the lumber that was in it. The club had quit meeting—people moved away and so forth.

In the forties another neighborhood group was organized, this one known as the Helping Hand Club. An undated Fox Hollow news item notes that the "Helping Hand Club held its meeting at Rose Johnson's home recently.

*Charlie Swaggart family
on a Sunday drive.
George Knox*

Lois Taylor won the hostess prize and a quilt was set together."

Then in 1952 another Spencer Butte Improvement Club was organized, with Florence Murdock being one of the organizers. That club incorporated so it could hold title to a 10-acre parcel of land donated by George Owen for a community center and park. While membership changes as oldtimers pass away and new people move into the area, that club still meets once a month.

Besides church and social functions which prompted neighbors to gather, there were farm organizations working in the area. Fred Knox was active in grange affairs for a good many years. Spencer Creek Grange was organized about 1936 according to Irene Carson Albro: "I was chaplain for many years. . . . I've been more than forty years in the grange. They always help you out if you need it. The grange got our electric light through here. They worked for that and they got the mail route through too. It was a long time before we got any mail service out here. Before that we went to Eugene about once a week, picked up a paper and any letters there might be."

Elsie Sutton told me: "My folks belonged to the Farmers' Union. There was some people named Butler lived over by Creswell. He was always Farmers' Union—always campaigning for the Farmers' Union. Whenever they'd have meetings why we'd go over on Camas Swale to the meetings. The grange was mostly down toward Lorane. Nobody campaigned my folks to belong to the grange. The Farmers' Union tried to help farmers get better prices for their crops, their wheat and stuff."

Within the memory of present-day residents there were some "characters" living here. Bert Judkins was one of them. Emory Pruett described Bert: "He was a bachelor who lived down behind Halbergs. Bert would go to town after his supplies in a wheelbarrow—a homemade wheelbarrow with a steel wheel. He'd push that to town and get his groceries, and then he'd push it back up this hill. You'd think it would be quite a chore to push that wheelbarrow up this hill. I used to haul him back and forth to town when he come walking by. My brother and I used to haul cordwood out to the road for Judkins. He cut it with a crosscut, had it all split to cordwood size. We'd haul it out there and stack it by the road, using our team and wagon. There used to be a log bridge across the creek down behind Halberg's house so Bert could get back and forth across the creek. That's what we hauled out wood over."□

CHAPTER 5

The Rural Schools

There were seven rural public schools serving the people within the boundaries of this study (see map on page 88).

When were these schools established? Who attended them? Who were their teachers? What was a school day like? Only partial answers to these questions have been uncovered.

Martha Ann Gay Masterson wrote in *The Sunset Trail* (p. 59):

"Time went on and we were to have a school. The neighbors were all assembled to talk the matter over. A site was chosen for the building which would be of logs, my father, Martin Baker Gay, having donated a corner of his land for this purpose.

"After it was finished a teacher was hired for five months. On the opening day we were happy as larks as we walked the mile to the school building. We were delighted to find there were about forty pupils in all. We had an interesting term of school and made progress in our studies. Pink was quite young for school but she wanted to go so the big brothers carried her when she got tired.

"Friday afternoons we usually had spelling matches. The teacher's oldest son and daughter were the best spellers in school, although some of my brothers were also good. We had several terms of school in the big log house and were thankful for the chance to learn."

Martha's brother James was more specific in his diary. A March 10, 1855, entry reads as follows: "I was at the school house today to organize the school district. . . ."

According to the *Atlas of Oregon* (p. 38), "The development of public education in Oregon was sporadic and late, partly because of the strong influence of denominational and private schools. Although the office of State Superintendent of Public Instruction was established by the State constitution, the first superintendent was not appointed until 1872."

In his first Biennial Report for 1871-1872 that superintendent wrote:

Too little attention has heretofore been paid to schoolhouse architecture in Oregon and to selection of proper location for school buildings. A great many of our people seem to have an idea that almost any kind of a house will do to teach school in, and that a schoolhouse should never be built upon a piece of land that is good for anything else. Hence, in many of the districts in Oregon the school houses are inferior in construction and in provision for the comfort of their inmates, to the barns of some of the farmers who live near them, and it is no uncommon thing to find the school house built upon the most barren and unsightly spot in the neighborhood. And to make the matter worse, no proper care is taken of these wretched and ill-located structures after they are built. They are used for all kinds of public gatherings from itinerant magic lantern exhibitions up, or down, to political meetings and caucuses. Every man and boy in the neighborhood who is the possessor of a "jack knife" and of the well-nigh universal Yankee propensity for "Whittling," feels at liberty to exercise his skill upon the doors and windows and furniture of the school house, and if he happens also to be the owner of a lead pencil, and is lucky enough to find a clean place on the wall, he tries his hand, occasionally, at drawing or scribbles some choice couplet of vulgar rhyme. The result is that some of our school houses are so delapidated and so befouled with obscene pictures and words that they are hardly fit for decent people to enter. And yet these are the places to which we send our boys and girls to have them trained up to become intelligent men and women.

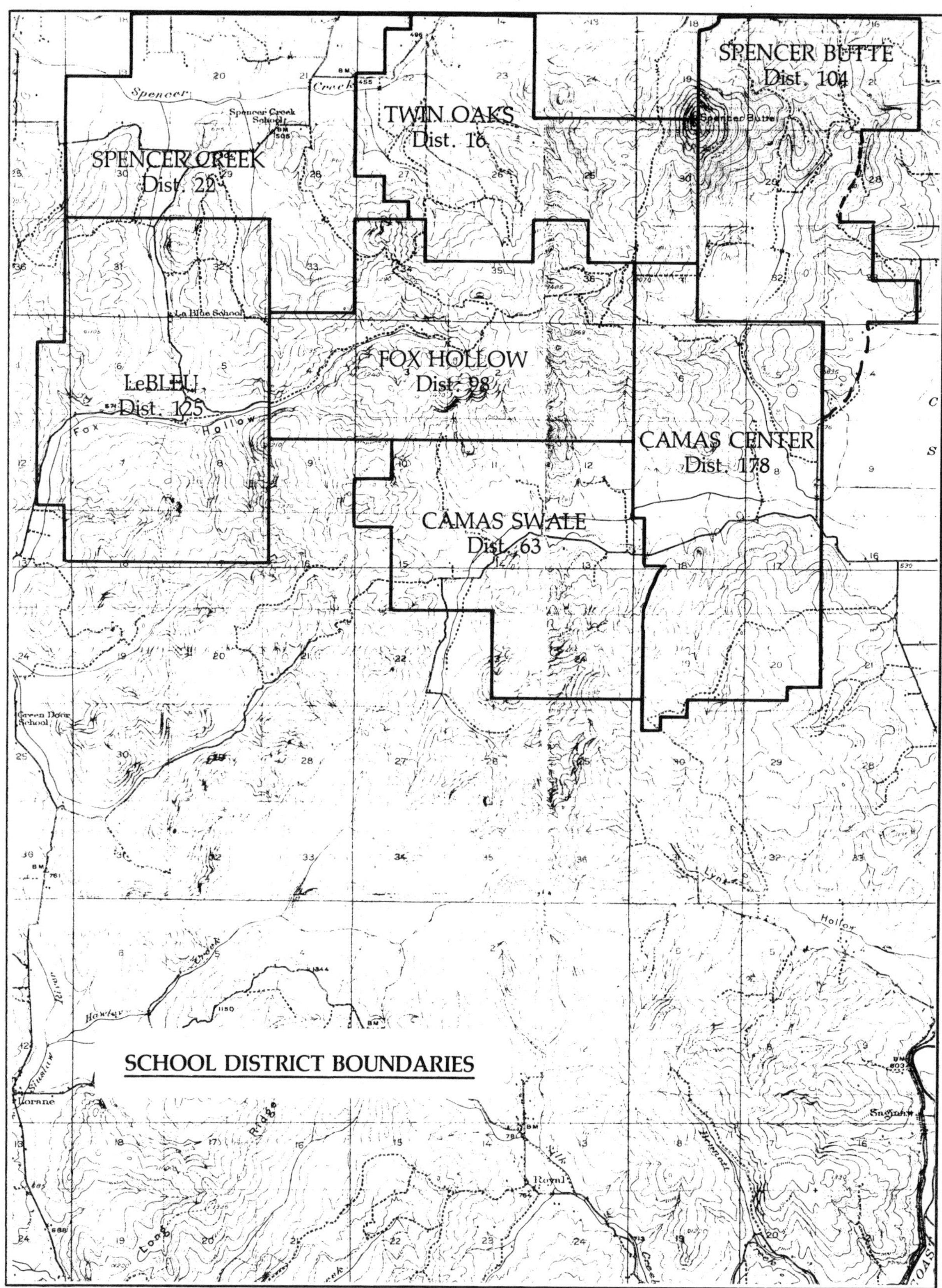

Boundaries of the seven rural school districts covered in this study.

First Twin Oaks School, 1885. Lower Spencer Creek and Twin Oaks students combined for the picture.
Irene Albro

Irene Carson Albro described the schoolhouse where she went to school. This would be the early Twin Oaks School, not the original log house, but a second building:

"The old schoolhouse I went to at first, they was some logs there, but it was mostly boards. But they were just them old kind of rough boards that went up and down this way. And then inside we used to get catalogs—they were a kind of magazines. I can't remember who put those out, but they was good-sized and they had color pictures in them. We pasted that all over our schoolhouse, and a lot of them had women's dresses and men's clothing and things. But they were pretty because they were colored. We had that paper on the inside of our old schoolhouse. We had long wide desks with two in a seat.

"I didn't go there more than a couple of years until they built the other school and I was pretty small at the time. We had one of those long wood stoves that opened on the end and then you put in a long piece of wood. We kids used to hover over that in cold weather. The room wasn't very tight."

The Biennial Report quoted earlier included these words from T. G. Hendricks, Lane County School Superintendent:

The conditions of the public schools of this county is slowly improving. Our schools need requirements that would cause attendance and prevent tardiness. I know of no way to reach the case except by compulsory education. Let our schools be made free and they will be well attended.

Private schools seemed to flourish between 1860 and 1872, according to a 1936 historical pamphlet prepared by the Eugene School District. The average tuition charges made in private schools per quarter were: Primary, $4.50; Common English, $5; Higher English, $7; Bookkeeping, $2; Music, $10; Plain or ornamental needlework, $4.50.

Early Lane County school records are incomplete. Some of them were destroyed by fire. Presumably the districts were established in order of their number. The 1873-1874 Biennial Report includes a paragraph submitted from Lane County noting that "there are about twenty frame, twenty box and seventeen log

"New" Twin Oaks building, 1925 or 1926. Grace Pasley, teacher. Front row, from left: May Davidson, Dale Davidson, Cecil Bragg, Hugh Smith, Fern Bailey, Dorothy Schnorenberg, Majory Baker, Opal Bailey, Agnes McNeil, Lucy Howard, Genivieve Baker, Ellen Taylor. Back row, from left: Clyde McNeil, Hugh McNeil, Elmer Albro, Frank Howard, Keney Mohey, Merl Albro, Edna Howard, Thelma Johnson, Fay Howard, Helen Chezem, Loretta Taylor, Howard Svarverud, Alton Baker, Mrs. Pasley.
Gertrude Albo

[schoolhouses] in the county. About 40 of them have been painted, more or less. A few are well-seated. Many of them are poorly seated."

In the statistical table from that report, only Twin Oaks (District 16) and Spencer Creek (District 22) of "our" seven districts are included. Apparently the others had not yet been established. An 1879 list of county schools receiving apportionment of school funds did not include District 16. District 22 had seventy-two pupils, which leads one to wonder whether they had been combined by that date.

From minutes of the District Boundary Board we learn that Spencer Butte (or East Spencer) was known as District 104 and was set up in 1906. There had been another school on Lake Creek earlier also known as District 104. Since the number was reassigned it is difficult to determine the order in which these schools were set up.

Since Fox Hollow School (District 98) is centrally located, its history may be representative. In my search for the Fox Hollow story I have talked with these former teachers and pupils: Janet Bell Brown, Maggie Kindt Toll, Jane Taylor Puett, Harry Taylor, Jr., Bertha Toll, Ralph Toll, Elsie Swaggart Sutton, Lester Swaggart, Flora Toll Getchell, Gertrude Knox Albro, Merl Albro, Irene Albro, Bill Kindt, Walter Kindt, Candis Haley Harris, Ruth McBeth Svarverud, Howard McBeth,

Children of Spencer Butte School. The teacher, Esther Burkett (Kommer) seated in front row at left.
John Kommer

Fox Hollow Student Body, 1916. Teacher, Vida McLain, in center with black bow at her neck. Front row, from left: Oscar Taylor, Lee Taylor. Second row: John Toll (partly hidden), Floyd Kindt, Walter Roberts. Third row: Lester Swaggart, Vida McLain, Gladys Roberts. Fourth row: Elsie Swaggart, Helen Sheridan, Bertha Toll. Back row: Rosie Taylor, Alice Roberts, Rose Kindt, Jane Taylor.
Elsie Sutton

Model Report Card

Monthly Report

Of *Flora Toll*

Apr. 3 Term, 189 9.

Studies. Etc.	1st m	2d m.	3d m.	4th m.	5th m.	6th m	Av
Reading.	G	E	E				
Spelling.	E	E	E				
Writing.	E	E	E				
Arithmetic.	E	G	E				
Geography.							
Language Grammar.	G	G	G				
History.							
Physiology.	G	G	E				
1-2 Days Absent.							
Deportment.	E	E	E				

All Rank is on the Scale of 100. Lower than 75 is unsatisfactory.

REMARKS: *E = excellent , G = good.*

Sadie. Baum Teacher.

MODEL REPORT CARD. COPYRIGHTED.

PUPIL'S MONTHLY REPORT.

Report of *Flora Toll*

For term ending *June 22* 1906

Fox Hollow School.

STUDIES, Etc.	1st Mo.	2nd Mo.	3rd. Mo.	4th Mo.	Total Average.
Spelling.					66
Reading.					
Writing.					9.
Grammar.					73
Arithmetic.					80
Geography.					95
History					62
Physiology					100
Civil Gov.					67
Deportment.					500
Times Tardy.					11
Days Absent.					2
Average.					

Highest degree of Excellence is denoted by 100, Perfect; 90 to 95, Very Good; 80 to 90, Medium; 70 to 80, Low; Under 70, Lowest. Parent please sign on reverse side and return to teacher.

Chas. A. Walker Teacher.

George and David Knox, Lee Taylor, and Martha and Henry Christensen.

When the first schoolhouse was built it was called the Maupin School. Boyd and Pauline Maupin homesteaded near the lower end of Fox Hollow Road around 1870 (see homestead map). The first school may have been located on their land. I found no one now living who remembers where the building was. Charles Swaggart and step-brother Frank Goodpasture, George Toll and two Robinson boys are said to have been among those who attended the Maupin School. One of their teachers was Annie Bowser who was a sister of J. L. Lombard's wife.

By the time the second building was erected, probably sometime in the late 1880s, the name was Fox Hollow school. Jess Breeding, Ruth Shepherd (Hill), Candis Haley (Harris) and Luella Toll (Swaggart) were some of the students at the "first" Fox Hollow School. That building was located in a little glade on the north side of Fox Hollow Road about midway along the north boundary line of Section 3. A creek ran through the school yard.

The third school house in the district was built in 1909 or 1910. George Toll was one of the builders. The location had been moved to the west edge of Nick Toll's homestead which was closer to the center of the district. Erosion of the creek bank undercut the earlier building, so something had to be done.

Bertha Toll, Lester Swaggart, Lee Walker and Gladys Roberts made up the first class of first-graders in that new building. Their teacher was William Wills. Lane County records show that he taught a twelve-week term beginning September 18, 1909, and another beginning January 10, 1910. He received forty dollars a month and began teaching with a Grade 3 certificate which he upgraded to Grade 2 in February 1910.

Jane Taylor attended the second Fox Hollow School, starting when she was five "because Rose was seven and they didn't want her

Report cards of 1899 and 1906 from Flora Toll Getchell's scrapbook. She explained that Charles Walker was not a popular teacher. His students gave him a hard time as the 1906 deportment grade, later altered, indicates.

Camas Center Schoolhouse (District 178). Roy Andrews, Oregon Collection, University of Oregon Library

to wait any longer. So they started me because it was dangerous for her to go through the woods alone on account of wild animals. Maggie Toll was our teacher to begin with. There was Janet Bell Brown and Tom Hedger and Mrs. Pasley and then Charlie Dawson. We went to Spencer Creek School when we moved over the hill." (From taped interview February 23, 1977.)

Elsie Sutton remembered the range cattle they sometimes encountered—"wild mean animals" that scared school children who had to detour around them to get home. She also spoke of school picnics on Spencer Butte: "Every year we went up there for end-of-school picnics." Twin Oaks' students did this too. The Christensen children remembered encountering timber wolves on their way to Spencer Butte School in the 1920s.

Irene Albro told about a neighbor's boar that threatened her walks to school: "I remember goin' to school one mornin' and I had to cross the bridge across the creek and here stood that hog. He was dangerous and when I seen him I came back and I got through the gate and

come up the road and run clear up the hill and told my Dad. Dad took his rifle and took me to school, but when we got down there he was gone. But he had tushes that long [three to four inches] that stuck out of his mouth and he'd chase the children if he saw us. He stood up like that [thirty inches]. He killed our dog. He got out and he got over here on our place. Our little dog wasn't very big and he just slit his neck right open with that tush. I sure was afraid of him. He ran right out in the pasture.

"Later I walked to school with the Wills boys, Bob and Joe and Don and Ed. And those boys was just as nice as they could be. . . . They'd come down and they'd always wait for me. They'd whistle and they waited for me to go to school. I was never afraid after they started."

Elsie Sutton recalled: "Fox Hollow was just three miles from here and we walked or rode horseback. Grandpa Toll lived about a quarter of a mile from the schoolhouse. When we rode in the wintertime we would tether our horses in Grandpa's barn and Papa would put oats in a sack for us to go up at noon to feed the horse."

Ralph Toll told about a barn at the "first" Fox Hollow School: "It was a log barn—a pole barn—Dad said. The kids, and even the teacher, rode a horse to school. It was back a'ways from the schoolhouse."

"One time we was riding over a stretch of corduroy road," according to Elsie, "about three or four blocks long, over on the other side of Gay Hill. My horse stumbled at the end of that road and threw me in the mud on the way to school. Was I ever a mess?" She chuckled at the memory but made sure I knew it wasn't funny at the time.

"The Taylor kids lived on the hill north of the schoolhouse. It was a very steep climb and their dad cut steps up that hillside so they could get up without fallin' in the mud so much in the winter," Bertha Toll remembered.

The school programs loom large in memories of school days. "Every single pupil had a part even if it was only a line or two. We all learned our pieces. We'd practice for the Christmas program that last week every day after the afternoon recess, 'cause we couldn't come back in the evening to practice," according to Irene Albro. Elsie remembered going to Christmas programs at both Spencer Butte School and at LeBleu. She walked four or five miles across country to the LeBleu program through the winter mud with her brothers.

Louis Kindt was one area resident who taught at three of the schools. He was at Fox Hollow in the spring of 1921, at Spencer Butte in the fall of that year and also at LeBleu some other term.

Here is part of what Janet Bell Brown had to say about teaching at Fox Hollow:

"I started teaching there in '22. I boarded with Guy and Eva Knox. I walked three miles to school. I lived in their household for two years, from '22 to '24. Their son, George, went to school [with] me. The girls weren't old enough. I had all the Taylors one year except Rosie and Jane who were in high school. I had Oscar and Isaac [now known as Lee] and Ellen. There were two little ones, Nora and Effie.

A school souvenir from Flora Toll Getchell's scrapbook.

They weren't old enough to go to school, but they used to run off and come to school. They were the ones that ate the candles off the Christmas tree. I missed 'em and there they were sittin' underneath there chewing that paraffin. . . .

"If there was only one lamp at Knox's I waited till the dishes were done, and usually helped with the dishes so I could use the kerosene lamp. I checked papers every night. I never had any aides. I had all eight grades. Sometimes I combined five and six, or three and four, but as a rule I [taught] the biggest part of them. Elsie Sutton and Oscar Taylor took ninth grade under me. They couldn't go to high school, so they came and I taught them four high school courses; Breasted's *History* and algebra and English, and then science was more or less nature study.

"We packed water to Fox Hollow. It had a pump but the water was not fit to drink. We carried [drinking water] from the Tolls. The school water had a mineral in it, like iron, that made a scum on the top and it was distasteful. You could wash your hands in it, which we did, but the taste of it was just vile. It was a dug well, had a pump on it, inside the cloak room. See, there was a cloak room on the

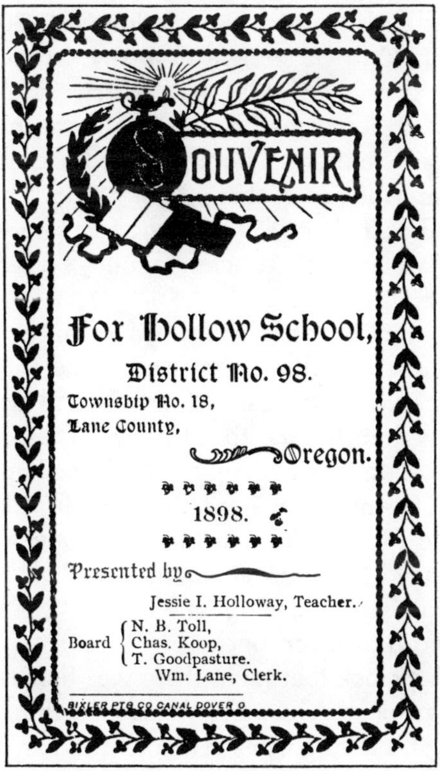

The old LeBleu School, 1911 or 1912. Roy Andrews, Oregon Collection, University of Oregon Library.

front. There was a sink there and the drain went down to the creek. The outhouses were down on the creek too. We packed water all the years I was there. We carried it downhill, and if the kids packed it they usually slopped most of it out.

"I got butcher paper for art work. I always bought the paint for them. In order to teach art you had to furnish all the material.

"I went back to teach Fox Hollow in 1930 and taught '30 to '35 straight in a row. I rode horseback every day. [She had married and homesteaded down the canyon in the meantime.] I had children at home. I hired a girl. Amy Rump was one of them. I got paid $85 a month one year. I got $50 another. I got warrants, and when I went to get my money I'd get $45 for a $50 warrant.

'The school burned the 9th of November, 1944. I know how the fire started. I did my own janitor work, and Calvin [her son] and his dad was waitin' for me to go home. They'd taken my car and gone to town. We cleaned up the school room and we put the trash in the stove. The fire was out, or so we thought. We'd warmed the soup at noon. We always had a gallon bucket of soup, and we'd get up a big fire and heat it for lunch.

"At six o'clock that night there was flames shootin' out of the chimney. When that thing was over and they got the settlement money, Bertha Toll told me that there was a brick loose in that chimney. Many times she'd seen fire shoot out. She told them (the school board) about it again and again. And she said that night fire was shooting out where that brick was loose.

"Before I was married I walked to school in the mud, and changed my shoes when I got there. One night my fiance picked me up and I lost one of my good shoes. We looked all night, using his seven-cell deer-hunting flashlight, but we never did find the shoe. He was concerned about my reputation because we were out all night, and not yet married.

"After the Taylors moved away the school ran out of kids. All they had left was Oscar Taylor's little girl, Beth. Then there was a group of people moved in and that's why they wanted me back to teach in '44. They remodeled it all on the inside, bought new desks. That's what made me so sad when it burned up, because it had all new books and everything. It was really very attractive. Well, you see, then they consolidated with LeBleu. We were District 98 and LeBleu was 125, and they consolidated and changed it all to 98. At that time they put on a bus that hauled the kids from Fox Hollow to LeBleu.

"I went to school one morning and there was a great big billy goat caught in the fence. His horns were caught on both sides. And I thought, 'Well, he's been here for some time.' I was deathly afraid of him, but I put my horse

Inside view of the LeBleu School, 1911 or 1912. The pictures were taken by Roy Andrews when he was Assistant Superintendent of Lane County for rural schools.

in the barn and went up. He'd got past the fighting stage, so I took this horn, and I took that horn and I loosened them from the fence. And you know, that confounded goat, if he could have got to me, he would have just tore me apart. He was on the other side of the fence, and he laid there and rested for a while.

He'd twisted and struggled till there was almost a groove in those horns.

"The Toll boys had a mill on the creek there. They had a lathe and John used to make all kinds of things—table legs and such—with waterpower. The school kids used to just love to watch him with that water going over that wheel, turning that wheel. You see it, a waterpower thing, doesn't go steady. It goes as the water comes over, and you have to be ready with the turning lathe to cut when the water comes. The kids always jumped when it began to turn. John was deaf and dumb. He tried to go to school to me one year, but I just couldn't make him understand well enough.

"The kids brought the soup for lunches from home. They'd take turns. You had to be sure the lid was loosened when you warmed it. One time we didn't loosen the lid and all our cocoa went to the ceiling. We had cocoa, potato soup, beef stew. We had beans several times a week. Something hot to go with the biscuit they brought. There was a calendar and they signed up. The seventh and eighth grade always took care of the soup calendar.

"We read aloud every day. Every class. Whether we did anything else or not, every-

---

XMAS EVENT IS PLEASING

TEACHER AND PUPILS SPENCER SCHOOL ENTERTAIN

(Register Lane County Special)

EAST SPENCER, Ore., Dec. 29.—A very delightful afternoon was provided those who attended the excellent Christmas program given by the pupils and teacher of the East Spencer school in district 104 on December 24th.

The following program was rendered:

I. Play, "Cosette's Christmas Eve," teacher and pupils.

II. "Old Kriss Kringle," Martha Christensen.

III. "The Little Christmas Tree," Albert and Henry Christensen and Robert Walter and Theodore Scharen.

IV. "The Day of Days," Henry Christensen.

V. "A Telephone Message," the teacher, Miss Esther Burkett.

VI. "A Merry Christmas and a Glad New Year," Albert Christensen.

Refreshments and presents were distributed immediately after the program.

This undated clipping tells of a Christmas program at District 104. Esther Burkett taught there in 1923 and 1924 and again in 1926.
Bertha Toll Scrapbook

A Joyce Kommer drawing, from memory, of Spencer Butte School, District 104.

body learned to read. I taught the Bacon method of sounding. It got results. I had all those kids reading before the year was out. Every one of them.

"We always planted a garden every spring. School was always out about the first week in May. We sprouted seeds to watch them sprout, and then the kids planted them down by the creek. The garden was there in the fall as a rule. If the plants didn't dry out. To me it was just an experience. They could go home and do the same thing at home after school was out. The kids had lots of fun.

"We worked awful hard, but we played hard too. We had to work hard because the state was giving tests at the time, and the eighth grade had to pass or you didn't get the contract the next year. I had to teach eighth grade and I had to teach first grade. . . . My eighth graders always helped the first and second. When they got their work done they went and listened to the little ones. And the first graders learned a lot about living just listening to the older ones. They had to wait for their older brothers and sisters. They weren't allowed to go home. They had to walk with the older ones, so those little kids had to be taught from 2:30 on."

Janet Brown spoke of combining grades sometimes. Elsie Sutton remembered one such occasion with another teacher: "I think my first teacher was Maggie Toll. I went to her to the fourth grade, and she kept me back. Rose [Kindt] was having a time gettin' through, so she held me back with Rose. Otherwise there'd

The last Fox Hollow School Building which burned in 1944. Roy Andrews, Oregon Collection, University of Oregon Library

Inside view of Fox Hollow School circa 1912. Teacher is Laura Jackson. The students, but not in this order, are: Candis Haley, Albert Walker, Lester Swaggart, Alice Roberts, Carl Toll, Maude Walker, Lee Walker, Gladys Roberts, George Haley, Bertha Toll, Elmer Roberts.

Above left: Camas Swale School, District 63. Marion Sutton attended this school. Pearl Ashby, teacher in 1919-1920, lived in the Sutton home while she was teaching there.
Roy Andrews, Oregon Collection, University of Oregon Library

Opposite: Interior view of Camas Swale School (District 63) circa 1912. Earliest boundary records available for this district are dated 1889.
Roy Andrews, Oregon Collection, Univesity of Oregon Library

Above right: Inside view of Camas Center building, circa 1912. Names of some of the families whose children attended this school: Napper, Singletary, Wakefield, Bush, Cowgil, Ziniker, Ruegger. Paul Ziniker told of one teacher who was "a mean one. He'd make the kids lie down on the floor and roll from side to side. Then he'd hit them with a rope. I watched him do it." Marie Ziniker Erdmann said of Harry Bush, an older boy in this picture who parts his hair in the middle, "He was very kind to us, helping us over the language barrier, writing things on the board for us."
Roy Andrews, Oregon Collection, University of Oregon Library

have been two classes with one in each class and she didn't want to do that. So she held me back to be with Rose and I know I resented it terrible. I wanted to be in the fourth grade and Rose was in the third. But Aunt Maggie was a good teacher 'n it didn't hurt me none, as far as that was concerned."

According to Merl Albro, Irene's son, who attended the Twin Oaks School in later years, the Spencer Creek School was consolidated with Twin Oaks. They built the present Twin Oaks building at the time of consolidation. It stands across McBeth Road from the Spencer Creek Grange Hall and is now used as a private residence.

Spencer Butte, District 104, was the first of the rural schools surrounding Eugene to consolidate with the Eugene district. A Eugene *Register Guard* story dated February 6, 1945, says, "The Spencer Butte district immediately south of the city pushed its proposition to a vote because of the imperative condition resulting from growth in that direction with only a one-room obsolete school house. Their school levy jumped to 32.4 mills on their valuation of $69,064. Their school will be continued the rest of the present year. After that their pupils may be brought to Edison in Eugene until growth trends in that area determine where a new primary school should be placed." The 1944 census for District 104 was thirty-five pupils.

Twin Oaks and LeBleu school district residents voted December 9, 1947, on merger. A later news story, May 14, 1957, reports that LeBleu asked Eugene for consolidation. The board voted favorably on that request June 14 of that year. Then on the 23rd of June, little more than a week later, vandals sacked the LeBleu building.

The lower Camas Swale School, known as Camas Center School, was organized May 11, 1908. An election was held at the home of W.

P. Napper, at which time John Ziniker, Ed. Ruegger and C. A. Reetz were elected directors, and Mary V. Reetz, clerk. The board accepted land for a building site from Mr. Wullschlager for twenty dollars. . . . An eight mill tax levy was instituted for building purposes. The plan and contract proposed by R. H. Parsons was accepted, by which he agreed to build a schoolhouse for $710, and a fence around the grounds for $42.50.

Other information from the Clerk's Record Book, which is now in the Creswell Museum, tells of a special meeting the following November when it was voted to permit the schoolhouse to be used for Sunday School and other meetings "if carried on in a decent and orderly manner and in accordance with the school law of Oregon."

Again from the Record Book: "The assets of the district that first year came from these sources: A loan from Henry Melton, $1000, State school fund, $64, County school fund, $258, Special tax $191.34, and Library fund, $3.20.

"Expenses included supplies, $201; the building, $710; insurance and an axe, $8.35; teacher's salary @ $40 per month for four months and on April 23rd, a payment of $120. A sink etc. cost $3.75; twice the fees of $4 for conducting eighth grade examination; a clerk's salary was $15; and $191.34 paid on note.

"June 21, 1909, annual meeting of the board elected directors, levied an eight-mill tax for the relinquishment of the debt, and sealed bids were ordered for ten ricks of fir and five ricks of oak wood. It was decided to let Mr. H. D. Myers furnish five corner posts for the fence @ 15¢ each. Woven wire fence with barbed wire at the top was to be built."

The Camas Swale schools were consolidated into the Creswell system about the same time consolidation was taking place around the Eugene district, bringing to an end the rural schools in the Spencer Butte country. □

CHAPTER 6

Building the Roads

Roads to serve the area were established quite early, but not entirely in the same location as present-day ones. At first, of course, access was very primitive. Elsie Sutton's grandfather said the route from Eugene south on the west side of the Butte was originally an Indian trail, used also by the deer and other wild animals, and that the only way you could tell where homes were located as you rode the trail was by hearing the roosters crow.

The traveler over South Willamette Street in 1982 would have a hard time visualizing road conditions of fifty or 100 years earlier. In the general area where the stoplight is at 46th Street, those who drove the route in 1910 stopped their teams and opened a gate into Lucas's cow pasture which they had to cross on their way up the hill. Any experienced stockman would instantly recognize the hazards of such access to his pasture. Uninformed or careless passersby often failed to secure the gate adequately, if they bothered to close it, and the animals which were normally kept at home by the fence and gate were free to explore beyond their normal limits. One supposes most of the travelers of that day had stock of their own and would have been reasonably careful.

The road was a dirt road which turned to mud in the rainy season. It ended some distance below the present Spencer Butte Park entrance in the winter time. From that point on they used a trail. An old-timer told of going to meet the doctor who had been summoned from town to attend a childbirth. He took two horses, one for the doctor to ride when he got to the end of the road and was obliged to abandon his rig.

Because the names attached to county records bring in the human element, specific de-

tails are included here from road applications. Among the earliest county records relating to roads in this area is a petition dated February 27, 1869, filed by G. J. Emerick and others, applying for a change in a county road as follows:

To the Honorable Board of County Commissioners of Lane County:

The Undersigned citizens of Lane County respectfully petition your Honorable Body to have the road changed leading from Eugene City running west of Spencers Butte to Camas Swale to Siuslaw as follows-viz-commencing at NW corner of DLC of Jonathan Riggs & running south on Section Line as near as practicable about 2½ miles to N. line of DLC of Chas. Martin running thence westerly one mile to Intersect the said road, and so much of the old road as may be rendered unnecessary by the change be vacated.

And your petitioners will ever pray

George J. Emerick	D. Daniels
Henry Padburg	Cyrus Hayes
David G. Gay	Jesse Bill
John H. Moore	John Rinehart
H. F. Bogart	M. L. Duncan
John H. Taylor	Lewis Rinehart
Robinson Morford	Milton Emerick
N. Moxley	C. Hager
J. A. Moore	G. C. Duncan
J. O. Chrisman	

A bond of $100 was posted by George J. Emerick. Road viewers appointed were Jesse Cox, James Breeding and William Masterson. They met the first Monday in April and made the following report: "It is located on the best ground and shortest route; that the same can be made a good public highway and we recommend it be so declared."

The report was read May 5 and 6, 1869, and the road declared a public highway. The field notes of the county surveyor read in part as follows:

> Commencing at the NW corner of Jonathan Riggs DLC #64, being also NW corner Sec. 31, T 18 S, R 3 W, running in a southerly direction . . . to where the line of the new road intersects the old road at Rinehart's gate . . . 59.65 ch to gate of Henry Padburg's cow lot, after crossing TWP line . . . top of hill at dug road [Murdock Road] . . . 2nd milestone in Gay's pasture . . . south line of the road in Scott Chrisman's pasture. This road is 3 miles and 57.51 chains in length and runs over a comparatively level country mostly prairie with scattering timber and grounds that will make a very good road.
> *April 6, 1869*   *R. E. Foley*, County Surveyor

This road remained in use into the 1930s or later. Elsie Sutton said Marion traveled that road when he was courting her.

Not long after the west-side road was established another petition was filed, dated May 5, 1869, to reroute the road south from Eugene on the East side of the Butte. This application is ascribed to W. R. Dillard, A. M. Osburn and others. The viewers appointed were G. J. Emerick, John Rinehart and Henry Padburg. The petition asked for:

> . . . a change in the County Road running south from Eugene City, said road being reviewed and surveyed by James R. Phillips, Titus and Huddleston. Commencing at the 4th mile post [south from Eugene via Alder St.] and follow said Phillips survey to an abandoned gate on the land of Wm. R. Dillard thence in a southerly direction to a sag some ten rds. west of NE corner of A. M. Osburn's enclosure. Thence in a SE direction to the line of said Dillard and Osburn thence south on said line to the SE cor of said enclosure. Thence in a SW dir. to the line of Wm. D. Renshaw & A. M. Osburn thence S on said line to the Twp. line thence on most practical route to NE cor of J. Killingsworth DLC thence S as near as practical to former survey of Phillips, Huddleston, Titus & Leon[?]

Signed

C. B. Stewart	A. M. Osburn
V.P. Quimby[?]	D. C. Fitch
Jonathan Butler	Wm. Russell
James Stewart	W. R. Dillard
Hiram Stewart	W. D. Renshaw

However, there was a conflict. E. and H. L. Chichester represented that their "premises will be injured and damaged in the sum of $50 by the change and opening the county road (as proposed). If the said change is made the peti-

tioners will be compelled to remove one string of fence near a mile in length and reset the same on the line of the proposed change. Wherefore petition & ask that such proceeding be had for the assessment of such damages as the law provides."

A later note requests a slight reroute, dated August 1, 1910, across Sec. 32, T 18 S, R 3 W, "approximately on the line of Rd. 269, the marks of which have disappeared," by petition of Webster Kincaid and W. J. Butler. The name of this road was changed in May, 1954, to Sher Khan Road.

That section of Fox Hollow Road south and west of Murdock Road was once called Welch Creek Road. In 1890 a petition was filed to lay out and establish a county road as follows:

> We, the undersigned petitioners, petition the Hon. County Court of Lane County, Oregon, to lay out and establish a County Road 40 feet wide, commencing in center of Siuslaw-Eugene road [Lorane Highway] in front of Conrad House, near line between Sec. 5 & 8, T 19 S, R 4 W, crossing to south side of Welch Creek, following around field and keeping on south side of said creek and crossing to the North side about 100 yards east of line between Conrad place and E. Knoop's House. Thence going up same creek North of Knoop Bros. sawmill, following private road from Knoop Bros. barn to line between W. Lane's and Herrington's place up north side of creek to line between Sec. 2 & 3, crossing south up to J. L. Toll's and north again through N. Toll's place, up to head of creek near center line of Sec. 2. Thence following old Road from J. Bonds to Goodpastures through Goodpasture's and Judkin's places and terminating in center of Camas-Swale-Eugene County Road at the gate going into E. Osburn's place about 1/2 mile NE of Goodpasture's house.

Ludwig Deiss[?]	William Lane
W. S. Westrope	L. D. Herrington
Jeremiah Pipes	S. N. Smith
I. L. Simpson	T. J. Calloway
John Simpson	Tony Sinay
E. A. Kloek [Klock?]	S. P. Calloway
W. O. Blanton	E. J. Crow
A. M. Osburn	L. P. Toll
C. E. Winter	J. W. Ware
A. Rogers	W. H. Calloway
J. Farron	N. B. Toll
W. D. Coleman	J. L. Toll
H. A. Mullin	J. H. Pickens
S. Lucas	W. D. Wood
E. Knoop	L. J. Deffenbacher
J. H. Baily	Geo. Landreth

*Cookshack with cooks Bess and Bertha Chetwood and the road building crew in the Fox Hollow neighborhood, circa 1910-11.
Leonard Clearwater*

[illegible]   K. M. Callison
John P. Anderson   C. Knoop
P. F. Blanton

The action for this road was filed July 5, 1890.

These were not the only travel lanes in use. Local residents established a road over "Bond Hill" southeast from the Toll home. That was the most direct route to the Trunnel mill in Creswell where they went to have their grain ground. The first gate in that road was still in place near John Toll's home in 1978. The road came out on what is now Toleman Road and was never used extensively because there were bad grades both going up and coming down on the south side of the ridge, according to local old-timers. The travel was by ox team and wagon around the turn of the century.

There was also a road from what is now Christmas Tree Land, on Murdock Road, down across the Ziniker place, connecting with what is now Sher Khan Road. The south end of this road was through the Ruegger property and involved several gates. Lee Taylor told me he stopped use of that road when he worked for Sher Khan in the forties. He would tell people it was private and that they should go around.

Another road—preceding the McBeth Road —went over the hill north and west from the homes on the prairie to which LeBleu Road now gives access. This probably connected with what is now known as Svarverud Road which intersects McBeth Road near the Lutheran Church south of Spencer Creek Grange.

The Christensen Road was established in May 1912 by petition of F. L. Chambers. The report on that road made to the County Court reads as follows:

> We are of the opinion that the proposed road should be established as described for the following reasons. . . :
> It is laid on a very easy and suitable grade, into an extensive country having no other practicable public highway. It is being opened and constructed by private parties who have intended to convey it to the public as a county road by executing the deeds from which the attached descriptions are copies. The required grading we found largely completed and culverts set. There is fine material for surfacing near the line almost everywhere—basalt boulders showing on strad [sic] surface.

This was originally described as Market Road Number 24 in Lane County. Deeds for the right of way were given by J. F. and Cora May, Hans T. Christensen and Harriet N., his wife, and from a Mr. Goddard.

Even though the right of way for this road was in place as early as 1912, Mollie Christensen recalled that it was not usable during the rainy season until some years after they began hauling products to market. They were obliged to go west from their buildings up through the former Riggs Donation Land Claim and out onto what is now known as Wildwood Creek Ranch Road which feeds into Murdock Road south of the Willamette-Fox Hollow intersection. Mollie Christensen said in a taped interview in 1976 that they had to build their own road up through their valley. They often needed to hitch two teams to the wagon or sled to get it through the mud. Those first years they either went the South Willamette road to town, a distance of nine miles, or went south through Creswell.

The section of Fox Hollow Road between South Willamette and the Alder Street extension was built in the 1920s by the local residents with some help from the county. It was called a market road and the petition for this one was dated November 8, 1921, and signed by W. S. Roberts, W. H. McBeth, C. A. Swaggart, C. H. Rice, Harry Taylor, Luella Swaggart, D. R. McBeth, O. G. Thornton, William Kindt, Louis Kindt, Belle Taylor, N. B. Toll, G. W. Toll, J. Davidson, Nancy F. Kindt and Margaret Redemer.

A road bond of $200 was posted November 26, 1921, signed by William Kindt and W. H. McBeth. The road viewers' report dated December 21, 1921, declares "this road is necessary in order to provide an outlet to terri-tory south and west of Spencers [sic] Butte. The present road west of the Butte cannot be relocated on good alignment and grade without excessive cost, while the proposed road can be graded at a very reasonable cost and will serve the people interested very much better than the present road."

This road was built within the memory of several people now living. Howard McBeth, son of W. H. who posted bond, said in a taped interview:

"My dad was responsible for getting the road built. In the spring it was awful bad trying to get through [the Willamette Road]. The mud started to dry and then it would ball on the wheels. There were some springy places there on the hill above Pruetts. When we first started building Fox Hollow Road we worked one day for pay and the next day for free. Just about the whole neighborhood worked on the road—everyone that had a team. A lot of equipment wasn't even the county's. The county paid us. The Fresnos and plows were county equipment, but the teams and all—it was one way of getting a road.

"Those big cuts below the Christensen Road, that was real rough country in there. You couldn't even get over it with a team to get the cuts started, see. So we went in there and drilled a lot of holes by hand and then we put dynamite in there and hooked 'em all up with wire and shot 'em all at once and cut that open so we could put a team down there. I took the first team over it after it was shot, with a big old road plow. It took four horses to the plow. The man that was driving the team next to the plow would ride the plow beam. You'd get throwed something fierce sometimes, especial-

W. H. McBeth and Walter Kindt arriving for work on Fox Hollow Road, circa 1921.
Howard McBeth

"Everyone in the neighborhood worked on the road." This picture was actually taken during the construction of Wolf Creek Road.
Ralph Petzhold

ly if you hit a rock. And then we used a Fresno to move the dirt. A long box with a long handle on it. The team would pull it. Sometimes four horses.

"A Redemer boy was powder monkey when we worked on the road. He left his crimpers on a stump near the set and blew them away. It got to be a joke. The county supplied the crimpers and dynamite. Dwayne Crow was Commissioner when Fox Hollow was built. I don't remember just how old I was. I worked on the road, but in those days you worked before you was old enough."

Ralph Petzhold of the county road department also worked on a crew of this kind, but in the Crow area. He recalls his father saying that the county would pay one dollar per day for a man and the same for his team. He also recalls that roads were often financed those days by a tax assessment in the district which had jurisdiction over the area. Another Fox Hollow resident of the period, eighteen-year-old Lester Swaggart, was a talented cartoonist. His father and mother were signers of the Fox Hollow Road petition. These cartoons reveal Swaggart's sentiments regarding a road bond issue which was coming up for a vote, and presumably represent the experience of folks in the area who were obliged to use the roads. This undated clipping from the Eugene City *Guard* gives background on Swaggart.

LOCAL BOY IS DRAWING CARTOONS FOR GOOD ROADS

The cartoon in today's issue of the *Guard* on the matter of good roads and the $2,000,000 road bond issue, was drawn by a local youth, Lester Swaggart, son of Charles Swaggart. He was born in Lane County 18 years ago, on a farm one mile east of Spencer's Butte, and it may almost be said that he has been drawing ever since. His passion for the pencil was very

Good Roads, Good Sense, Good Markets, Less Expense

Good Roads, Good Sense, Good Markets, Less Expense
Marketing when prices are right beats marketing when roads are ready—or, not, at all.
Vote 318 X Yes and 302 X Yes For Good Roads.
LANE COUNTY GOOD ROADS ASSOCIATION
FRED FISK, Pres.

Good Roads, Good Sense, Good Markets, Less Expense
We have proved it folly to temporize with poor roads, but wise to construct good ones.
Vote 318 X Yes and 302 X Yes
For Good Roads.
LANE COUNTY GOOD ROADS ASSOCIATION
FRED FISK, Pres.

Lester Swaggart's cartoons promoting the road bond issue.

apparent at the time he started to school when he was six years of age, and the work has been developing rapidly ever since. Young Swaggart then started a course in the Federal School of Applied Cartoonists, and since coming under the supervision of capable instructors his work has been better than ever. He has, during the past few years done considerable work for local firms including comic lines and "joke stuff."

One other proposed route through this area should be noted in this chapter. The Eugene City *Guard* of January 22, 1870, carried the following editorial:

RAILROAD SURVEY—The Citizens of our town have realized the fact, that unless something is done to induce Haliday to adopt a line for his Railroad through this place, the Burrage line running by Springfield will be selected. Quite an amount of funds have been raised to carry on a survey under the superintendence of Jesse Applegate. He began at a point one and a half miles North of Maxwell's ferry and one quarter of a mile east of the offset Meridian in T. 18S R. 5W in the prairie leading to Albany and ran in a southerly direction on the highest

The cut below Christensen Road, 1921.
Howard McBeth

ground, crossing the river a few yards above the ferry, then SSW to the farm formerly owned by Hen. Ownes. Thence in a Southerly course to town, keeping between the road and the river. A survey was also made from here through the ridge east of Spencer's Butte, down the swale, running past Mrs. Gays. This is the shortest route to get to Hamiltons' but a tunnel will have to be made three quarters of a mile through the ridge. Mr. A. then came back, connected onto the old survey running up eleventh street, and ran a line on a grade by Mr. Judkins, across J. H. D. Henderson's farm, through the gaps West of the McVay point to the Coryell hill. By this route the top of the Coryell hill is reached without cutting but little, saving also running through the Springfield low bottom and about a mile in distance. The line then goes on to Hamilton's cutting off considerable of the distance by the Burrage survey from the Coryell hill to the last named place.

The Town and Country column of the *Guard* for the following week carried these items:

This was Fox Hollow south of Spencer Butte in 1979.
David Herrick

A CARD: *1-27-1870*—At a meeting of citizens held this day the undersigned were appointed a committee to solicit grants of right of way along the proposed RR route, recently surveyed by Jesse Applegate. It is so well known that this obstacle must sooner or later be removed either by litigation or otherwise and the sooner it is done the greater inducement to adopt any given route, and the right of way having been generally offered nearly the whole line of the Burrage survey, we trust no further effort than this announcement will be required to obtain it along these lines. The necessary papers will be found in the hands of the Postmaster at Eugene City, and each of the undersigned. Those interested will please call without delay.

S. Ellsworth
J. H. D. Henderson

RAILROAD MEETING—According to adjournment the Railroad Meeting convened at the courthouse Thursday p.m. to hear the report of the survey made by Hon. Jesse Applegate. Mr. A. filed his report which was received and the city papers were requested to publish it. Mr. Applegate says that the survey made, running east of Spencer's Butte is a shorter and better route than the Burrage route which runs by Springfield.

The February 5, 1870, *Guard* carried this item:

REPORT OF THE LATE RAILROAD SURVEY THROUGH EUGENE

To A. S. Patterson, Esq., Chairman of a Railroad Meeting of the Citizens of Eugene City.

Sir: Under the instructions of your Committee, and with the assistance of Hon. Henry Gilfry and John McClung, Esq., both competent Engineers, I have, after due exploration of the country, run with one of Young's construction of Transits the following line, to wit:

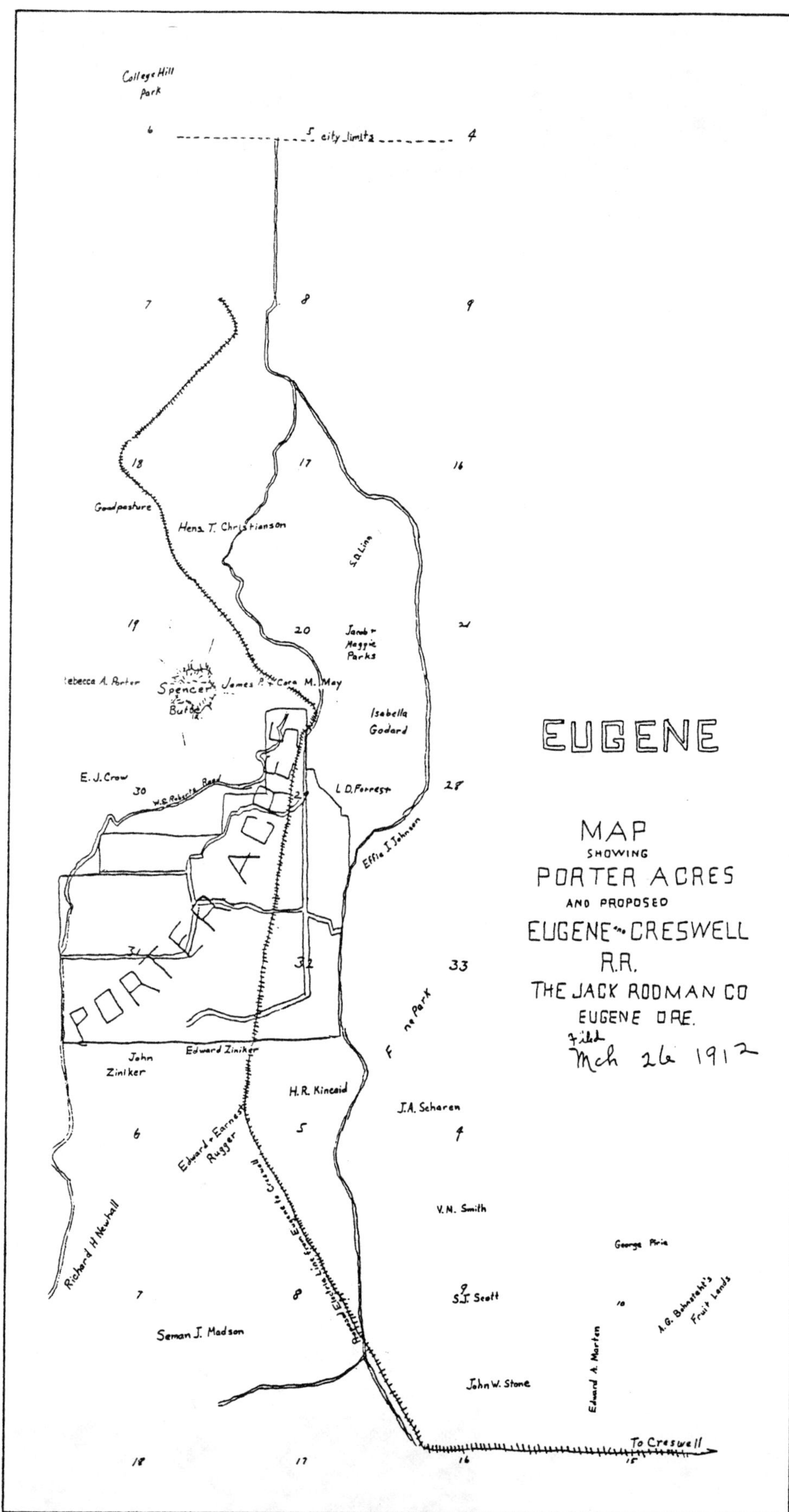

The proposed rail route through Christensen Valley, surveyed by Jesse Applegate and later considered for electric rail route, circa 1912.
Hal Barton personal library

1st. A line beginning at a point about one mile and a half north of Maxwell's Ferry, to station No. 76 (in Mr. Pacard's orchard) near the corporate limits of Eugene City.

2nd. A line starting at said station 76 and running southerly to Coast Fork valley, crossing the mountain spur east and near Mount Spencer.

3d. A line through the City, connecting station 76 with the Burrage survey through Eleventh Street, at his station No. 43, east of Eugene City (Near Mr. Chichester's blacksmith shop).

4th. A line starting at the Burrage line, Station No. 43, and curving through the foothills east and south to the Coast Fork valley.

Full details of the character of the ground over which these lines pass are given in the plats and field notes herewith submitted, and a brief notice of each is only necessary in this report. . . .

Then follows a discussion of the problems likely to be encountered in crossing the Willamette, after which he discusses the route near Mount Spencer:

To gain the full advantage of this line it should, as indicated by the red line on the map, leave the surveyed line at Station No. 61 in the farm of L. Davis, one and one half miles north of Eugene, touch Eugene City on the west, and pass over the low hills west of the little valley followed by the survey. The tunnel would thus be reached by a line nearly straight, and upon the right course. The surveyed line follows the little valley which lies smoothly from the city up to the pass—goes over the ridge and descends Gay's creek to the valley of the Coast Fork; but a railroad at a grade of 80 feet to the mile cannot climb the ridge without being more expensive than to go through it by a tunnel. This will be about three quarters of a mile in length and at a high grade towards the south, as the valley of Gay's creek lies considerably higher than the valley north of the ridge.

This route is obviously the shortest and best, and it is probable it will ultimately be adopted, but at present the tunnel may be considered too expensive and tedious a work to be undertaken.

*THE SURVEY OVER THE FOOTHILLS
EAST OF SPENCER*

Cheaper than the tunnel and shorter than the Burrage line, is the survey over the foothills. This line should also leave the survey from Maxwell's Ferry at Station 63, thence (as indicated by the red line on the map) along the southerly base of Skinner's Butte, looping the mill race and reaching the Burrage line through Eleventh street at station 43, and going over the hills by the way of Judkins, Henderson's Bennett's etc. and to the Coast Fork valley at a pro-

per point to pass on a straight line west of Stony or Bowie's butte, and east of the Petree point. Where the survey first climbs the hills after leaving the city, there is about one mile of road that will require considerable cutting and filling, and some trestle work across Mes/rs Judkins' and Henderson's valleys; but in every way this line is superior to that chosen by Mr. Burrage in his survey through Eugene City. By going further to the east he places his line in a low bottom, which, as it approaches its easterly point opposite Springfield, is washed by a powerful current. With the material at hand permanent embankments cannot be made; and consequently a long line of trestles must support the road. A road crossing the river at or near Springfield must necessarily cross the low bottom and encounter the strong current that washes it, and be too low to gain the plain below Coryell hill; hence, Mr. Burrage was under the necessity of following the Coast Fork in a long bend to the east which this survey avoids. No grade exceeding 50 feet to the mile need be made on this line, and except for the mile alluded to, by a judicious location the cost of cutting and filling for the remainder of the distance need not exceed that of making the roadway on level ground.

Since Albany has been made a point on the OCRR and Eugene City is directly south of Albany, and the objective point in Umpqua valley is to the west; no route lying east of Eugene City can be as short as one passing through that place, and it is evident the route through or by the city is practicable and not more expensive than the present surveyed route by Springfield.

I recommend that the plats and field notes herewith returned be forwarded at once to Mr. Holiday, at Washington City, so that in case he files a plat of the OCRR in order to withdraw the public land from market through which it passes, he may adopt the survey made by your order as part of it.

Respectfully,
Jesse Applegate
Eugene City
January 21, 1871

It is interesting to speculate what the Christensen valley would look like today if the railroad had gone through the Butte area instead of by the Judkins route. According to this map, the city fathers considered building an electric railway from Eugene to Creswell along this route. □

CHAPTER 7

Area Landmarks

BUTTE AREA POST OFFICES

The earliest application for a post office in the Spencer Butte area was made by Milton S. Riggs, and was dated March 18, 1853. The application reads, "The proposed office will be called Spencers [sic] Butte and it is located in Twp. 18S, Range 3W, being on or near the route from Salem to Pleasant Hill on which mail is now carried once per week. The location is described as five miles west of Pleasant Hill and six miles east of Skinners. It is one mile west of the coast fork of the Willamette river and there are seven families residing within two miles."

According to the directory of Lane County Post Offices compiled by Dave Ramstead and Clarin Lewis, this post office was established July 14, 1853, and discontinued April 2, 1855. The first postmaster is listed as Milton Riggs and the location was probably near the present Goshen. (Ramstead and Lewis, *Lane County, Oregon, Post Offices*, p. 11.)

In point of time the next post office to be established was one known as Spencer Creek. The date of establishment is given as July 21, 1874. It was discontinued December 12, 1879. It was located in the northwest quarter of Sec. 28, Twp. 18S, R. 4W, and south of Spencer Creek, which would put it very near the location of the Spencer Creek School. James F. Amis, who married Hollen Bailey's widow, is listed as postmaster. The application says this was on the route from Eugene City to Franklin over which mail was carried once a week. The Siuslaw Post Office was about six miles south and Eugene City nine miles northeast. About 40 families were to be served by this post office.

A third post office was established in the area in 1922. Oregon *Geographic Names*, page 292, states, "There was at one time a Fox Hollow post office near the road junction in Section 5, Twp. 19S, r. 4W, with Mrs. Aslaug I. Knox postmistress. This office was in service

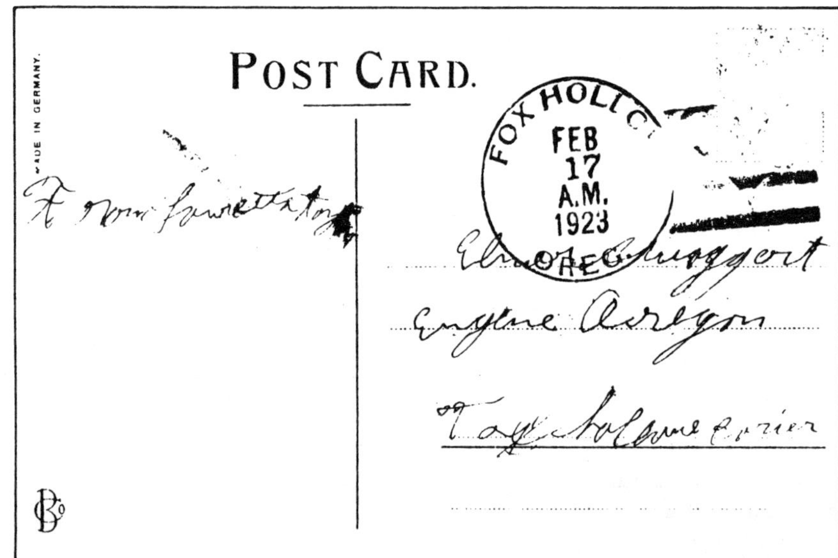

A postcard which was part of the neighborhood campaign to save the Fox Hollow Post Office.

Fred Knox and Aslaug Knox, Postmistress of Fox Hollow Post Office.

from November 27, 1922 to September 1, 1924, in the Fred G. Knox farm house, and was closed by the extension of rural route 3 from Eugene."

Harry Taylor Jr., in an interview in 1977, said: "As I remember it the first mail route they had through Fox Hollow was carried by Elmer Roberts on horseback. He had mailbags, you know. In about 1919 or 1920 they started that Star Route through Fox Hollow and in order to keep the route going why everybody wrote all the letters they could. I mean they wrote extra letters so the mailman would have enough mail to justify the run. Anyway, I think that ran for a couple of years. . . . I remember he used to stop at the school house and talk to the kids."

Janet Brown recalled when Eva Knox carried the mail: "She had a cart and a horse. A two-wheeled cart. And she packed it from the Lorane Highway clear through to the Spencer Creek schoolhouse and on up to Hilliard Street road. All through there in the mud. She had a real light horse with a good action to its feet. She borrowed mine once and it got mud fever all over its legs. She picked up the mail at the post office at Knox's. She got so much a mile for the carrying. . . ."

LOCATION OF PROPOSED POST OFFICE

DIVISION OF
POSTMASTERS' APPOINTMENTS

Post Office Department

FIRST ASSISTANT POSTMASTER GENERAL

Washington, June 26, 1922

IN REPLYING
MENTION INITIALS AND DATE

AF-2d

JUL 24 1922

Mr. W. S. Roberts,

Eugene, Oregon.

5661

SIR: With reference to the proposed establishment of a post office at the point named below, and in order that the office, if established, may be accurately represented upon the post-route maps, it is requested that you furnish accurately the information called for below and prepare a sketch according to instructions on opposite side of paper, which should be returned to the First Assistant Postmaster General, Division of Postmasters' Appointments, as soon as possible.

Respectfully,

FIRST ASSISTANT POSTMASTER GENERAL.

Proposed post office, _Fox Hollow_ (Name.), _Lane_ (County.), _Oregon_ (State.)

If the town, village, or site of the post office be known by another name than that of the post office, state that other name here: _none_

The post office would be situated in the _S.W._ quarter of section No. _8_, in Township _19_ (N. or S.) Range _4_ _W_ (E. or W.), of the _Willamette_ principal meridian, County of _Lane_

State of _Oregon_

The name of the nearest river is _Willamette_, and the post-office building would be at a distance of _14 miles_, on the _S_ (N., S., E., or W.) side of it.

The name of the nearest creek is _Coyote_, and the post-office building would be at a distance of _120 yds_, on the _S_ (N., S., E., or W.) side of it.

The name of the nearest office on the same route as this proposed post office is _Eugene_ and its distance is _13_ miles, by the traveled road, in a _N_ (N., S., E., or W.) direction from the site of this proposed office.

The name of the nearest office on the same route, on the other side, is _none_ and its distance is _______ miles, in a _______ (N., S., E., or W.) direction from the site of this proposed office.

The name of the nearest office not on the same route as this proposed post office is _Creswell_ and its distance is _9½_ miles, by the traveled road, in a _S_ (N., S., E., or W.) direction from the site of this proposed office.

The post-office building would be on the _S_ (N., S., E., or W.) side of the _S. P._ Railroad. and at a distance of _13_ from the track. The railroad station name is _Eugene_

The post office would be _10 miles_, air-line distance, _N_ (N., S., E., or W.) from the nearest point of my county boundary.

Signature of Applicant for Postmaster _(Mrs.) Aslaug L. Knox_

Date: _July 15th 1922_

1031   1—6001

Application to establish the Fox Hollow Post Office.

THE BIG SLIDE

Old-timers in the area still talk about the big slide on Spencer Butte during the late 1880s. It tore away the vegetation leaving a raw yellow scar two-thirds of the way up the south slope. This scar was a prominent feature of the landscape for fifteen or twenty years. The memory lingers.

Elsie Sutton recalled seeing the scar plainly from their front porch on a moonlit night when they used to sit listening to the coyotes yapping on the Butte. Paul Ziniker's mother told many times how she had heard the rumbling of the rocks down the mountain. She lived on the north slope of Camas Swale several miles away. Paul's Ruegger cousins were puzzled by the very muddy water in their creek the next day until they learned of the major disturbance upstream.

When the first settlers came to Lane County the Butte was largely bald—few trees except in the gullies. People climbed up there for the view, even in the early days. This story from Walling's *Illustrated History of Lane County* tells of an early climber:

> During the "early days" when the Hudson's Bay Company's men were almost the sole white occupants of Oregon, it was their custom to send out parties in every direction to hunt, trap and trade with the Indians during each recurring summer. Usually some one of these were commissioned to go through to California and return with horses, cattle, etc., purchased from the Spanish residents of that country. With one of these parties passing up the Willamette valley was a young Englishman, named Spencer. This party camped one afternoon, near the old Indian trail that crosses Spencer creek some six or eight miles west of where Eugene City now stands, and Spencer announced to his comrades that he would go hunting and intended to ascend the large Butte to the eastward of the camp in order to obtain a good view of the surrounding country. This was the last seen of him alive.
>
> Not returning to camp his companions started out the next morning to search for him. They tracked him to the butte in question and, about half-way up its western slope, found his lifeless body, stripped naked, shot full of arrows and otherwise mutilated. They buried his remains as best they could, by covering it with loose stones, and sadly took their departure southward, calling the mountain Spencer Butte, which name it still bears. . . .
>
> Mr. Bristow remembering the story of the

Fan of rubble from the Big Slide visible from Bennett Stephensen's pasture.

> Hudson Bay men, made inquiry concerning the matter of the Indians whom he encountered upon first settling in the county. Of these he found but one who would acknowledge having any information concerning it. This was "Old Tye Tom," well known by nearly all the old settlers, and who was then the chief of the Chifen tribe, inhabiting that portion of the country adjacent to Spores point. This venerable Indian stated that he was then but a young man, and was one of the party that killed Spencer, boasting of the prodigies of valor he performed on that occasion. His story briefly told was: that discovering the party of whites traveling through the country they hovered near them waiting an opportunity to capture their horses, and observing Spencer to leave the camp alone they followed him to *Champ-a-te* (the Indian name of the butte, which signifies Rattlesnake mountain) and as he was ascending it, way-laid [and] killed him, carrying away as trophies his scalp, firearms and clothing. (Lewis A. McArthur, *Oregon Geographic Names*, Oregon Historical Society, 4th Edition revised by Lewis L. McArthur, 1974, p. 687.)

There is public record of other climbers over the years. A Eugene City *Guard* story dated May 9, 1885, reads: "A party of young folks from this city and Springfield ascended Spencer's [sic] Butte last Sunday." Then after the slide, which probably occurred in late fall of 1889, the Eugene City *Guard* carried this story datelined:

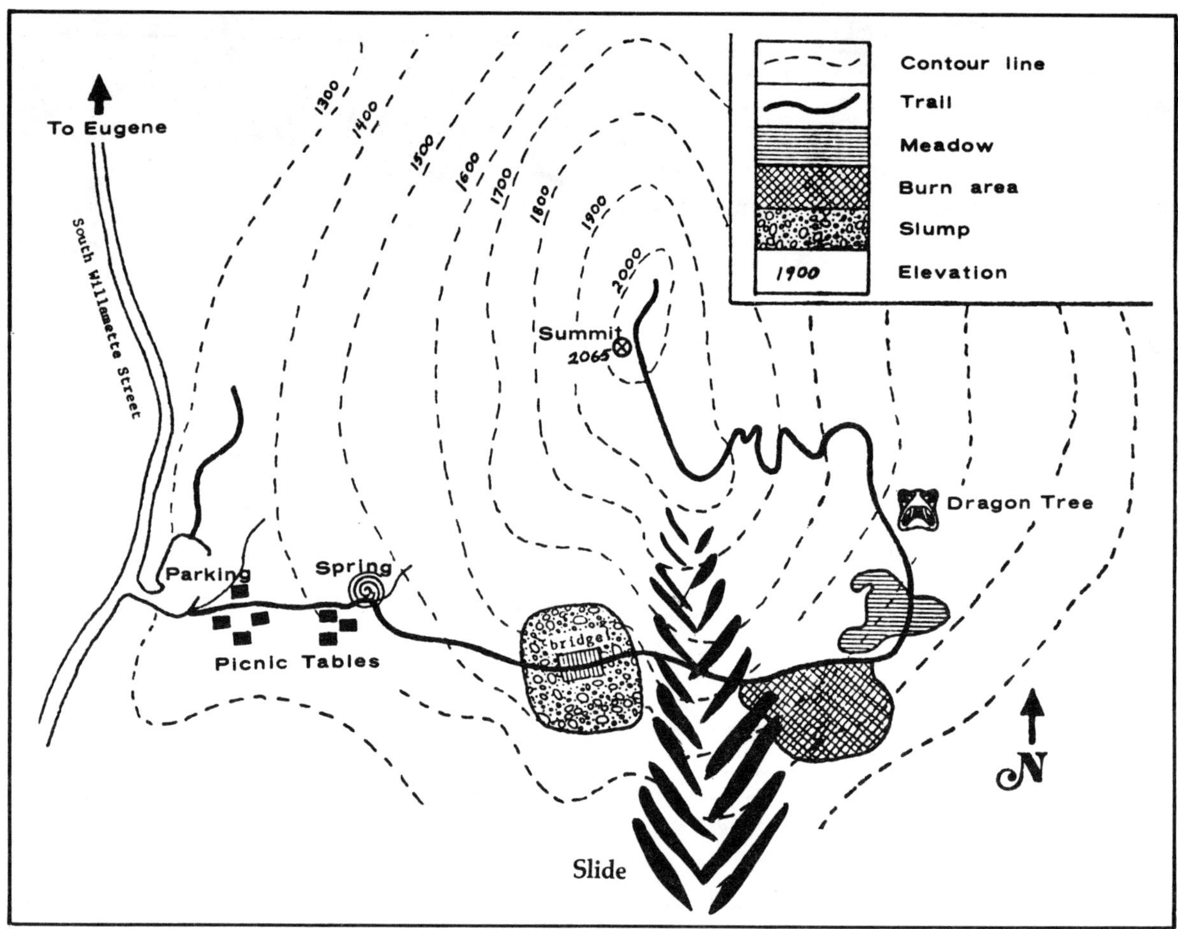

Spencer Butte Trail Map with Big Slide area indicated.
Lane County IED

GOSHEN: *Feb. 15, 1890*—Several visited the Spencer Butte slide last Sunday.

The late Walter Dillard (County Commissioner at the time) told Bennett Stephenson—present owner in whose pasture the remnants of the slide are evident—that it had been an exceptionally rainy fall and slides were common throughout this part of the state.

Mother Nature has healed the scar. Stately firs disguise the evidence from the casual passerby, except for the fan formation at the base of the slide which even today is clearly visible from Fox Hollow Road in an open meadow which belongs to Bennett Stephenson. The upper part lies within the boundaries of the city park. The enormous pile of tumbled boulders crests just below the trail which skirts the south side of the Butte. Several large trees with charred bark grow along the trail at that point. A careful observer can distinguish the upper section of the slide by locating the huge old-growth Douglas firs which border it. This contour map prepared by Lane Intermediate

Education District's Environmental Education Department has had slide details added.

THE BOY SCOUT CAMP

In the southeast quarter of Section 31, T 18 S, R 3 W, are the remains of a log cabin with a sturdy chimney still standing. Small cedar trees have begun to hide the crumbling remnants of the log walls.

This cabin was built in the mid-thirties, sponsored and grubstaked by the American Legion scouting committee, for Troop 1 Boy Scouts. The Legion put up food for an unemployed man who built it with help from the scouts. It was common practice in those days for each troop to have its "hideaway" camp somewhere in the area. Troop 2 had such a camp northeast of Springfield near Jasper.

There was no direct road access to this cabin. The scouts hiked about three miles from the "end of the gravel" where Christensen Road intersects with Fox Hollow. Cars were parked there and the troop proceeded on foot,

Looking east across the ruin of the Boy Scout cabin.

carrying their packs on their backs.

Harvey Blythe was scout master and Bill Rossen his assistant. These men were in the ROTC program at the University. Rossen went on from there to become the youngest general in the U.S. Army during World War II according to one account.

Troop 1 was organized in 1924 and some of the members over the years have been Jess W. Barr, Warren Strasser, Paul Brabham, Cecil Armes, Frank N. Rhodes, Kenneth T. O'Neil, L. L. Erdmann, George Evans, T. V. Stockman, Max L. Dudley, Warren Smith, Douglas Spencer, Don and Dan England, Harvey Speck, Bob Rogers, John Alltucker and Ehrman Guistina.

In 1977 enough remained of the cabin to reveal some significant features of its design. It was built of logs with small poles used as chinking. There was a fireplace built of native stone and lined with firebrick. The gable ends and roof were shaked and the roof was supported by unpeeled pole rafters. Former scouts told of a loft across the fireplace end which was visible upon entering through the door. Remains of a ladder up the wall indicate access to

this loft where the boys undoubtedly slept.

John Taylor recalled that he and his father were building a fence along their north line sometime in the mid-thirties when the boys came along and requested permission to cross the Taylor property to reach their cabin. Permission was granted with a caution about keeping gates closed at all times.

Warren Smith recalled one trip when a cougar followed his troop as they hiked into camp. He was about twelve or fourteen years old at the time.

Use of the cabin was discontinued during World War II. The property changed hands several times in the next few years. A small sawmill was built in the clearing a few hundred feet south of the cabin by "a man from Oklahoma." Then Oral Suttlee built a slab house across the creek and lived there during the summer for a few years. He logged for John Taylor one or two summers from that location. During the rainy season, the Suttlees lived on River Road. Joanne Suttlee Taylor told of a time when she was milking the family cow there. The cow stood, eating from a bucket of feed, just out in the open pasture. A cougar yowled somewhere in the area and the cow took off across country—leaving the milkmaid sitting with her pail between her knees. She followed the cow's example and headed for shelter.

Sometime later the property became part of the Christensen Brothers Ranch where it remained through the 1950s.

Corner detail of the Scout's log cabin.

Left: Lillie. Daughter of J. and V. Ziniker. January 29, 1888 - July 25, 1902.

Below: Martha Ann Gay. Born Nov. 8, 1837. Died Dec. 12, 1916.

PIONEER CEMETERIES

There are three "pioneer" cemeteries of record within the boundaries of this study: the Mary Gay Cogswell cemetery, the Moxley cemetery and the Toll cemetery.

An unpublished manuscript titled *Lane County, Oregon, Cemeteries*, compiled by Lane County Historical Society (no date, p. 93) locates the Moxley cemetery as follows: Four miles northwest of Creswell, Oregon turn to the right and go about one-third of a mile to a new gravelled road. This road on the left leads to a farm. Drive through the field up a slope about one-eighth of a mile to the foot of a small hill. In June 1940 the cemetery was advertised for sale for unpaid taxes. (It is reported that this cemetery has been destroyed.)

Those buried there are listed as T. J. Moxley, M. E. Moxley, John H. Taylor, his wife Almira Taylor and Clarence G. Taylor. Joseph Milliken reports this cemetery as being at the end of Tolman Road.

The Toll cemetery is located off Fox Hollow Road in Section 2, T 19 s, R 4 W. The Tolls came to Oregon in 1882. They purchased the John R. Ellison homestead (Certificate 1198) from Keeler Farrington June 28, 1883. The homestead consisted of the north half of the northwest quarter of Section 2 as above. The burial plot is about 25 paces from the south line, on the crest of the hill east of Fox Hollow Road. Sarah Almira Applegate Toll and three of Nick and Melissa Toll's daughters are buried there. The girls died in infancy. One was stillborn and the other two lived only briefly. Caroline and June were their names. Their surviving sister, Bertha Toll, thinks they were "blue babies."

Family members have kept the area cleared of brush and occasionally carried flowers to decorate the graves over the years even though ownership of the land has passed out of the family. The original grave markers are gone and the family acknowledges that the location they have tended is only approximate.

The Mary Gay Cogswell cemetery is on a

hill northwest of the north end of Sher Khan Road. The land was originally donated by Martin Gay. The acre is fenced off from the Christensen pasture which surrounds it now. These pictures give some visual description of the spot. Many of the gravestones carry the names of families mentioned in this book. □

Top left: MARY ANN. Died Apr. 4 1857. Aged 3 yrs. 10 mos. 24 days. FLORILLA. Died Sep. 30 1857. Aged 1 yr. 8 mos. 25 days. Daughters of John & Mary F. Cogswell.

Top right: Mary Gay Cogswell. Pioneer Cemetery. D.A.R. Recorded

Lower left: Gay. Ann Stewart. Born Feb. 3, 1808. Died Jan. 1874.
Martin Baker. Born Oct. 24, 1803. Died Mar. 17, 1867.

Lower right: Albert Ruegger. 1842-1902. Rosena. 1848-Obscured. Gone but not forgotten.

Epilogue

In the Preface I asked the question, "Was this land good to the pioneers who made the long trek across the Oregon Trail?" The hundred years covered by this book embodies the end of an era when the majority of American families were farm-based and knew a degree of self-sufficiency—foreign to most of us today. This small section of Lane County is only a sample of the larger whole. My childhood experience on my parents' Ohio farm gave me an appreciation for the quality of life a family develops when the work they do together is seen to benefit the children as well as the grown-ups. It has been a satisfaction to record "how it was" for a few others here in Lane County.

Even though this foothill land was not very productive, and even though such family farms are a passing way of life, I regret the loss of cleared fields which could be cultivated and the fading of a community spirit which bolstered those hardworking people. They were isolated from much of the world and dependent on each other for social contacts as well as emergencies. Howard McBeth said, "Some families were more successful financially, but others were competent, independent, took care of themselves, were hardworking and clever. These days they'd be on welfare, but *then* they were proud of getting along." Gertrude Albro said, "It was a pretty wonderful way of life when you stop to think back on it." I agree.

Another generation will harvest the timber which has taken over the fields. Trees are what this land grows best. Who knows? Perhaps when Mother Nature has built more topsoil, some future generation may clear and plant again. □

Appendix I

ALPHABETICAL LIST OF HOMESTEADERS

Name	Place of Birth	Section	Township S.	Range W.	Settled on Claim
Anderson, James H.	Canada	32	18	4	1898
Anderson, Wm. H.	Canada	32	18	4	1902
Bailey, Hollen & Eliz.	Kentucky	28,29,32,33	18	4	1853
Blanton, John & Catherine	Missouri	5,6	19	3	1854(?)
Bond, John H. & Mary	Iowa	2	19	4	1890
Bowden, James F. & Mary	England	17,20	18	3	1853
Bowers, Solomon & Lucinda	Germany	10	19	4	?
Bruce, David C.	Indiana	25	18	4	1871
Butler, James & Isabella	Missouri	15,16	19	3	1854*
Butler, Jonathan & Mary	Ohio	20	18	3	1855(?)
Calloway, Chas. & Eliz.	Kentucky	21,28	18	4	1853
Carson, Andrew J.	N. Carolina	27	18	4	1854
Conkle, Philip	Unknown	34	18	4	1883 patent rec'd.
Daniels, N. N. & Rachel	Unknown	29	18	3	1868 sold
Davis, Isaac S. & Marg.	Missouri	10,11	19	4	1854
Edia, Jasper & Martha	Unknown	33	18	4	1871
Eddy, Isaac & Sarah (Edia)	Indiana	27	18	4	1872
Ellison, John R. & Nancy	Unknown	2	19	4	1866
Emerick, Geo. J. & Sophia	Virginia	4	19	3	1853
Emerick, James M.	Iowa	1,12	19	4	1866
Engley, Dexter & Emma	Unknown	24	18	4	1871
Gay, James W. & Frances	Kentucky	4,5,8,9	19	3	1852
Gay, Martin B. & Ann	Virginia	5,8,17	19	3	1852
Herrington, Lorenzo & Alice	Unknown	27	18	4	1899
Hutchins, John & Susan	Illionis	26	18	4	1855
Jewett, Washington	Indiana	28	18	3	1855
Jones, Joseph M. & Polly	S. Carolina	8,9	19	3	1853
Killingsworth, John & Ann	Tennessee	5,8	19	3	1853
Kindt, Louis & Alice	Kansas	36	18	4	1923*
Knoop, Charles & Anna	Germany	4	19	4	1893
Knoop, Ernest	Germany	4	19	4	1893
Lombard, Atmer & Lizzie	Maine	34	18	4	1891
Lombard, James L. & Sarah	Maine	35	18	4	1891
Martin, Charles G. & Rachel	Kentucky	18,7,12,13	19	3,4	1850
Martin, Gustin & Marg.	N. Carolina	8,9,10,16,15	19	3	1854*
Malone, Jas. R. & Eliz.	Virginia	29,35	18	4	1854
Mathany, Robert & Marg.	Kentucky	12	19	4	1854
Maupin, Boyd & Amanda	Missouri	18,19	18	4	1853
Mercer, John H. & Sarah	Unknown	34	18	4	1901
Moore, Caleb & Jane	Pennsylvania	14,15	19	4	1853
Moore, James & Eliz.	Tennessee	7,8,17,18	19	3	1853
Morgan, Wm. H. & Ruth	Kentucky	26,27	18	4	1855
Mulkey, J. Thos. & Ann	Kentucky	23	18	4	1853
Osburn, Wm. T. & Sarah	Iowa	13	19	3	1854
Padburg, Henry & Martha	Germany	31	18	3	1870 patent rec'd.
Park, Azariah & Eliz.	Virginia	21	18	3	1854
Phelps, Orville	New York	19,30	18	3	1877
Renshaw, Wm. D. & Mary	Tennessee	32,33	18	3	1852
Riggs, Garnett & Nancy	Missouri	29,30,31	18	3	1853
Riggs, Jonathan & Mary	Kentucky	31	18	3	1853

Rinehart, Geo. W. & Martha	Illinois	29,32	18	2	1854
Rinehart, James H. & Alcinda	Illinois	2,10,11	19	4	1854
Rinehart, Lewis & Eliz.	Illinois	11	19	4	1854
Ritchie, Geo. W. & Mary	Indiana	31,32	18	3	1854
Robinson, James C.	Ohio	8,9,16,17	19	3	1850*
Sinay, Tony	Unknown	35	18	4	1892
Stewart, James & Marg.(?)	Tennessee	27,28	18	3	1854
Stibbens, Daniel W.	Unknown	34	18	4	1898
Sweeney, G.	Unknown	29	18	3	1869
Toll, Carl	Oregon	3	19	4	1936
Toll, Nicholas & Melissa	Illinois	2	19	4	1883(?)
Walker, Wm. & Mary	Tennessee	3,4,9,10	19	3	1853
Walker, Wm. Thomas & Ardelia	Tennessee	33	18	3	1854
Ware, James H.	Unknown	4	19	4	1895
Ware, Joel & Eliz.	Ohio	26	18	4	?
Ware, Thos. & Mariah	Kentucky	21,22	18	4	1853
Whitmore, P. P.	Unknown	25	18	4	1871

*Section 16 & 36 in each township was reserved for school lands and later sold by the state to original private owner of that acreage.

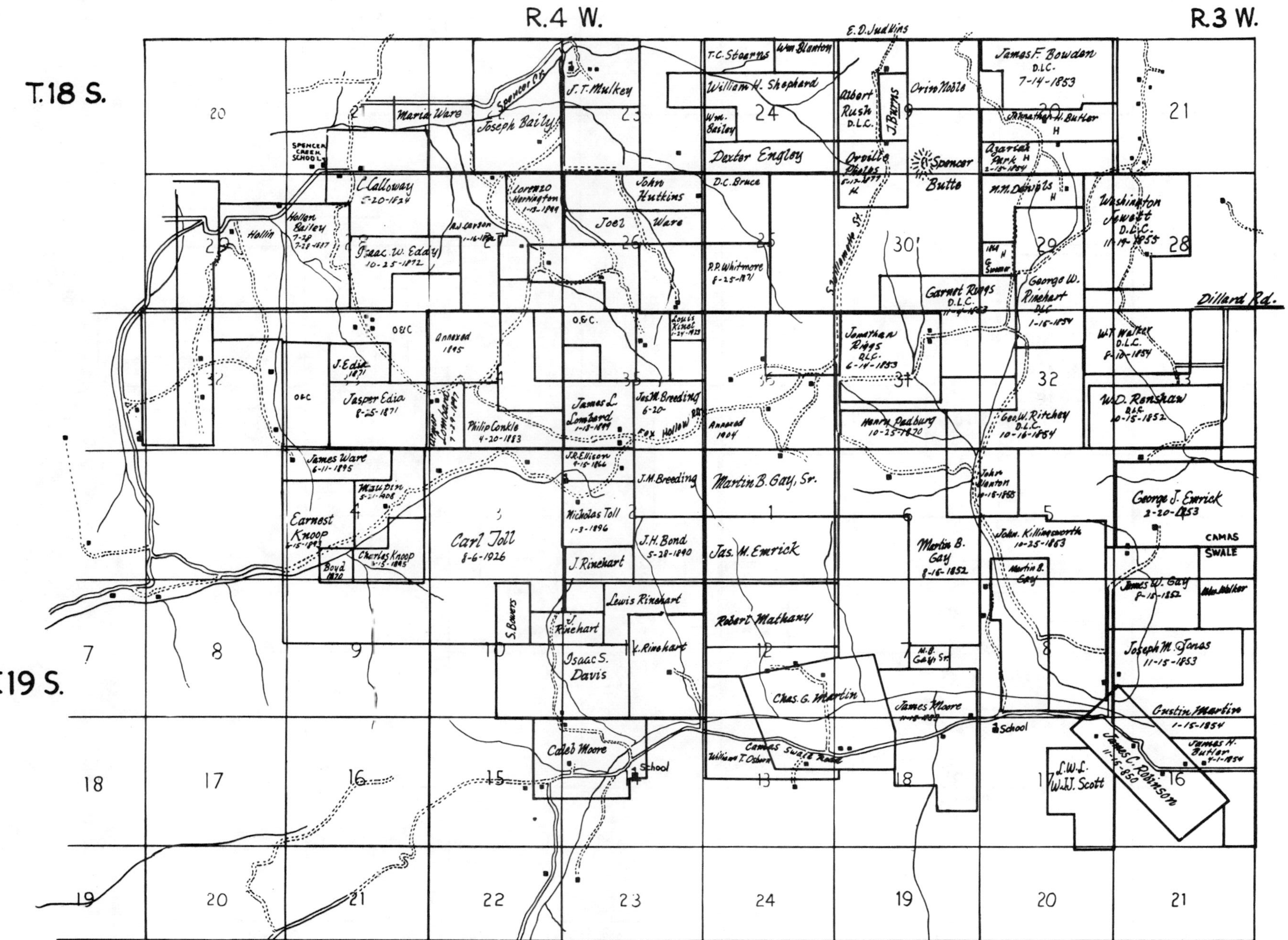

ORIGINAL HOMESTEADS 1852-1926: *This map represents the 67 original homesteads settled between 1852 and 1926 when the major use of the land was timber harvesting and small family farming. See Chapters I and II.*

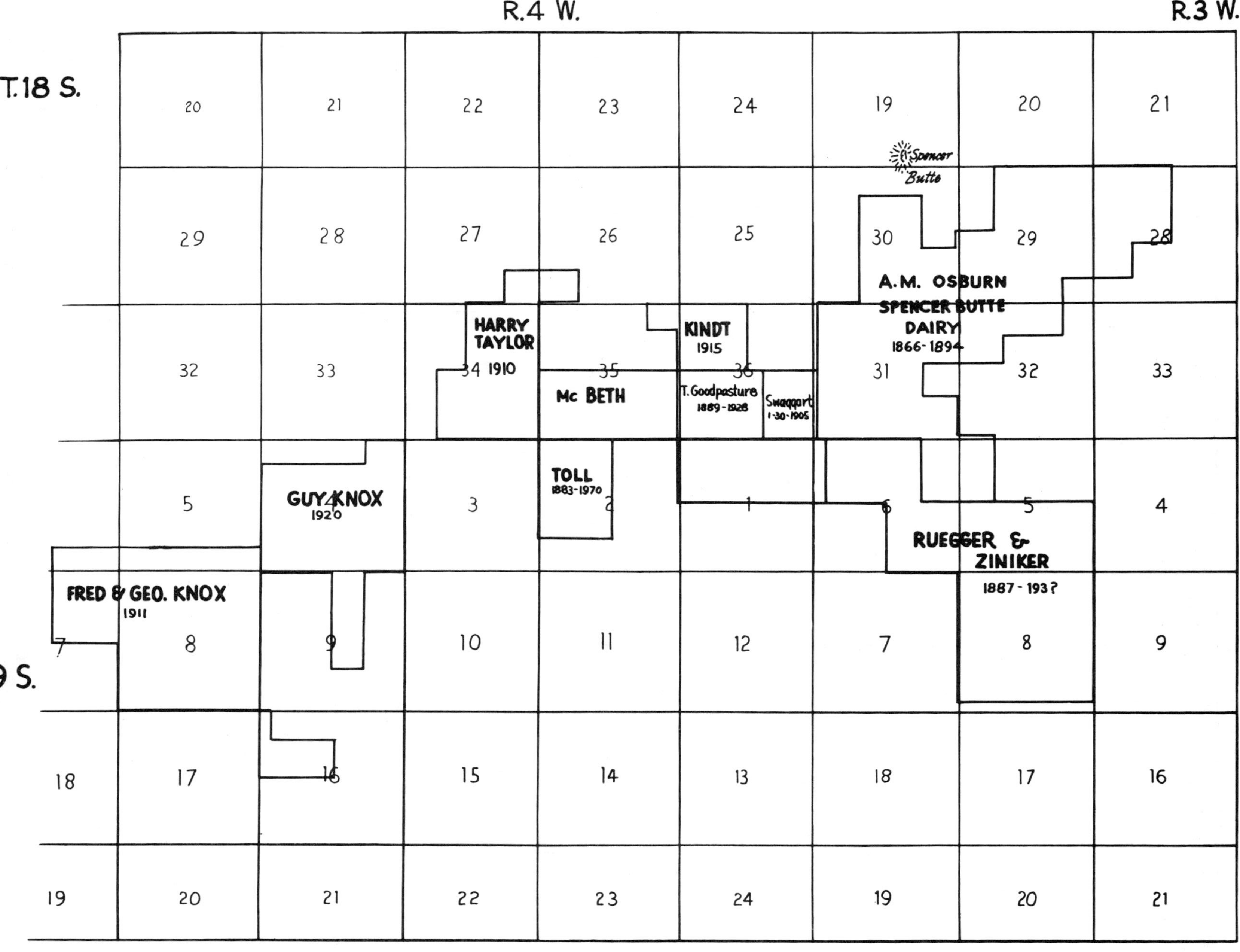

BIG RANCHES 1866-1930: *This map indicates the location of the eight major sheep and cattle ranches and the pattern of land consolidation which developed during the era of the big ranches, 1866-1930. See Chapter III.*

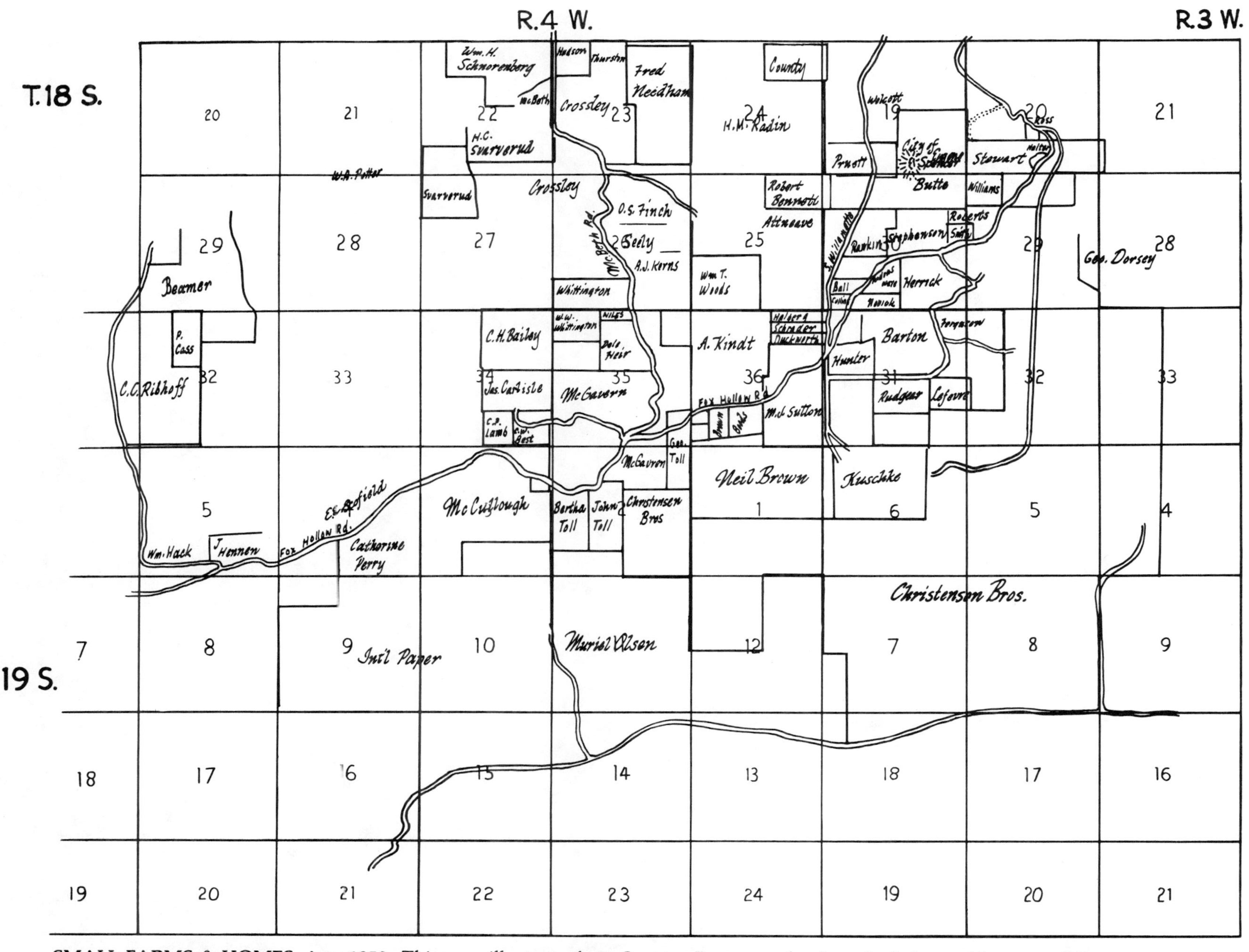

SMALL FARMS & HOMES circa 1950: *This map illustrates how Spencer Butte area land use had changed by 1950. What had earlier been timberland and small family farms (1852-1900), then large sheep and cattle ranches (1866-1930), had by 1950 evolved into more than 70 small tree farms and home sites—with much less emphasis on traditional small family farming.*

Bibliography

Editorial note: When Lois Barton talks about her eight years' work of researching and writing *Spencer Butte Pioneers*, it is clear that her fondest and most vivid memories are of the many people whose lives are the living history which makes this book so vital. Her approach to gathering oral history has been sensitive and incisive demonstrating how rich and valuable this technique can be for contemporary scholars and lay historians. It is only fitting that the names of those who contributed so willingly to the oral history sections of this book be listed first in the bibliography.

TAPE-RECORDED INTERVIEWS—1976-1978
(Transcripts donated by the author to the Lane County Historical Society, Eugene, Oregon.)

Irene Carson Albro—Spencer Butte area, Oregon.
Merl and Gertrude Knox Albro—Eugene, Oregon.
Janet Bell Brown—Florence, Oregon.
Mollie and Henry Christensen—Spencer Butte area, Oregon.
Marie Ziniker Erdmann—Eugene, Oregon.
Candis Haley Harris—Longview, Washington.
Bill Kindt—Eugene, Oregon.
Walter Kindt—Eugene, Oregon.
George and Molly Knox—Coburg, Oregon.
Howard and Dorothy McBeth—Spencer Butte area, Oregon.
Helen Osburn Meador—Portland, Oregon.
Florence Murdock—Eugene, Oregon.
John Napper—Creswell, Oregon.
Jane Taylor Puett—Eugene, Oregon.
Emory and Mildred Pruett—Spencer Butte area, Oregon.
Ralph and Earnest Ruegger—Gresham, Oregon.
Elsie and Marion Sutton—Spencer Butte area, Oregon.
Lester Swaggart—Eugene, Oregon.
Harry Taylor, Jr.—Eugene, Oregon.
Bertha Toll—Spencer Butte area, Oregon.
Maggie Kindt Toll and Ralph Toll—Waldport, Oregon.
Ed Ziniker, Jr.—Eugene, Oregon.
Leonard Ziniker—Creswell, Oregon.
Paul and Gladys Ziniker—Eugene, Oregon.

INFORMAL INTERVIEWS

Ambrose Canaday—Veneta, Oregon.
Dr. Eva Johnson—Eugene, Oregon.
David Knox—Eugene, Oregon.
Clarence Lombard—Eugene, Oregon.
Cecil Robe—Eugene, Oregon.
Bennett Stephenson—Spencer Butte area, Oregon.
Ruth McBeth Svarverud—Spencer Butte area, Oregon.
Curtis Thornton, Boy Scouts of America—Eugene, Oregon.

CORRESPONDENCE

Ethel Briggs—New Martinsville, West Virginia.
Helene Kerr Brown—Pasco, Washington.
Ruth Lombard Kerr—Portland, Oregon.
Alice Whitmore Sousa—Veneta, Oregon.
Mrs. Albert Ziniker—Washougal, Washington.
Emma Ziniker—San Francisco, California.

UNPUBLISHED MANUSCRIPTS

Conners, Fern, "Butler Genealogical Study." From the personal library of Fern Connors, Columbia Falls, Montana, circa 1975.

Gay, James Woods, "Oregon Trail Diary." From the library of Arthur Sperling (grandson), Eugene, Oregon, circa 1851.

Masterson, Martha Gay, "The Sunset Trail." Oregon Historical Society, Portland, Oregon, circa 1900.

Rinehart, James H. (?), "The Rinehart Story." From the personal library of Charles Wallace, Eugene, Oregon, circa 1950.

Ruegger, Albert, "Account Book, 1878-1930." From the personal library of Ralph Ruegger (grandson), Gresham, Oregon.

Swaggart, Lester, "Nicholas Barnett Toll." From the personal library of Lester Swaggart, Eugene, Oregon, circa 1970.

Taylor, Harry, "J. O. Taylor." From the personal library of Mrs. Harry Taylor, Jr. (daughter-in-law), Eugene, Oregon, circa 1950.

NEWSPAPERS

The Eugene City *Guard*, Eugene, Oregon.

The Eugene *People's Press*, Eugene, Oregon, published 1858-1861.

The Eugene *Register Guard*, Eugene, Oregon.

The *Oregonian*, Portland, Oregon.

DOCUMENTS

Bureau of Land Management, *Land Records* (microfilm file). Portland, Oregon.

Camas Center School District 178, *Clerk's Record Book.* Creswell Museum, Creswell, Oregon.

Lane County, Oregon, *Deed Books.* Lane County Courthouse, Eugene, Oregon.

_______________ , *Road Records.* Lane County Surveyor's Office, Eugene, Oregon.

_______________ , *School District Boundary Board Minutes.* Archives of Lane Educational Service District, Eugene, Oregon.

National Archives, *Homestead Records.* Washington, D.C.

Oregon Historical Society Library, *Pioneer File Index.* Portland, Oregon.

Prescott, H. W., Surveyor, *Field Notes, 1853-54.* Map Room, Condon Hall, University of Oregon, Eugene, Oregon.

Sheldon, A. C., Naturalist, *Field Notes, 1915.* Museum of Natural History, University of Oregon, Eugene, Oregon.

State Superintendent of Public Instruction, *Biennial Report, 1871-72.* Oregon Collection, University of Oregon Library, Eugene, Oregon.

PERIODICALS

Lane County Historian, Vol. I-XXVI, Lane County Historical Society, 1958-1981.

Oregon Historical Quarterly Index, Vol. I-XL (1939) and XLI to LXI (1967), Lane County Museum, Eugene, Oregon.

BOOKS

Gaston, Joseph, *Centennial History of Oregon, 1811-1912.* Chicago: S. J. Clark Publishing Company, 1912.

Helm, Mike, compiler and editor, *Conversations with Bullwackers, Muleskinners, Pioneers, Prospectors, '49ers, Indian Fighters, Trappers, Ex-Barkeepers, Authors, Preachers, Poets, & All Sorts & Conditions of Men (The Lockley Files).* Eugene, Oregon: Rainy Day Press, 1981.

Loy, William, *Atlas of Oregon.* Eugene, Oregon: University of Oregon Press, 1976.

McArthur, Lewis A., *Oregon Geographic Names.* Portland, Oregon: Oregon Historical Society, 1974.

Ramstead, David A. and Lewis, Claren A., *Lane County Post Offices.* Eugene, Oregon: Mid-Oregon Postal History Group, 1980.

Unruh, John D., *The Plains Across.* Champaign, Illinois: University of Illinois Press, 1979.

Walling, A. G., *Illustrated History of Lane County.* Eugene, Oregon, 1884.

Youngberg, Elsie, transcriber, *1850 Oregon Territorial Census.* Lebanon, Oregon: End of Trail Researchers, 1970.

Creswell Centennial in Pictures, 1873-1973. Creswell, Oregon: Creswell Area Historical Society, 1976.

Eugene and Lane County Directory, 1892-93. Eugene, Oregon: Lane County Museum.

Introduction to Oregon Donation Land Claim Records. Vol. I to IV, Genealogical Forum of Portland, Oregon, Inc., 1957-1967.

A Piece of the Old Tent. Eugene, Oregon: Lane County Pioneer Museum, 1976.

Portrait and Biographical Record of the Willamette Valley. Oregon. Chicago: Chapman Publishing Company, 1903.

1860 Federal Census of Lane County, Oregon. Oregon Genealogical Society, 1972.

1870 Federal Census of Lane County, Oregon. Oregon Genealogical Society, 1972.

Index

About the author

Lois Barton and Spencer Butte.
William Kunkle

Lois Barton has lived on the same land south of Spencer Butte for over 30 years where she and Hal Barton raised eight children and "countless goats, chickens, rabbits and cattle." She has edited the *Lane County Historian* for five years and recently indexed 25 years of that journal. She has published a family history covering 300 years and tracing her Quaker ancestors from England and Ireland to colonial and midwestern America. Her poetry and articles have appeared in local newspapers, church magazines and *Harper's Weekly*.

Born a few months before the Armistice in 1918, she grew up in rural Ohio. During the Depression, she traveled with her family for four winters to sharecrop in the Florida Everglades to help make payments on the Ohio farm. She attended Olney Friends School and Schauffler College in Ohio. She supported her studies as a telephone operator and bookkeeper and later taught at Tunesassa, a Quaker school for Indian children in New York state. In 1944 she joined an American Friends Service Committee project at Philadelphia State Hospital for the Insane and became the project director in 1945.

The Bartons moved to their 80-acre Spencer Butte farm in 1948. Their goal was to sustain their family (eventually five daughters and three sons) on the land—which they have done by 30 years of gardening and raising stock. Six of the Barton children returned to Ohio to attend Olney Friends School and seven of the eight now live in Lane County, Oregon. One daughter married an Ohio schoolmate. Five children were born on the farm and Lois assisted at the home birthing of three of her seven grandchildren.

Lois became one of the area's best-known peace educators during the 1960s and 1970s. She directed the World Without War Council for 10 years and was a member of a church peace mission to Southeast Asia in 1974. She served five years as a regional officer in the Religious Society of Friends and is a former president of the Spencer Butte Improvement Assocation. She has been active in 4H and as a precinct committeewoman and election board member.

Colophon

This book was edited and produced by Charlotte Mills and Caroline Parke of Northwest Matrix, Eugene, Oregon.

The cover and text were designed by Gwen Thomsen of Vesta Creative Services, Eugene, Oregon, assisted by the author.

The cover photo was by Grant Rose, Eugene, Oregon.

The text was phototypeset in 11 point Paladium by Connie Maske of ProtoType, Eugene, Oregon.